VEGETARIAN

the best-ever recipe collection

VEGETARIAN

the best-ever recipe collection

LINDA FRASER

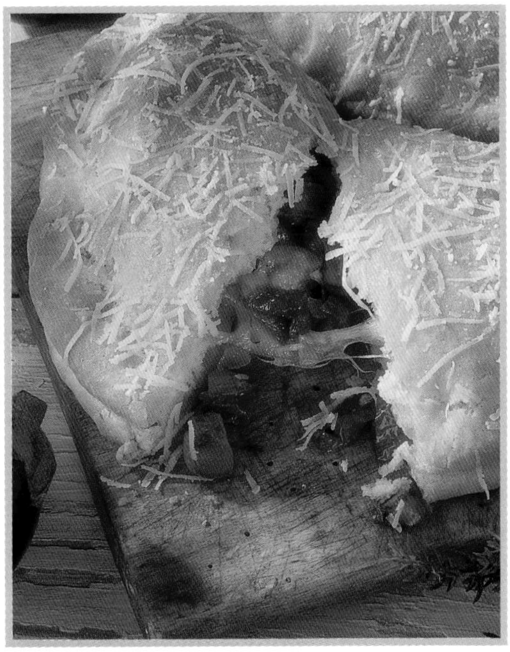

HERMES HOUSE

This edition produced by Hermes House
an imprint of
Anness Publishing Limited
Hermes House, 88–89 Blackfriars Road, London SE1 8HA

A CIP catalogue record for this book is available from the British Library

Publisher: Joanna Lorenz
Senior Cookery Editor: Linda Fraser
Project Editor: Sarah Duffin
Designer: Bill Mason
Illustrator: Anna Koska

Also published as the *Best Ever-Vegetarian*

3 5 7 9 10 8 6 4

NOTES

For all recipes, quantities are given in both metric and imperial measures and, where appropriate, measures are also given in standard cup and spoon sizes. Follow one set but not a mixture, because they are not interchangeable

Standard spoon and cup measurements are level.
1 tsp = 5ml, 1 tbsp = 15ml, 1 cup = 250ml/8fl oz

Australian standard tablespoons are 20ml. Australian readers should use 3 tsp in place of 1 tbsp for measuring small quantities of gelatine, cornflour, salt etc.

Medium eggs should be used unless otherwise stated.

Contents

Introduction

WHETHER FOR HEALTH REASONS or due to ethical concerns, more and more people are rejecting animal products and turning instead to a vegetable-based diet and realizing that there is life after meat, after all. With the plentiful supply of fresh vegetables, fruit, herbs, nuts, grains, pulses (dried beans, peas and lentils) and pasta that is available to us, the possibilities of creating exciting and varied recipes have never been greater.

It is not only vegetarians who can enjoy vegetarian food. The fresh, light and innovative recipes that have come to the forefront of new-style vegetarian cuisine provide a tempting departure from many of the heavier, nonvegetarian dishes. This book gathers together some of the best recipes in the world, all of them packed with fabulous tastes and textures.

You are what you eat, and we are constantly being urged to choose a diet rich in complex carbohydrates found in cereals, grains, fruits and vegetables, which are abundant in vegetarian cooking. If you include dairy products in your diet, restrict your intake by choosing skim or low-fat milk and low-fat yogurts and cheeses. By limiting the use of oils to polyunsaturated types such as olive, sunflower, corn and peanut, you can reduce the level of fat in your diet considerably.

With options for everything from light snacks to special occasion dinners, every recipe here is delicious proof that eating the vegetarian way is not only nutritious, but entertaining and exciting too. Try them and enjoy them.

Fresh Vegetables

Thanks to the range of fresh produce now available, the choice for vegetarians has expanded enormously.

Asparagus
Asparagus spears have an intense, rich flavor—delicious served with melted butter.

Beans
Fava beans, green beans and runner beans can be steamed or lightly boiled in salted water until al dente.

Broccoli
Quick and easy to prepare, broccoli can be eaten raw with dips, or cooked.

Cabbage
There are many varieties of cabbage. Care should be taken not to overcook this vegetable.

Carrots
Carrots have a sweet and fragrant flavor. They are just as delicious eaten raw as they are cooked.

Cauliflower
Cauliflower has a pleasant, fresh flavor.

Celeriac
Celeriac has a hint of sweet celery.

Celery
With its distinctive flavor, celery is an ideal ingredient for soups.

Chiles
Members of the capsicum family, these can be very fiery.

Corn
Eaten on the cob with salt and butter, corn is absolutely delicious.

Cucumber
This has a crisp, refreshing taste.

Eggplant
Eggplant has a smoky flavor when cooked.

Fennel
Aniseed-flavored and delicious.

Garlic
These firm, round bulbs have a very distinctive flavor.

Leeks
A versatile vegetable with a subtle, oniony flavor.

Lettuce
There are many varieties of lettuce available. Most salads include this vegetable.

Mushrooms
Whether cultivated or wild, mushrooms are an essential ingredient for vegetarian cooking.

Onions
Onions come in many different varieties. They can be sautéed, roasted or eaten raw in salads.

Parsnips
A sweet root vegetable with a distinct earthy flavor.

Peas
Sweet tender peas are unbeatable. Make the most of them when they are in season.

Peppers
Green bell peppers have a fresh "raw" flavor, whereas red, yellow and orange peppers are sweeter.

Potatoes
Rich in carbohydrates, potatoes can be baked, boiled, fried, sautéed, mashed or roasted.

Pumpkins/Squashes
These have a fibrous flesh with a mild, slightly sweet flavor.

Rutabagas
These are ideal for adding to soups and casseroles.

Shallots
These small bulbs are ideal for using in sauces.

Spinach
Rich in iron, spinach can be eaten raw in salads or cooked.

Tomatoes
These come in a variety of sizes and form the basis of many vegetarian dishes.

Turnips
Sweet and with a nutty flavor, turnips range from very small to large, mature vegetables.

Zucchini
These are succulent and tender, with a delicate flavor.

Dairy Products

Both local and imported dairy products are now widely available. Most have low-fat versions.

Butter/Margarine
Butter is a natural dairy product made from cream. Margarine is a butter substitute made from vegetable fat.

Buttermilk
This is skim or low-fat milk with an added bacterial culture, to give it a natural tangy flavor.

Cheeses (hard and semi-hard)
Hard cheeses are often essential for cooking, and of course Parmesan is an important ingredient for many dishes.

Cheeses (soft)
Cottage cheese, curd cheese, mascarpone and ricotta are all soft, moist cheeses used in many dishes. Other soft cheeses of culinary note are mozzarella and tangy feta.

Cheeses (blue)
Blue cheeses such as Gorgonzola, Roquefort and Stilton are among some of the most popular cheeses used for sauces, soups and tarts.

Cream
This is available in many forms, including light, heavy, whipping, sour and crème fraîche.

Eggs
Rich in protein, eggs are used in both savory dishes and desserts.

Fromage frais
A creamy, fresh white cheese sold in pots.

Milk
This is available as skim, low-fat and full-fat, as well as condensed, powdered, and evaporated.

Quark
This soft white cheese is made from fermented skim milk.

Yogurt
Yogurt is available in various forms including active culture, low-fat, nonfat and strained plain ("Mediterranean-style").

Beans, Peas and Lentils

Dried beans, peas and lentils (pulses) are a good source of protein. They all need to be washed, and beans and peas should be soaked overnight before cooking. Beans should initially be boiled hard for ten minutes to destroy their toxins. Do not add salt until they are nearly cooked, as this toughens their skins.

Dried Beans and Split Peas

Black-eyed peas
These are the only peas or beans that do not need soaking.

Lima beans
These are ideal for soups or pâtés, as they have a velvety texture.

Chickpeas
These round, beige-colored pulses have a strong, nutty flavor when cooked.

Navy beans
These are small, white and oval. They are ideal for slow cooking, as they absorb the flavor of herbs and spices easily.

Kidney beans
Kidney beans are dark red-brown beans with a strong flavor.

Green and yellow split peas
These tasty and nutritious peas are ideal for hearty soups and are frequently used in Indian cooking.

Lentils

Brown and green lentils
These small lentils have a delicate flavor and retain their shape during cooking. Green lentils have a slightly stronger taste.

Red split lentils
Popular and easy to cook, these lentils are often used in vegetarian dishes.

Tofu

This is an unfermented soybean curd that is available in firm and silken varieties and can be used in all kinds of sweet and savory dishes as an alternative to dairy products.

Spices

The inclusion of spices in a recipe can literally transform a meal.

Cardamom
These pods are often used whole to add flavor to rice dishes.

Chili powder
The dried seeds of chiles are ground to make a very hot and spicy powder.

Cinnamon
Cinnamon is available whole or ground. The sticks are used for flavor and are not eaten.

Cloves
Cloves are used in spice mixtures for both sweet and savory dishes.

Coriander seeds
These are the roasted, dried seeds of the plant.

Cumin
Available as whole dark brown seeds and ground.

Fennel seeds
Small, light green seeds, similar in smell and taste to aniseed.

Fenugreek seeds
Fenugreek is used in many fish dishes and curries.

Ginger
Both fresh and ground ginger have a sharp, refreshing flavor. Fresh ginger root should be peeled before use.

Mustard seeds
Often used with vegetables and pulses, these have a nutty flavor.

Nutmeg
Whole or ground, nutmeg has a sweet, nutty flavor.

Peppercorns
Used in virtually all savory cooking, pepper has the capacity to enhance other flavors.

Saffron
This expensive spice is used for its aroma and color.

Turmeric
Turmeric is a bright yellow powder and is primarily used for its coloring properties.

Herbs

Beautiful fresh herbs from around the world are readily available. This herb checklist highlights both familiar and less well known items.

Basil
Well known for its affinity for tomatoes, basil has a spicy aroma that is a pungent mixture of cinnamon and anise.

Bay leaves
These are one of the oldest herbs used in cooking. When used fresh, they have a deliciously sweet flavor.

Chives
This herb has a very delicate, oniony flavor.

Cilantro (fresh coriander)
An intense, aromatic, sweet and spicy herb. The leaves can be used as a garnish.

Dill
A pungent, slightly sweet-tasting herb with anise overtones.

Marjoram
This is very similar to oregano, though more delicate in flavor.

Mint
A very versatile herb with a distinctive scent, mint is used in both sweet and savory dishes.

Oregano
An aromatic and highly flavored herb, oregano features strongly in Italian cooking.

Parsley
Both flat-leaf and curly varieties have a slightly bitter flavor.

Rosemary
Rosemary, with its dark, needle-like leaves, has an intense flavor and should be used sparingly.

Sage
The aromatic oils in sage impart a distinct and powerful flavor.

Savory
With its peppery flavor, savory makes a good seasoning.

Tarragon
This has a sweet, aniseed flavor.

Thyme
A robust aromatic herb with a warm, earthy flavor.

Dry Goods

Building up a pantry of everyday items such as flours, grains and pasta will ensure that you can produce a speedy meal at short notice.

Barley
With its distinctive flavor and slightly chewy texture, barley is used in soups or as an alternative to rice in risottos.

Buckwheat
Nutty in texture, this tasty alternative to rice is actually a grass.

Bulgur
This whole-wheat grain is steam-dried and cracked before sale, so it only needs a brief soaking before use. Keep it cool and dry in the pantry, and it will last for a few months.

Couscous
Also made from wheat, this grain is a staple in North Africa and is prepared in exactly the same way as bulgur.

Dried fruit
Rich in dietary fiber, vitamins and minerals, dried fruits are delicious in a wide selection of dishes, including muesli and pies. Because of their intense sweetness, they can be used as a healthy alternative to sugar in cooking.

Flours
As well as the usual white refined flour, try experimenting with other types including whole-wheat, buckwheat, soy, rice or rye for a more interesting, nutty flavor in your baking. Cornstarch is often used as a thickening agent for sauces.

Millet
High in protein, millet is used extensively in Southeast Asia and is cooked in the same way as rice.

Nuts and seeds
Nuts and seeds such as almond, cashew, brazil, sunflower, pumpkin and flax are a valuable source of protein, calcium and Omega 3 fatty acids. Bought in bulk for economy, they will keep in the freezer for several months.

Oats
Available as rolled, quick-cooking or steel-cut, this grain is an excellent source of complex carbohydrates, vitamins and minerals.

Pasta
While fresh pasta is generally preferred both for flavor and for speed of cooking, the dried product is a very valuable pantry ingredient. Italian pasta and Asian noodles are both useful.

Quinoa
Another good source of protein, quinoa is a soft grain from South America.

Rice
There are many different types of rice. Basmati is thought to have a superior flavor, fragrance and texture, and a mixture of basmati and wild rice (not a true rice, but the seeds of an aquatic grass) works well.

Sugars
Used sparingly, you can impart a distinctive flavor to your sweet dishes by adding dried sugars such as demerara, raw cane and confectioners' sugar, or liquid varieties including blackstrap molasses, honey and natural maple syrup.

Wheat, barley and rye flakes
These can be used in savory or sweet crumbles and biscuits to provide a variety of tastes and textures.

Bottled and Canned Goods

The pantry should be the backbone of your vegetarian kitchen. Stock it sensibly, and you'll always have the wherewithal to make a tasty, satisfying meal.

Canned beans, peas and lentils
Chickpeas, cannellini beans, green lentils, navy beans and red kidney beans survive the canning process well. Wash in cold running water and drain well before use.

Canned vegetables
Although fresh vegetables are best for most cooking, some canned products are very useful. Artichoke hearts have a mild, sweet flavor and are great for adding to stir-fries, salads, risottos or pizzas. Pimientos are canned sweet red peppers, seeded and peeled. Canned tomatoes are an essential ingredient to have in the pantry. Additional useful items to include are corn and water chestnuts.

Mustard
Whole-grain or Dijon mustards are widely used both in cooking and in salad dressings.

Oils
Peanut or sunflower oils are bland and will not mask or overpower delicate flavors. They are ideal for deep-frying. Fiery chili oil will liven up vegetable stir-fries, while tasty sesame oil will give them a rich, nutty flavor. A good olive oil will suit most purposes, except deep-frying; extra-virgin olive oil, being more expensive, is best kept for salads.

Olives
Green or black olives now come in a variety of marinades. Olive paste is useful for pasta sauces.

Passata
This thick sauce is made from sieved tomatoes. It is mainly used in Italian cooking.

Pesto
This classic Italian sauce combines fresh basil, pine nuts, Parmesan, garlic and olive oil and is useful for pasta or grilled or roasted vegetables.

Soy sauce/Shoyu
Soy sauce is a thin, salty black liquid made from fermented soybeans. Shoyu, or naturally brewed soy sauce, is fermented for far longer and so has fewer additives than soy sauce.

Stocks and flavorings
There are three kinds of vegetable stocks. Granules are ideal for light soups and risottos, bouillon cubes have a stronger flavor suited to hearty soups, while vegetable extracts have a robust taste that is delicious in casseroles.

Sun-dried tomatoes
These deliciously sweet tomatoes, baked in the sun and dried, are sold in bags or in jars, steeped in olive oil.

Tahini paste
Made from ground sesame seeds, this paste is used in Middle Eastern cooking.

Tomato paste
This is a concentrated tomato purée that is sold in cans, jars or tubes. A version made from sun-dried tomatoes is now available.

Vinegars
White or red wine and sherry vinegars are ideal for salad dressings. Balsamic has a very distinctive sweet/sour flavor that can be used in salad dressings or to liven up roasted vegetables and cooked grains.

MURCIA
CONSERVAS
MAILLE.
1747

SOUPS

Wild Mushroom Soup

Wild mushrooms are expensive, but dried porcini have an intense flavor, so only a small quantity is needed.

INGREDIENTS

Serves 4

1 ounce dried porcini mushrooms
2 tablespoons olive oil
1 tablespoon butter
2 leeks, thinly sliced
2 shallots, roughly chopped
1 garlic clove, roughly chopped
8 ounces fresh wild mushrooms
5 cups vegetable stock
½ teaspoon dried thyme
⅔ cup heavy cream
salt and freshly ground black pepper
sprigs of fresh thyme, to garnish

1 Put the dried porcini in a bowl, add 1 cup warm water and let soak for 20–30 minutes. Lift out of the liquid and squeeze over the bowl to remove as much of the soaking liquid as possible. Strain all the liquid and reserve to use later. Finely chop the porcini.

2 Heat the oil and butter in a large saucepan until foaming. Add the sliced leeks, chopped shallots and garlic and cook gently for about 5 minutes, stirring frequently, until softened but not colored.

3 Chop or slice the fresh mushrooms and add to the pan. Stir over medium heat for a few minutes, until they begin to soften. Pour in the stock and bring to a boil. Add the porcini, soaking liquid, dried thyme and salt and pepper. Lower the heat, half-cover the pan and simmer gently for 30 minutes, stirring occasionally.

4 Pour about three-quarters of the soup into a blender or food processor and process until smooth. Return the processed soup to the soup remaining in the pan, stir in the cream and heat through. Check the consistency and add more stock if necessary. Season with salt and pepper. Serve hot, garnished with thyme sprigs.

COOK'S TIP

Porcini are cépes, or boletus mushrooms. Italian cooks would make this soup with a combination of fresh and dried porcini, but if fresh ones are difficult to obtain, you can use other wild mushrooms, such as chanterelles.

Tomato and Fresh Basil Soup

A pungent soup for late summer, when fresh tomatoes are at their most flavorful.

INGREDIENTS

Serves 4–6

1 tablespoon olive oil
2 tablespoons butter
1 medium onion, finely chopped
2 pounds ripe Italian plum tomatoes, roughly chopped
1 garlic clove, roughly chopped
about 3 cups vegetable stock
½ cup dry white wine
2 tablespoons sun-dried tomato paste
2 tablespoons shredded fresh basil
⅔ cup heavy cream
salt and freshly ground black pepper
whole basil leaves, to garnish

1 Heat the oil and butter in a large saucepan until foaming. Add the onion and cook gently for about 5 minutes, stirring, until the onion is softened but not brown.

2 Stir in the chopped tomatoes and garlic, then add the stock, white wine and sun-dried tomato paste, with salt and pepper to taste. Bring to a boil, then lower the heat, half-cover the pan and simmer gently for 20 minutes, stirring occasionally to keep the tomatoes from sticking to the bottom of the pan.

3 Process the soup with the shredded basil in a blender or food processor, then press through a sieve into a clean pan.

4 Add the cream and heat through, stirring. Do not allow the soup to approach the boiling point. Check the consistency and add more stock if necessary, then season with salt and pepper. Pour into heated bowls and garnish with basil. Serve at once.

Cream of Zucchini Soup

The beauty of this soup is its delicate color, rich and creamy texture and subtle taste. If you prefer a more pronounced cheese flavor, use Gorgonzola instead of dolcelatte.

INGREDIENTS

Serves 4–6

2 tablespoons olive oil
1 tablespoon butter
1 medium onion, roughly chopped
2 pounds zucchini, trimmed and sliced
1 teaspoon dried oregano
about 2½ cups vegetable stock
4 ounces dolcelatte cheese, rind removed, diced
1¼ cups light cream
salt and freshly ground black pepper
fresh oregano, extra dolcelatte and cream, to garnish

1 Heat the oil and butter in a large saucepan until foaming. Add the onion and cook gently for about 5 minutes, stirring frequently, until softened but not brown.

COOK'S TIP

To save time, trim off and discard the ends of the zucchini, cut them into thirds, then chop in a food processor fitted with a metal blade.

2 Add the zucchini and oregano with salt and pepper to taste. Cook over medium heat for 10 minutes, stirring frequently. Pour in the stock and bring to a boil, stirring.

3 Lower the heat, half-cover the pan and simmer gently, stirring occasionally, for about 30 minutes. Stir in the diced dolcelatte until melted.

4 Process the soup in a blender or food processor until smooth, then press through a sieve into a clean pan.

5 Add two-thirds of the cream and stir over low heat until hot but not boiling. Add more stock or water if the soup is too thick. Season with salt and pepper. Pour into heated bowls. Swirl in the remaining cream. Serve, garnished with oregano, extra cheese, cream and pepper.

Garlic, Chickpea and Spinach Soup

This delicious, thick and creamy soup is richly flavored and makes a great one-pot meal.

INGREDIENTS

Serves 4

2 tablespoons olive oil
4 garlic cloves, crushed
1 onion, roughly chopped
2 teaspoons ground cumin
2 teaspoons ground coriander
5 cups vegetable stock
12 ounces potatoes, peeled and finely chopped
15-ounce can chickpeas, drained
1 tablespoon cornstarch
⅔ cup heavy cream
2 tablespoons light tahini (sesame seed paste)
7 ounces spinach, shredded
cayenne pepper
salt and freshly ground black pepper

1 Heat the oil in a large saucepan and cook the garlic and onion for 5 minutes, or until they are softened and golden brown.

2 Stir in the cumin and coriander and cook for another minute.

3 Pour in the stock and add the chopped potatoes to the pan. Bring to a boil and simmer for 10 minutes. Add the chickpeas and simmer for 5 minutes more, or until the potatoes and chickpeas are just tender.

4 Blend together the cornstarch, cream, tahini and plenty of seasoning. Stir into the soup with the spinach. Bring to a boil, stirring, and simmer for another 2 minutes. Season with cayenne pepper, salt and black pepper. Serve immediately, sprinkled with a little cayenne pepper.

Classic French Onion Soup

When French onion soup is made slowly and carefully, the onions caramelize to a deep mahogany color. The soup has a superb flavor and is a perfect winter supper dish.

INGREDIENTS

Serves 4

4 large onions
2 tablespoons sunflower or olive oil, or 1 tablespoon of each
2 tablespoons butter
3¾ cups vegetable stock
4 slices French bread
1½–2 ounces Gruyère or Cheddar cheese, grated
salt and freshly ground black pepper

1 Peel and quarter the onions and slice or chop them into ¼-inch pieces. Heat the oil and butter in a deep, medium-size saucepan, so that the onions form a thick layer.

2 Sauté the onions briskly for a few minutes, stirring constantly.

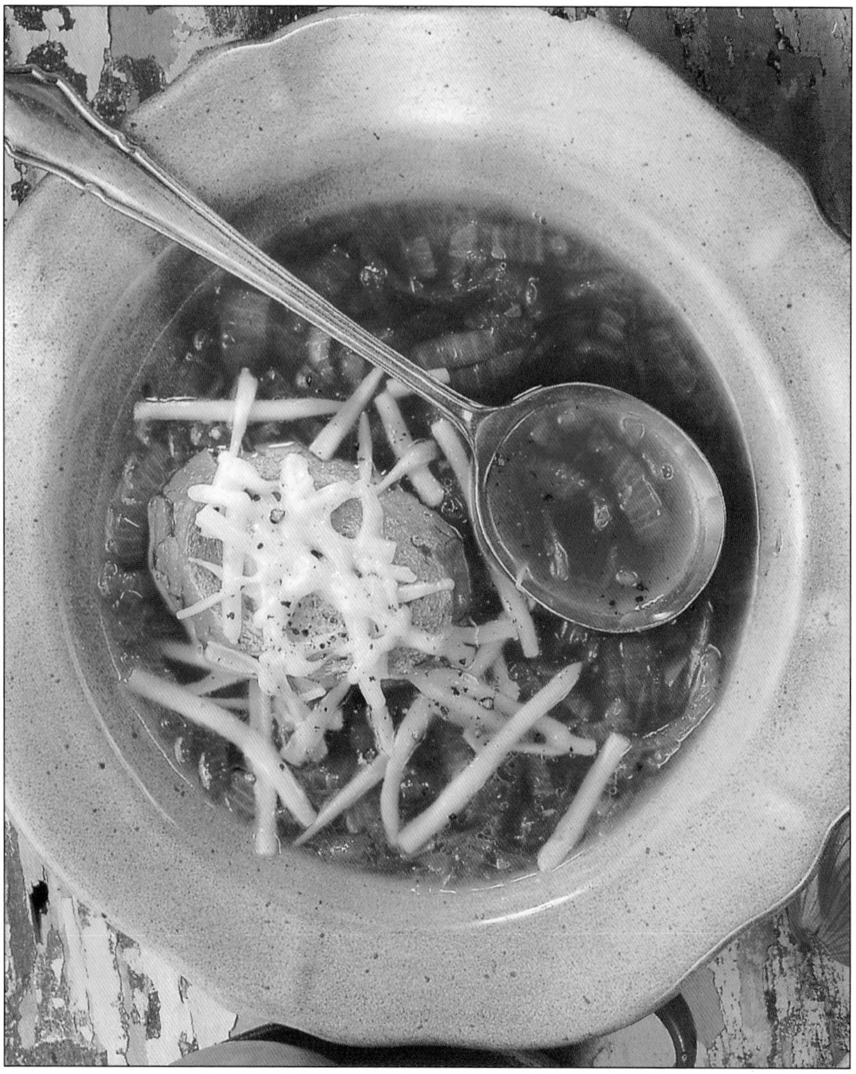

3 Reduce the heat and cook gently for 45–60 minutes. At first the onions need to be stirred only occasionally, but as they begin to color, stir frequently. The color of the onions gradually turns golden and then more rapidly to brown, so take care to stir constantly at this stage so that they do not burn on the bottom.

4 When the onions are a rich mahogany brown, add the vegetable stock and a little seasoning. Simmer, partially covered, for 30 minutes, then season with salt and pepper.

5 Preheat the broiler and toast the French bread. Spoon the soup into four ovenproof serving dishes and place a piece of bread in each. Sprinkle with the cheese and broil for a few minutes, until golden. Season with plenty of freshly ground black pepper.

White Bean Soup

A thick purée of cooked dried beans is at the heart of this substantial country soup from Tuscany. It makes a warming lunch or supper dish.

INGREDIENTS

Serves 6

1½ cups dried cannellini or other white beans
1 bay leaf
5 tablespoons olive oil
1 medium onion, finely chopped
1 carrot, finely chopped
1 celery rib, finely chopped
3 medium tomatoes, peeled and finely chopped
2 cloves garlic, finely chopped
1 teaspoon fresh thyme leaves or ½ teaspoon dried thyme
3 cups boiling water
salt and freshly ground black pepper
olive oil, to serve

1 Pick over the beans carefully, discarding any stones or other particles. Rinse thoroughly in cold water to ensure that they are clean. Soak in a large bowl of cold water overnight. Drain the beans and place them in a large saucepan of water, bring to a boil and cook for 20 minutes. Drain. Return the beans to the pan, cover with cold water and bring to a boil again. Add the bay leaf and cook for 1–2 hours, until the beans are tender. Drain again. Remove the bay leaf.

2 Purée about three-quarters of the beans in a food processor or pass through a food mill, adding a little water if necessary, to create a smooth paste.

3 Heat the oil in a large saucepan. Stir in the onion and cook until it softens. Add the carrot and celery, and cook for 5 minutes more.

4 Stir in the tomatoes, garlic and thyme. Cook for 6–8 minutes more, stirring often.

5 Pour in the boiling water. Stir in the beans and the bean purée. Season with salt and pepper. Simmer for 10–15 minutes. Serve in individual soup bowls, sprinkled with a little olive oil.

COOK'S TIP

Canned cooked beans, such as cannellini or borlotti, may be substituted in this recipe. Simply drain the beans and omit Step 1.

Asparagus Soup

Home-made asparagus soup has a delicate flavor, quite unlike that from a can. This soup is best made with young asparagus, which are tender and blend well. Serve it with wafer-thin slices of bread.

INGREDIENTS

Serves 4

1 pound young asparagus
3 tablespoons butter
6 shallots, sliced
1 tablespoon all-purpose flour
2½ cups vegetable stock or water
1 tablespoon lemon juice
1 cup milk
½ cup light cream
2 teaspoons chopped fresh chervil
salt and freshly ground black pepper

1 Cut 1½ inches off the tops of half the asparagus and set aside for a garnish. Slice the remaining asparagus.

2 Melt 2 tablespoons of the butter in a large saucepan and sauté the sliced shallots for 2–3 minutes, until soft.

3 Add the asparagus and sauté over low heat for 1 minute.

4 Stir in the flour and cook for 1 minute. Stir in the stock or water and lemon juice and season with salt and pepper. Bring to a boil, half-cover the pan, then simmer for 15–20 minutes, until the asparagus is very tender.

5 Cool slightly and then process the soup in a food processor or blender until smooth. Press the puréed asparagus through a sieve into a clean saucepan. Add the milk by pouring and stirring it through the sieve with the asparagus so as to extract the maximum amount of asparagus purée.

6 Melt the remaining butter and sauté the reserved asparagus tips gently for 3–4 minutes, to soften.

7 Heat the soup gently for 3–4 minutes. Stir in the cream and the asparagus tips. Continue to heat gently, then serve sprinkled with chopped fresh chervil.

Fresh Tomato, Lentil and Onion Soup

This delicious, wholesome soup is ideal served with thick slices of whole-wheat bread.

INGREDIENTS

Serves 4–6

2 teaspoons sunflower oil
1 large onion, chopped
2 celery ribs, chopped
¾ cup split red lentils
2 large tomatoes, peeled and roughly chopped
3¾ cups vegetable stock
2 teaspoons dried herbes de Provence
salt and freshly ground black pepper
chopped parsley, to garnish

1 Heat the oil in a large saucepan. Add the onion and celery and cook for 5 minutes, stirring occasionally. Add the lentils and cook for 1 minute.

2 Stir in the tomatoes, stock, dried herbs, salt and pepper. Cover, bring to a boil and simmer for about 20 minutes, stirring occasionally.

3 When the lentils are cooked and tender, set the soup aside to cool slightly.

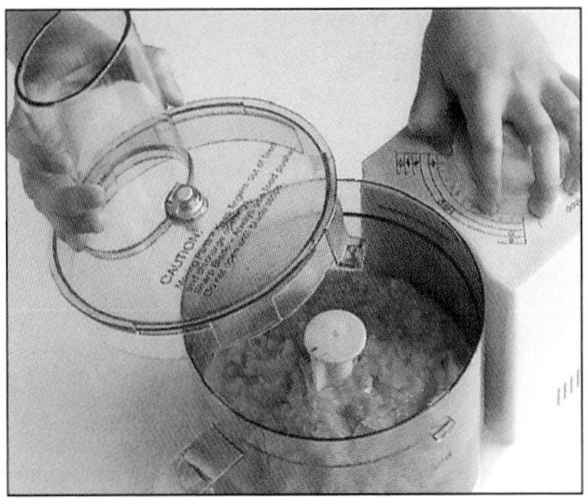

4 Purée in a blender or food processor until smooth. Season with salt and pepper, return to the saucepan and reheat gently until piping hot. Ladle into soup bowls to serve and garnish each with chopped parsley.

Minestrone with Pesto

Minestrone is a thick, mixed vegetable soup using almost any combination of seasonal vegetables. Short cuts of pasta or rice may also be added. This version includes pesto sauce.

INGREDIENTS

Serves 6

3 tablespoons olive oil
1 large onion, finely chopped
1 leek, sliced
2 carrots, finely chopped
1 celery rib, finely chopped
2 cloves garlic, finely chopped
2 potatoes, peeled and cut into small dice
6¼ cups hot vegetable stock or water, or a combination of both
1 bay leaf
1 sprig of fresh thyme, or ¼ teaspoon dried thyme
¾ cup peas, fresh or frozen
2–3 zucchini, finely chopped
3 medium tomatoes, peeled and finely chopped
2 cups cooked or canned beans, such as cannellini
3 tablespoons pesto sauce
salt and freshly ground black pepper
freshly grated Parmesan cheese, to serve

1 Heat the oil in a saucepan. Stir in the onion and leek, and cook for 5–6 minutes. Add the carrots, celery and garlic, and cook over moderate heat for 5 minutes. Add the potatoes and cook for 2–3 minutes more.

2 Pour in the hot stock or water and stir well. Add the herbs and season with salt and pepper. Bring to a boil, reduce the heat and cook for 10–12 minutes.

3 Stir in the peas, if fresh, and the zucchini. Simmer for 5 minutes. Add the frozen peas, if using, and the tomatoes. Cover the pan and simmer for 5–8 minutes.

4 About 10 minutes before serving, uncover the pan and stir in the beans. Simmer for 10 minutes. Stir in the pesto sauce. Simmer for another 5 minutes. Remove from the heat and let stand for a few minutes. Serve with the grated Parmesan cheese.

Pumpkin Soup

This beautifully flavored, golden-colored soup would be perfect for an autumn dinner.

INGREDIENTS

Serves 4

1-lb piece of peeled pumpkin
4 tablespoons butter
1 medium onion, finely chopped
3 cups vegetable stock or water
2 cups milk
pinch of grated nutmeg
1½ ounces spaghetti broken into small pieces
6 tablespoons freshly grated Parmesan cheese
salt and freshly ground black pepper

1 Chop the piece of pumpkin into 1-inch cubes.

2 Heat the butter in a saucepan. Add the onion and cook over moderate heat until it softens, 6–8 minutes. Stir in the pumpkin pieces and cook for 2–3 minutes more.

3 Add the stock or water and cook until the pumpkin is soft, about 15 minutes. Remove from the heat.

4 Process the soup in a blender or food processor. Return it to the pan. Stir in the milk and nutmeg. Season with salt and pepper. Bring the soup back to a boil.

5 Stir the broken spaghetti into the soup. Cook until the pasta is done. Stir in the Parmesan, sprinkle with nutmeg and serve at once.

Split Pea and Zucchini Soup

Rich and satisfying, this tasty and nutritious soup will warm a chilly winter's day.

INGREDIENTS

Serves 4

6 ounces (2 cups) yellow split peas
1 medium onion, finely chopped
1 teaspoon sunflower oil
2 medium zucchini, finely diced
3¾ cups vegetable stock
½ teaspoon ground turmeric
salt and freshly ground black pepper
crusty bread, to serve

1 Place the split peas in a bowl, cover with cold water and let soak for several hours or overnight. Drain, rinse in cold water and drain again.

2 Cook the onion in the oil in a covered pan, shaking occasionally, until soft. Reserve a handful of diced zucchini to use later.

3 Add the remaining zucchini to the pan. Cook for 2–3 minutes. Add the stock and turmeric and bring to a boil. Reduce the heat, cover and simmer for 30–40 minutes. Season.

4 When the soup is almost ready, bring a large saucepan of water to a boil, add the reserved diced zucchini and cook for 1 minute. Drain and add to the soup. Serve hot with warm crusty bread.

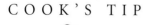

COOK'S TIP

For a quicker alternative, use red split lentils for this soup—they need no presoaking and cook very quickly. Adjust the amount of stock, if necessary.

Carrot and Cilantro Soup

Nearly all root vegetables make excellent soups, as they purée well and have an earthy flavor that complements the sharper flavors of herbs and spices. Carrots are particularly versatile. This simple soup is elegant in both flavor and appearance.

INGREDIENTS

Serves 4–6

1 pound carrots, preferably young and tender
1 tablespoon sunflower oil
3 tablespoons butter
1 onion, chopped
1 celery rib, plus 2–3 pale leafy celery tops
2 small potatoes, peeled
4 cups vegetable stock
2–3 teaspoons ground coriander
1 tablespoon chopped fresh cilantro
1 cup milk
salt and freshly ground black pepper

1 Trim and peel the carrots and cut into chunks. Heat the oil and 2 tablespoons butter in a large flameproof casserole or heavy saucepan and sauté the onion over gentle heat for 3–4 minutes, until slightly softened.

2 Slice the celery and chop the potatoes. Add them to the onion in the pan, cook for a few minutes and then add the carrots. Cook over gentle heat for 3–4 minutes, stirring, and then cover.

3 Reduce the heat even further and sweat for about 10 minutes. Shake the pan or stir occasionally so the vegetables do not stick to the bottom.

4 Add the stock and bring to a boil. Half-cover the pan and simmer for another 8–10 minutes, until the carrots and potatoes are tender.

5 Remove 6–8 tiny celery leaves for garnish and finely chop the remaining celery tops (about 1 tablespoon once chopped). Melt the remaining butter in a small saucepan and sauté the ground coriander for about 1 minute, stirring constantly.

6 Reduce the heat, add the chopped celery tops and cilantro and sauté for about 1 minute. Set aside.

7 Process the soup in a food processor or blender and pour into a clean saucepan. Stir in the milk and the cilantro mixture. Season, heat gently, taste and adjust seasoning. Serve garnished with the reserved celery leaves.

COOK'S TIP

For a more piquant flavor, add a little lemon juice just before serving.

Curried Celery Soup

An unusual combination of flavors, this soup is excellent served with warm whole-wheat rolls or whole-wheat pita bread.

INGREDIENTS

Serves 4–6

2 teaspoons olive oil
1 onion, chopped
1 leek, washed and sliced
1½ pounds celery, chopped
1 tablespoon medium or hot curry powder
8 ounces potatoes, washed and diced
3¾ cups vegetable stock
1 bouquet garni
2 tablespoons chopped fresh mixed herbs
salt
celery seeds and leaves, to garnish

1 Heat the oil in a large saucepan. Add the onion, leek and celery, cover and cook gently for about 10 minutes, stirring occasionally.

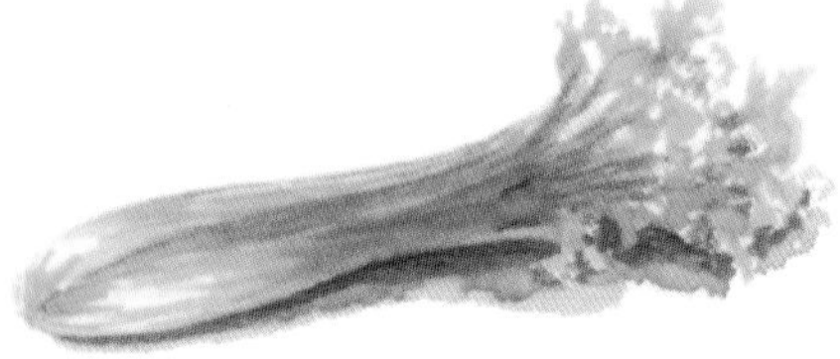

2 Add the curry powder and cook for 2 minutes more, stirring occasionally.

3 Add the potatoes, stock and bouquet garni, cover and bring to a boil. Simmer for 20 minutes, until the vegetables are tender.

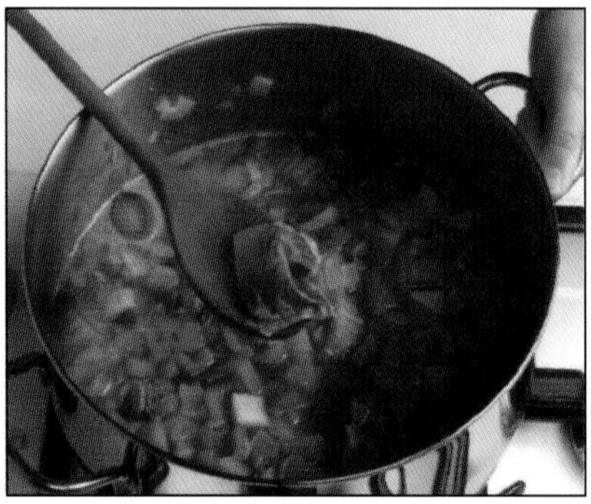

4 Remove and discard the bouquet garni and set the soup aside to cool slightly.

5 Purée in a blender or food processor until smooth.

6 Add the mixed herbs, season to taste and process briefly. Return to the saucepan and reheat gently until piping hot. Ladle into soup bowls and garnish each with a sprinkling of celery seeds and some celery leaves.

VARIATION

For a tasty change, use celeriac and sweet potatoes in place of the celery and standard potatoes.

Fresh Pea Soup

This soup is known in France as Potage Saint-Germain, a name that comes from a suburb of Paris where peas used to be cultivated in market gardens. If fresh peas are not available, use frozen peas, but thaw and rinse them before use.

INGREDIENTS

Serves 2–3

2 tablespoons butter

2 or 3 shallots, finely chopped

3 cups shelled fresh peas (from about 3 pounds garden peas) or thawed frozen peas

3–4 tablespoons whipping cream (optional)

salt and freshly ground black pepper

croutons, to garnish

1 Melt the butter in a heavy saucepan or flameproof casserole. Add the shallots and cook for about 3 minutes, stirring occasionally.

2 Add 2 cups water and the peas, and season with salt and pepper.

3 Cover and simmer for 12 minutes for young or frozen peas and up to 18 minutes for large or older peas, stirring occasionally.

4 When the peas are tender, ladle them into a food processor or blender with a little of the cooking liquid and process until smooth.

5 Strain the soup into the saucepan or casserole, stir in the cream, if using, and heat through without boiling. Season with salt and pepper and serve hot, garnished with croutons.

Pea, Leek and Broccoli Soup

A delicious and nutritious soup, ideal for warming those chilly winter evenings.

INGREDIENTS

Serves 4–6

1 onion, chopped
8 ounces leeks (trimmed weight), sliced (about 2 cups)
8 ounces unpeeled potatoes, diced
$3\frac{3}{4}$ cups vegetable stock
1 bay leaf
8 ounces broccoli florets
$1\frac{1}{2}$ cups frozen peas
2–3 tablespoons chopped fresh parsley
salt and freshly ground black pepper
parsley leaves, to garnish

1 Put the onion, leeks, potatoes, stock and bay leaf in a large saucepan and mix together. Cover, bring to a boil and simmer for 10 minutes, stirring.

2 Add the broccoli and peas, cover, return to a boil and simmer for another 10 minutes, stirring occasionally.

3 Set aside to cool slightly and remove and discard the bay leaf. Purée in a blender or food processor until smooth.

4 Add the parsley, season with salt and pepper and process briefly. Return to the saucepan and reheat gently until piping hot. Ladle into soup bowls and garnish with parsley leaves.

Gazpacho

This cold soup is popular all over Spain, where there are hundreds of variations. It uses tomatoes, tomato juice, green pepper and garlic, and is served with a selection of garnishes.

INGREDIENTS

Serves 4

3–3½ pounds ripe tomatoes
1 green bell pepper, seeded and roughly chopped
2 garlic cloves, crushed
2 slices white bread, crusts removed
4 tablespoons olive oil
4 tablespoons tarragon wine vinegar
⅔ cup tomato juice
good pinch of sugar
salt and freshly ground black pepper
ice cubes, to serve

For the garnishes

2 tablespoons sunflower oil
2–3 slices white bread, diced
1 small cucumber, peeled and finely diced
1 small onion, finely chopped
1 red bell pepper, seeded and finely diced
1 green bell pepper, seeded and finely diced
2 hard-boiled eggs, chopped

1 Peel and quarter the tomatoes, then remove the cores.

2 Place the green pepper in a food processor and process for a few seconds. Add the tomatoes, garlic, bread, olive oil and vinegar and process again. Add the tomato juice, sugar, salt and pepper and process.

3 The mixture should be thick but not too heavy. Continue processing until it is the right consistency. Press the liquid through a sieve into a bowl and chill for at least 2 hours but no more than 12 hours, or the texture will deteriorate.

4 To prepare the bread cubes to use as a garnish, heat the oil in a frying pan and sauté them over moderate heat for 4–5 minutes, until golden brown. Drain well on paper towels.

5 Place each garnish in a separate small dish, or alternatively arrange them in rows on a large plate.

6 Just before serving, stir a few ice cubes into the soup and then spoon into serving bowls. Serve with the garnishes.

Cold Leek and Potato Soup

Serve this flavorful soup with a dollop of crème fraîche or sour cream to add richness to the broth. Sprinkle with a few snipped fresh chives.

INGREDIENTS

Serves 6–8

1 pound potatoes, peeled and cubed
6¼ cups vegetable stock
4 medium leeks, trimmed
⅔ cup crème fraîche or
sour cream
salt and freshly ground black pepper
3 tablespoons snipped fresh chives,
to garnish

1 Put the potatoes and stock in a saucepan or flameproof casserole and bring to a boil. Reduce the heat and simmer for 15–20 minutes.

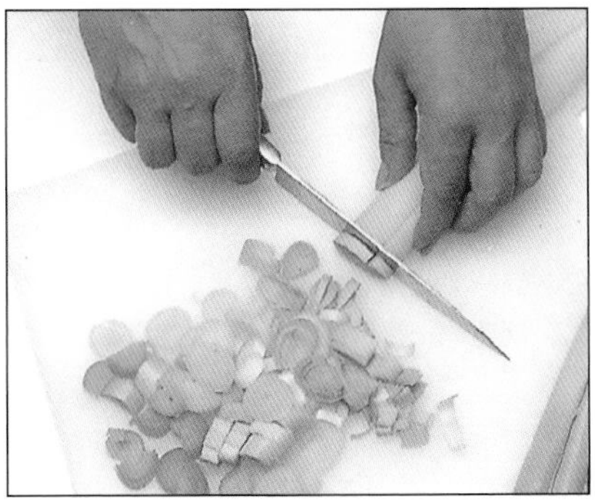

2 Make a slit along the length of each leek and rinse well under cold running water. Slice thinly.

3 When the potatoes are barely tender, stir in the leeks. Season with salt and pepper and simmer for 10–15 minutes, until the vegetables are soft, stirring occasionally. If the soup appears too thick, thin it with a little more of the stock or water.

4 Purée the soup in a blender or food processor, in batches if necessary. If you would prefer a very smooth soup, pass it through a food mill or press through a coarse sieve. Stir in most of the cream, cool and then chill. To serve, ladle into chilled bowls and garnish with a swirl of cream and some snipped chives.

VARIATION

To make a low-fat soup, use low-fat fromage frais instead of crème fraîche or sour cream, or simply thin the soup with a little skim milk.

APPETIZERS

Guacamole

This is quite a fiery version, although nowhere near as hot as you would be served in Mexico!

INGREDIENTS

Serves 4

2 ripe avocados, peeled and pitted
2 tomatoes, peeled, seeded and finely chopped
6 scallions, finely chopped
1–2 fresh chiles, seeded and finely chopped
2 tablespoons fresh lime or lemon juice
1 tablespoon chopped cilantro
salt and freshly ground black pepper
cilantro sprigs, to garnish

1 Put the avocado halves in a large bowl and mash them roughly with a large fork.

2 Add the remaining ingredients. Mix well and season with salt and pepper. Serve garnished with cilantro sprigs.

Lima Bean, Watercress and Herb Dip

This is a refreshing dip that is especially good served with fresh vegetable crudités and breadsticks.

INGREDIENTS

Serves 4–6

1 cup cottage cheese
14-ounce can lima beans, rinsed and drained
1 bunch scallions, chopped
2 ounces watercress, chopped
¼ cup mayonnaise
3 tablespoons chopped fresh mixed herbs
salt and freshly ground black pepper
watercress sprigs, to garnish
vegetable crudités and breadsticks, to serve

1 Put the cottage cheese, lima beans, scallions, watercress, mayonnaise and herbs in a blender or food processor and blend until fairly smooth.

2 Season with salt and pepper and spoon the mixture into a dish.

3 Cover and chill for several hours before serving.

4 Transfer to a serving dish (or individual dishes) and garnish with watercress sprigs. Serve with vegetable crudités and breadsticks.

COOK'S TIP

Try using other canned beans such as cannellini beans or chickpeas in place of the lima beans.

Saffron Dip

Serve this mild dip with fresh vegetable crudités—it is particularly good with florets of cauliflower.

INGREDIENTS

Serves 4

small pinch of saffron strands
7 ounces fromage frais
10 fresh chives
10 fresh basil leaves
salt and freshly ground black pepper
vegetable crudités, to serve

1 Pour 1 tablespoon boiling water into a small heatproof bowl and add the saffron strands. Let infuse for 3–4 minutes, stirring occasionally.

2 Beat the fromage frais until smooth, then stir in the infused saffron liquid.

3 Use a pair of scissors to snip the chives into the dip. Tear the basil leaves into small pieces and stir them in.

4 Season with salt and pepper. Serve immediately with vegetable crudités.

VARIATION

Leave out the saffron and add a squeeze of lemon or lime juice instead. Alternatively, replace the saffron strands with ground saffron powder.

Spiced Carrot Dip

This is a delicious dip with a sweet and spicy flavor. Serve wheat crackers or tortilla chips as accompaniments for dipping.

INGREDIENTS

Serves 4

1 onion
3 carrots, plus extra to garnish
grated zest and juice of 2 oranges
1 tablespoon hot curry paste
⅔ cup plain yogurt
handful of fresh basil leaves
1–2 tablespoons fresh lemon juice, to taste
red Tabasco sauce, to taste
salt and freshly ground black pepper

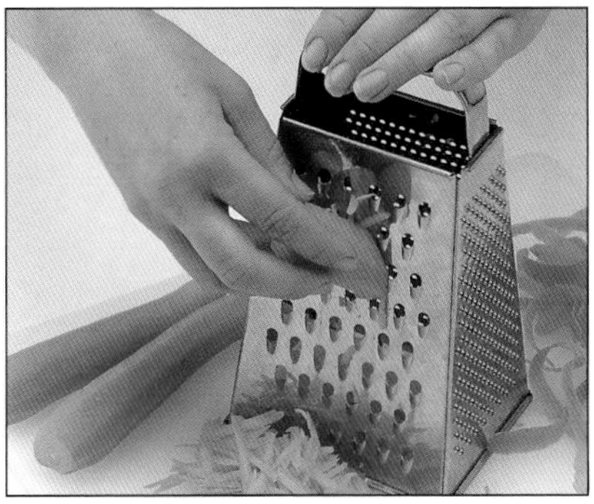

1 Finely chop the onion. Peel and grate the carrots. Place the onion, carrots, orange zest and juice and curry paste in a small saucepan. Bring to a boil, cover and simmer gently for 10 minutes, until tender.

2 Process the mixture in a blender or food processor until smooth. Let cool completely.

3 Stir in the yogurt, then tear the basil leaves roughly into small pieces and stir them into the carrot mixture.

4 Add the lemon juice and Tabasco and season with salt and pepper. Serve within a few hours at room temperature. Garnish with grated carrot.

Eggplant Dip with Crisp Bread

This delectable Middle Eastern dish is flavored with tahini (sesame seed paste), which gives it a subtle flavor.

INGREDIENTS

Serves 6

2 small eggplants
1 garlic clove, crushed
4 tablespoons tahini
¼ cup ground almonds
juice of ½ lemon
½ teaspoon ground cumin
2 tablespoons fresh mint leaves
2 tablespoons olive oil
salt and freshly ground black pepper

Lebanese flatbread
4 pita breads
3 tablespoons toasted sesame seeds
3 tablespoons fresh thyme leaves, chopped
3 tablespoons poppy seeds
⅔ cup olive oil

1 Start by making the Lebanese flatbread. Split the pita breads through the middle and carefully open them out. Mix the sesame seeds, chopped thyme and poppy seeds in a mortar. Crush them lightly with a pestle to release the flavor.

2 Stir in the olive oil. Spread the mixture lightly over the cut sides of the pita bread. Broil until golden brown and crisp. When completely cool, break into pieces and set aside.

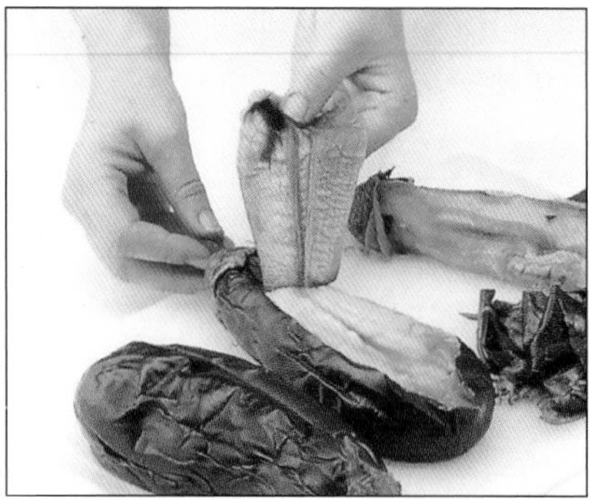

3 Broil the eggplant, turning them frequently, until the skin is blackened and blistered. Remove the skin, chop the flesh roughly and let drain in a colander. Wait for 30 minutes, then squeeze out as much liquid from the eggplant as possible.

4 Place the eggplant flesh in a blender or food processor. Add the garlic, tahini, almonds, lemon juice and cumin. Season, then process to a smooth paste. Chop half the mint and stir in.

5 Spoon into a bowl, sprinkle the remaining mint leaves on top and drizzle with olive oil. Serve with the Lebanese flatbread.

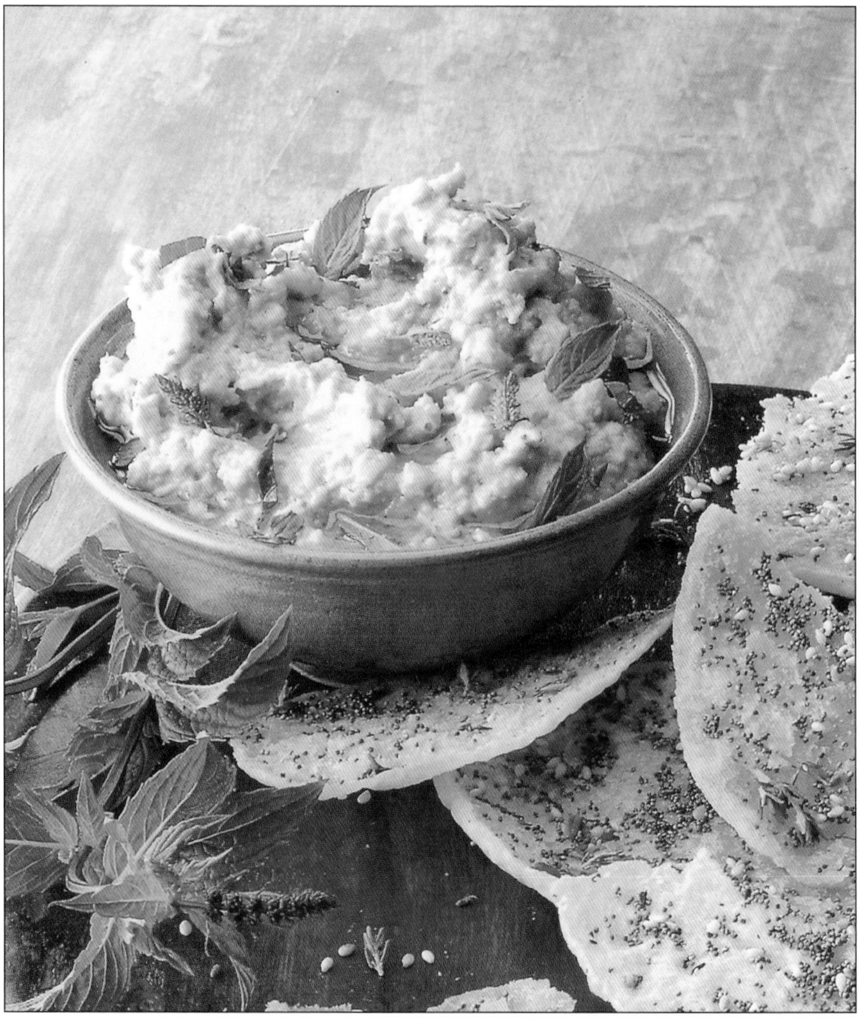

Chickpea Falafel with Cilantro Dip

Little balls of spicy chickpea purée, deep-fried until crisp, are served with a zesty cilantro-flavored mayonnaise.

INGREDIENTS

Serves 4

14-ounce can chickpeas, drained
6 scallions, finely chopped
1 egg
½ teaspoon ground turmeric
1 garlic clove, crushed
1 teaspoon ground cumin
4 tablespoons chopped cilantro
oil for deep-frying
1 small fresh red chile, seeded and finely chopped
3 tablespoons mayonnaise
salt and freshly ground black pepper
sprig of cilantro, to garnish

1 Put the chickpeas in a food processor or blender. Add the scallions and process to a smooth purée. Add the egg, ground turmeric, garlic, cumin and about 1 tablespoon of the chopped cilantro. Process briefly to mix, then season with salt and pepper.

2 Working with clean, wet hands, shape the chickpea mixture into about 16 small balls.

3 Heat the oil for deep-frying to 350°F, or until a cube of bread added to the oil browns in 30–45 seconds. Deep-fry the falafel in batches for 2–3 minutes, or until golden. Drain the falafel on paper towels. Place in a serving bowl and keep warm.

4 Stir the remaining chopped cilantro and the chile into the mayonnaise. Garnish with the cilantro sprig and serve alongside the falafel.

Hummus with Panfried Zucchini

Panfried zucchini are perfect for dipping into homemade hummus, served with pita bread and olives.

INGREDIENTS

Serves 4

8-ounce can chickpeas
2 garlic cloves, coarsely crushed
6 tablespoons lemon juice
4 tablespoons tahini (sesame seed paste)
5 tablespoons olive oil, plus extra to serve
1 teaspoon ground cumin
1 pound small zucchini
salt and freshly ground black pepper
paprika to garnish
pita bread and black olives, to serve

1 Drain the chickpeas, reserving the liquid from the can, and put them in a blender or food processor. Blend to a smooth paste, adding a small amount of the reserved liquid, if necessary.

2 Mix the garlic, lemon juice and tahini together and add to the blender or food processor. Process until smooth. With the machine running, gradually add 3 tablespoons of the olive oil through the feeder tube or lid.

3 Add the cumin. Season with salt and pepper. Process to mix. Scrape the hummus into a bowl. Cover and chill until required.

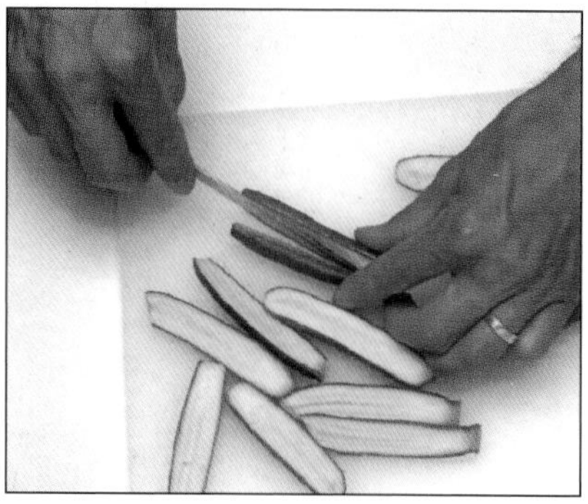

4 Remove the ends from the zucchini. Slice the zucchini lengthwise into even-size pieces.

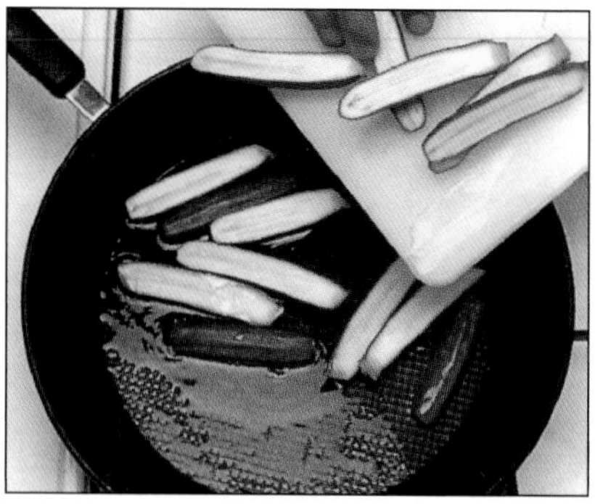

5 Heat the remaining oil in a large frying pan. Season the zucchini with salt and pepper and cook them for 2–3 minutes on each side, until just tender.

6 Divide the zucchini among four individual plates. Spoon a portion of hummus onto each plate and sprinkle with paprika. Add two or three pieces of sliced pita bread and serve with olives.

VARIATION

For a stronger nutty flavor, substitute smooth peanut butter for the tahini paste. This is also delicious served with panfried or broiled eggplant or red pepper slices.

Marinated Vegetable Antipasto

This colorful selection of fresh vegetables and herbs makes a great appetizer when served with fresh crusty bread.

INGREDIENTS

Serves 4

For the peppers

3 red bell peppers
3 yellow bell peppers
4 garlic cloves, sliced
handful of fresh basil
½ cup olive oil
salt and freshly ground black pepper

For the mushrooms

1 pound portobello mushrooms, thickly sliced
¼ cup olive oil
1 large garlic clove, crushed
1 tablespoon chopped fresh rosemary
1 cup dry white wine
fresh rosemary sprigs, to garnish

For the olives

1 dried red chile, crushed
grated zest of 1 lemon
½ cup olive oil
8 ounces (1⅓ cups) Italian black olives
2 tablespoons chopped fresh flat-leaf parsley
basil leaves, to garnish
1 lemon wedge, to serve

1 Place the peppers under a hot broiler. Cook until they are black and blistered all over. Remove from the heat and place in a large plastic bag to cool.

2 When the peppers are cool, remove their skins, halve the flesh and remove the seeds. Cut into strips lengthwise and place them in a bowl with the sliced garlic and basil leaves. Season, then cover with oil and marinate for 3–4 hours, tossing occasionally. Garnish with basil leaves.

3 Place the mushrooms in a bowl. Heat the oil in a pan and add the garlic, rosemary and wine. Bring to a boil, then simmer for 3 minutes. Season. Pour over the mushrooms.

4 Mix well and let cool, stirring occasionally. Cover and marinate overnight. Serve at room temperature, garnished with rosemary sprigs.

5 Place the chile and lemon zest in a small pan with the oil. Heat gently for about 3 minutes. Add the olives and heat for 1 minute more. Pour the olive mixture into a bowl and let cool. Marinate overnight. Before serving, sprinkle with parsley and garnish with basil leaves. Serve with the lemon wedge.

Spicy Potato Wedges with Chili Dip

The spicy crust on these potato wedges makes them irresistible, especially when served with a zesty chili dip.

INGREDIENTS

Serves 2

2 baking potatoes, about 8 ounces each
2 tablespoons olive oil
2 garlic cloves, crushed
1 teaspoon ground allspice
1 teaspoon ground coriander
1 tablespoon paprika
salt and freshly ground black pepper

For the dip

1 tablespoon olive oil
1 small onion, finely chopped
1 garlic clove, crushed
7-ounce can chopped tomatoes
1 fresh red chile, seeded and finely chopped
1 tablespoon balsamic vinegar
1 tablespoon chopped cilantro, plus extra to garnish

1 Preheat the oven to 400°F. Wash the potatoes. Cut them in half and then into 8 wedges.

2 Place the potato wedges in a saucepan of cold water. Bring to a boil, then lower the heat and simmer gently for 10 minutes, or until the potatoes have softened slightly. Drain well and pat dry on paper towels.

3 Mix the oil, garlic, allspice, coriander and paprika in a roasting pan. Season with salt and pepper. Add the potatoes and shake to coat thoroughly. Roast for 20 minutes, turning occasionally.

4 Meanwhile, make the chile dip. Heat the oil in a saucepan, add the onion and garlic and cook for 5–10 minutes, until soft and golden. Add the tomatoes with their juice and stir in the chile and vinegar.

5 Cook gently for 10 minutes, until the mixture has reduced and thickened. Season with salt and pepper. Stir in the cilantro and serve hot, with the potato wedges. Season with salt and freshly ground black pepper and garnish with cilantro.

Crisp Spring Rolls with Sweet Chili Dip

Dainty miniature spring rolls make delicious appetizers or perfect party finger food.

INGREDIENTS

Makes 20–24

1 ounce rice vermicelli noodles
peanut oil
1 teaspoon finely grated fresh ginger root
2 scallions, finely shredded
2 ounces carrot, finely shredded
2 ounces snow peas, shredded
1 ounce young spinach leaves
2 ounces fresh bean sprouts
1 tablespoon fresh mint, finely chopped
1 tablespoon finely chopped cilantro
2 tablespoons light soy sauce
20–24 spring roll wrappers, each 5 inches square
1 egg white, lightly beaten

For the dipping sauce

¼ cup sugar
¼ cup rice vinegar
2 fresh red chiles, seeded and finely chopped

1 First make the dipping sauce. Place the sugar and vinegar in a small saucepan with 2 tablespoons water. Heat gently, stirring until the sugar dissolves, then boil rapidly until it forms a light syrup. Stir in the chiles and let cool thoroughly.

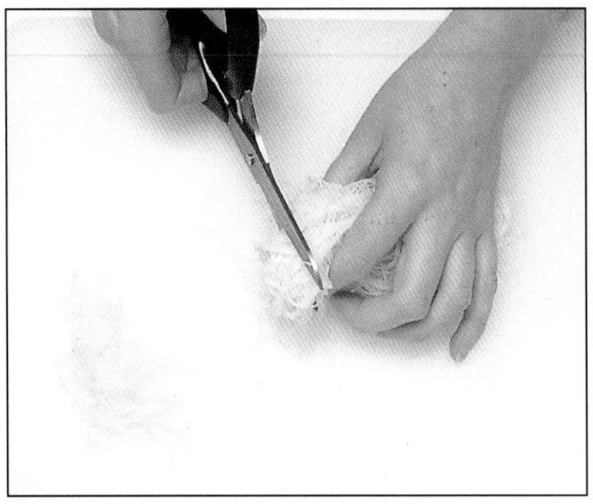

2 Soak the noodles according to the package instructions. Rinse and drain well. Using scissors, snip the noodles into short lengths.

3 Heat a wok until hot. Add 1 tablespoon oil. Add the ginger and scallions and stir-fry for 15 seconds. Add the carrot and snow peas and stir-fry for 2–3 minutes. Add the spinach, bean sprouts, mint, cilantro, soy sauce and noodles and stir-fry for another minute. Set aside to cool.

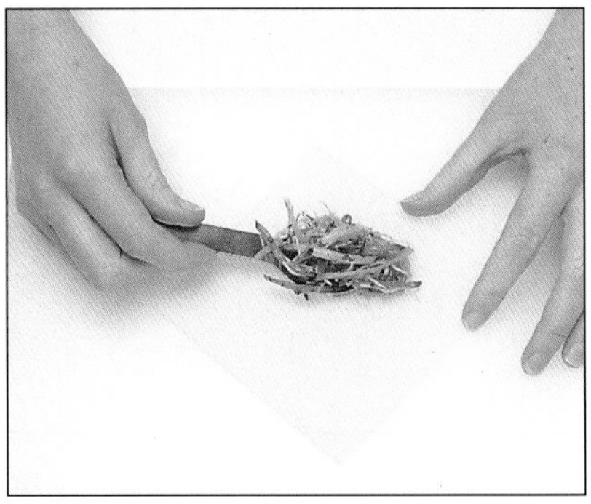

4 Place a spring roll wrapper on the work surface. Put a spoonful of filling in the middle. Fold to encase the filling.

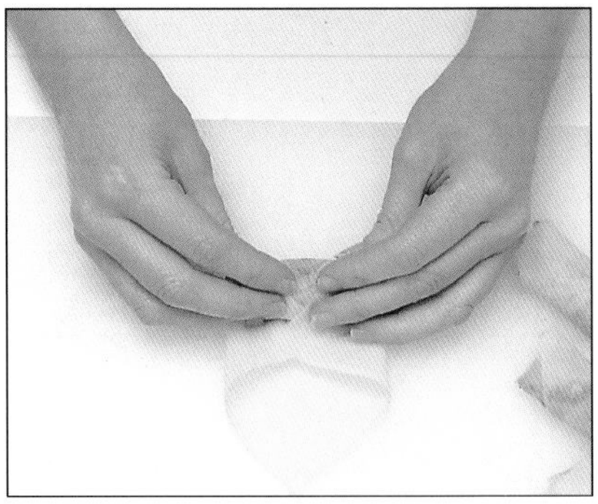

5 Fold in each side, then roll up tightly. Brush the end with beaten egg white to seal. Repeat until all the filling has been used.

6 Half-fill a wok with oil and heat to 350°F. Deep-fry the spring rolls in batches for 3–4 minutes, until golden and crisp. Drain on paper towels. Serve hot, with the sweet chile dipping sauce.

COOK'S TIP

You can cook the spring rolls 2–3 hours in advance. Then all you have to do is reheat them on a foil-lined baking sheet at 400°F for about 10 minutes, until they are ready to eat.

Potted Stilton with Herbs and Melba Toast

This appetizer is a great time-saver, as the potted Stilton can be made the day before, and the Melba toast will keep in an airtight container for up to two days.

INGREDIENTS

Serves 8

8 ounces (1 cup) Stilton or other blue cheese
4 ounces (½ cup) cream cheese
1 tablespoon port
1 tablespoon chopped fresh parsley
1 tablespoon snipped fresh chives, plus extra to garnish
½ cup finely chopped walnuts
salt and freshly ground black pepper

For the Melba toast

12 thin slices of white bread

1 Put the Stilton or other blue cheese, cream cheese and port in a blender or food processor and process until smooth.

2 Stir in the remaining ingredients and then season with salt and pepper.

3 Spoon into individual ramekins and level the tops. Cover with plastic wrap and chill until firm. Sprinkle with snipped chives just before serving.

4 To make the Melba toast, preheat the oven to 350°F. Toast the bread on both sides.

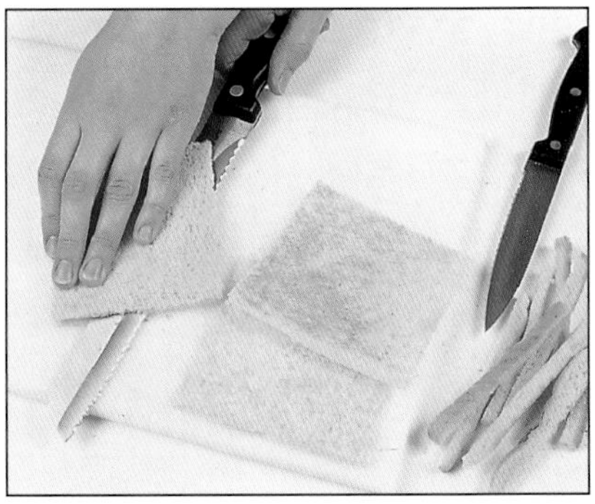

5 While the toast is still hot, cut off the crusts and cut each slice horizontally in two. While the bread is still warm, place it in a single layer on baking sheets and bake for 10–15 minutes, until golden brown and crisp. Continue with the remaining slices in the same way. Serve warm with the potted Stilton.

Mushroom and Bean Pâté

A light and tasty pâté, delicious served on whole-wheat bread or toast.

INGREDIENTS

Serves 12

1 pound mushrooms, sliced
1 onion, chopped
2 garlic cloves, crushed
1 red bell pepper, seeded and diced
2 tablespoons vegetable stock
2 tablespoons dry white wine
14-ounce can red kidney beans, rinsed and drained
1 egg, beaten
1 cup fresh whole-wheat bread crumbs
1 tablespoon chopped fresh thyme
1 tablespoon chopped fresh rosemary
salt and freshly ground black pepper
lettuce and tomatoes, to garnish

1 Preheat the oven to 350°F. Lightly grease and line a nonstick 9x5x3-inch (8-cup) loaf pan. Put the mushrooms, onion, garlic, pepper, stock and wine in a saucepan. Cover and cook for about 10 minutes, stirring occasionally.

2 Set aside to cool slightly, then purée the mixture with the kidney beans in a blender or food processor until smooth.

3 Transfer the mixture to a bowl, add the egg, bread crumbs and herbs and mix thoroughly. Season with salt and pepper.

4 Spoon the mixture into the prepared pan and level the surface. Bake for 45–60 minutes, until lightly set and browned on top. Place on a wire rack and allow the pâté to cool completely in the pan. Once cool, cover and refrigerate for several hours. Turn out of the pan and serve in slices, garnished with lettuce and tomato.

Garlic Mushrooms with a Parsley Crust

These garlic mushrooms are perfect for dinner parties, or you could serve them in larger portions as a light supper dish with a green salad.

INGREDIENTS

Serves 4

12 ounces large mushrooms, stems removed
3 garlic cloves, crushed
12 tablespoons (1½ sticks) butter, softened
1 cup fresh white bread crumbs
1 cup chopped fresh parsley
1 egg, beaten
salt and cayenne pepper
8 cherry tomatoes, to garnish

1 Preheat the oven to 375°F. Arrange the mushrooms cup side up on a baking sheet. Mix together the garlic and butter in a small bowl and divide 8 tablespoons of the butter among the mushrooms.

2 Heat the remaining butter in a frying pan and lightly sauté the bread crumbs until golden brown. Place the chopped parsley in a bowl, add the bread crumbs, season with salt and cayenne pepper and mix well.

3 Stir in the egg and use the mixture to fill the mushroom caps. Bake for 10–15 minutes, until the topping has browned and the mushrooms have softened. Garnish with quartered cherry tomatoes.

COOK'S TIP

If you are planning ahead, stuffed mushrooms can be prepared up to 12 hours in advance and kept in the refrigerator before baking.

Asparagus Rolls with Herb Butter Sauce

For a taste sensation, try tender asparagus spears wrapped in crisp phyllo pastry. The buttery herb sauce makes the perfect accompaniment.

INGREDIENTS

Serves 2

4 sheets of phyllo pastry
4 tablespoons butter, melted
16 young asparagus spears, trimmed

For the sauce

2 shallots, finely chopped
1 bay leaf
⅔ cup dry white wine
12 tablespoons (1½ sticks) butter, softened
1 tablespoon chopped fresh herbs
salt and freshly ground black pepper
chopped chives, to garnish

1 Preheat the oven to 400°F. Cut the phyllo sheets in half. Brush a half sheet with melted butter. Fold one corner of the sheet down to the bottom edge to give a wedge shape.

2 Lay 4 asparagus spears on top at the longest edge, and roll up toward the shortest edge. Using the remaining phyllo and asparagus spears, make three more rolls in the same way.

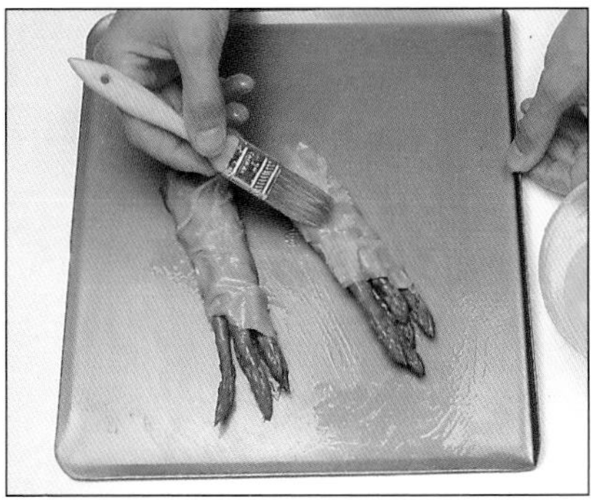

3 Lay the rolls on a greased baking sheet. Brush with the remaining melted butter. Bake for 8 minutes, until golden brown.

4 Meanwhile, put the shallots, bay leaf and wine in a pan. Cover and cook over high heat until the wine is reduced to 3–4 tablespoons.

5 Strain the wine mixture into a bowl. Whisk in the butter a little at a time until the sauce is smooth and glossy.

6 Stir in the herbs and add salt and pepper to taste. Return to the pan and keep the sauce warm. Serve the rolls on individual plates with a salad garnish, if desired. Serve the sauce separately, sprinkled with chopped chives.

Fried Mozzarella

These crispy cheese slices make an unusual and tasty appetizer. They must be cooked just before serving.

INGREDIENTS

Serves 2–3

12 ounces mozzarella cheese
oil for deep-frying
2 eggs
flour seasoned with salt and freshly ground black pepper
plain dry bread crumbs
flat-leaf parsley, to garnish

1 Cut the mozzarella into slices about ½ inch thick. Gently pat off any excess moisture with paper towels.

2 Heat the oil to 360°F, or until a small piece of bread sizzles as soon as it is dropped in. While the oil is heating, beat the eggs in a shallow bowl. Spread some seasoned flour on one plate and some bread crumbs on another.

3 Press the cheese slices into the flour, coating them evenly with a thin layer of flour. Shake off any excess. Dip them into the egg, then into the bread crumbs. Dip them once more into the egg, then again into the bread crumbs.

4 Fry immediately in the hot oil until golden brown. (You may have to do this in two batches, but do not let the breaded cheese wait for too long, or the bread crumb coating will separate from the cheese while it is being fried.) Drain on paper towels and serve hot, garnished with parsley.

Greek Cheese and Potato Patties

Delicious little fried morsels of potato and feta cheese, flavored with dill and lemon juice.

INGREDIENTS

Serves 4

1¼ pounds potatoes
4 ounces feta cheese
4 scallions, chopped
3 tablespoons chopped fresh dill
1 tablespoon lemon juice
1 egg, beaten
flour for dredging
3 tablespoons olive oil
salt and freshly ground black pepper

1 Boil the potatoes in their skins in lightly salted water until soft. Drain, then peel while still warm. Place in a bowl and mash. Crumble the feta cheese into the potatoes and add the scallions, dill, lemon juice and egg. Season with salt and pepper (the cheese is salty, so taste before you add salt). Stir well.

2 Cover the mixture and chill until firm. Divide the mixture into walnut-size balls, then flatten them slightly. Dredge in the flour. Heat the oil in a frying pan and fry the patties until golden brown on each side. Drain on paper towels and serve at once.

Cheese-Stuffed Pears

These pears, with their scrumptious creamy topping, make a sublime dish when served with a simple salad.

INGREDIENTS

Serves 4

- ¼ cup ricotta cheese
- ¼ cup dolcelatte (Gorgonzola dolce) cheese
- 1 tablespoon honey
- ½ celery rib, finely sliced
- 8 green olives, pitted and roughly chopped
- 4 dates, pitted and cut into thin strips
- pinch of paprika
- 4 ripe pears
- ⅔ cup apple juice

1 Preheat the oven to 400°F. Place the ricotta in a bowl and crumble in the dolcelatte. Add the rest of the ingredients except for the pears and apple juice and mix well.

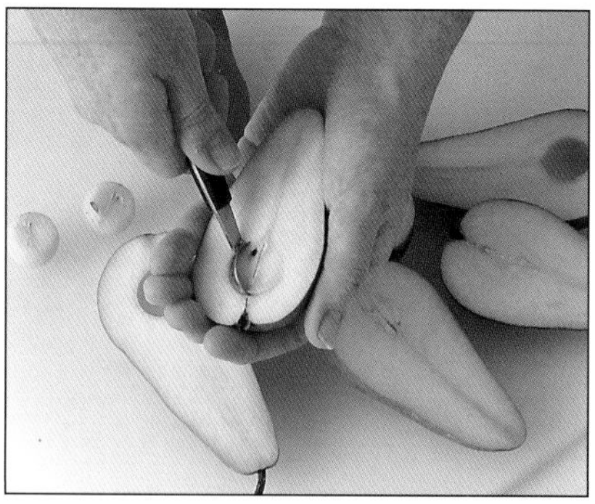

2 Halve the pears lengthwise and use a melon baller to remove the cores. Place in an ovenproof dish and divide the filling equally among them.

3 Pour the apple juice carefully into the dish and cover with foil. Bake for 20 minutes, or until the pears are tender.

4 Remove the foil and place the dish under a hot broiler for 3 minutes. Serve immediately.

COOK'S TIP

Choose ripe pears in season such as Bosc, Bartlett or Comice.

Mushroom Croustades

The rich mushroom flavor of this filling is heightened by the addition of mushroom ketchup.

INGREDIENTS

Serves 2–4

1 short French bread, about 10 inches
2 teaspoons olive oil
9 ounces portobello mushrooms, quartered
2 teaspoons mushroom ketchup
2 teaspoons lemon juice
2 tablespoons skim milk
2 tablespoons snipped fresh chives
salt and freshly ground black pepper
snipped fresh chives, to garnish

3 Place the mushrooms in a small saucepan with the mushroom ketchup, lemon juice and milk. Simmer for about 5 minutes, or until most of the liquid is evaporated.

4 Remove from the heat, then add the chives and season with salt and pepper. Spoon into the bread croustades and serve hot, garnished with snipped chives.

1 Preheat the oven to 400°F. Cut the French bread in half lengthwise. Cut a scoop out of the soft middle of each half, leaving a thick border all the way around.

2 Brush the bread with oil, place on a baking sheet and bake for 6–8 minutes, until golden and crisp.

Tomato Pesto Toasts

The flavor of pesto is so powerful that it can be used in very small amounts to good effect, as in these tasty snacks.

INGREDIENTS

Serves 2

2 thick slices crusty bread
3 tablespoons cream cheese or fromage frais
2 teaspoons red or green pesto
1 beefsteak tomato
1 red onion
salt and freshly ground black pepper
chopped basil, to garnish

1 Toast the bread slices until golden brown on both sides. Let cool.

2 Mix together the cheese and pesto in a small bowl until well blended, then spread thickly on the toasted bread.

3 Using a large, sharp knife, cut the tomato and red onion crosswise into thin slices.

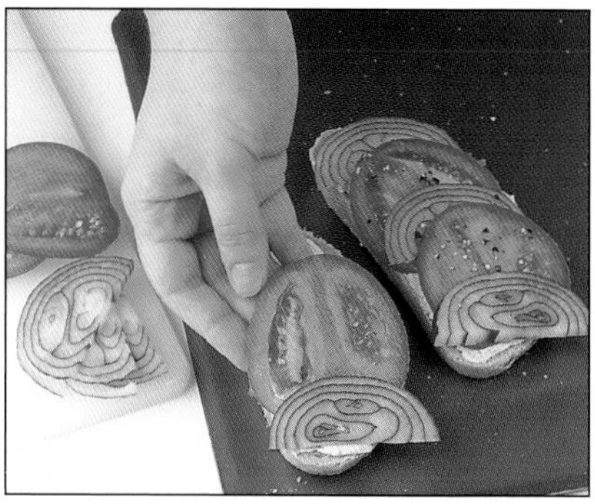

4 Arrange the tomato and onion slices, overlapping, on the toast and season with salt and pepper. Transfer to a broiler rack and heat through under a hot broiler. Serve, garnished with chopped basil.

COOK'S TIP

Almost any type of crusty bread can be used for this recipe, but Italian olive oil bread and French bread will give the best flavor.

Asparagus with Eggs

The addition of fried eggs and grated Parmesan turns asparagus into something even more special.

INGREDIENTS

Serves 4

1 pound fresh asparagus
5 tablespoons butter
4 eggs
4 tablespoons grated fresh Parmesan cheese
salt and freshly ground black pepper

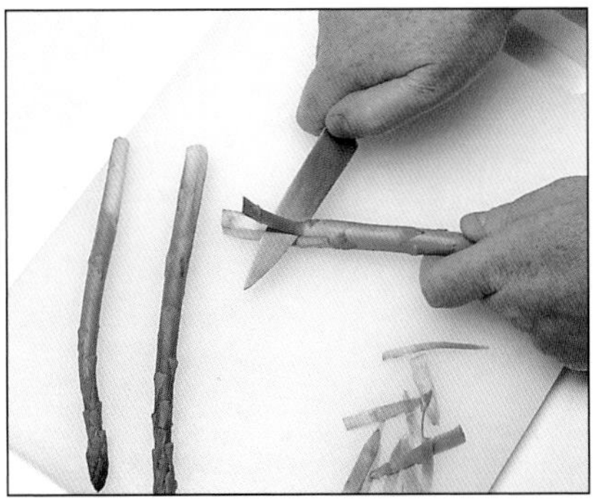

1 Cut off any woody ends from the asparagus. Peel the lower half of the spears by inserting a knife under the thick skin at the base and pulling up toward the tip. Wash the asparagus in cold water.

2 Bring a large pan of water to a boil. Boil the asparagus until just tender.

3 While the asparagus is cooking, melt a third of the butter in a frying pan. When bubbling, break in the eggs and cook them until the whites have set but the yolks are still soft.

4 As soon as the asparagus is cooked, remove it from the water with two slotted spoons. Place it on a wire rack covered with a clean dish towel to drain. Divide the spears among warm individual serving plates. Place a fried egg on each and sprinkle with the grated Parmesan.

5 Melt the remaining butter in the frying pan. As soon as it is bubbling, but before it browns, pour it over the cheese and eggs on the asparagus. Season with salt and pepper and serve at once.

Curried Eggs

Hard-boiled eggs are served on a bed of mild, creamy sauce with a hint of curry.

INGREDIENTS

Serves 2

4 eggs
1 tablespoon sunflower oil
1 small onion, finely chopped
1-inch piece of fresh ginger root, peeled and grated
½ teaspoon ground cumin
½ teaspoon garam masala
1½ teaspoons tomato paste
2 teaspoons tandoori paste
2 teaspoons lemon juice
¼ cup light cream
1 tablespoon chopped cilantro
salt and freshly ground black pepper
cilantro sprigs, to garnish

1 Put the eggs in a pan of water. Bring to a boil, lower the heat and simmer for 10 minutes.

2 Meanwhile, heat the oil in a frying pan. Cook the onion for 2–3 minutes. Add the ginger and cook for 1 minute more.

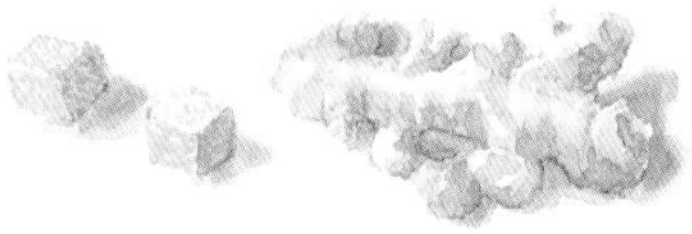

3 Stir in the ground cumin, garam masala, tomato paste, tandoori paste, lemon juice and cream. Cook for 1–2 minutes, then stir in the cilantro. Season with salt and pepper.

4 Drain the eggs, remove the shells and cut each egg in half. Spoon the sauce into a serving bowl, top with the eggs and garnish with cilantro sprigs. Serve at once.

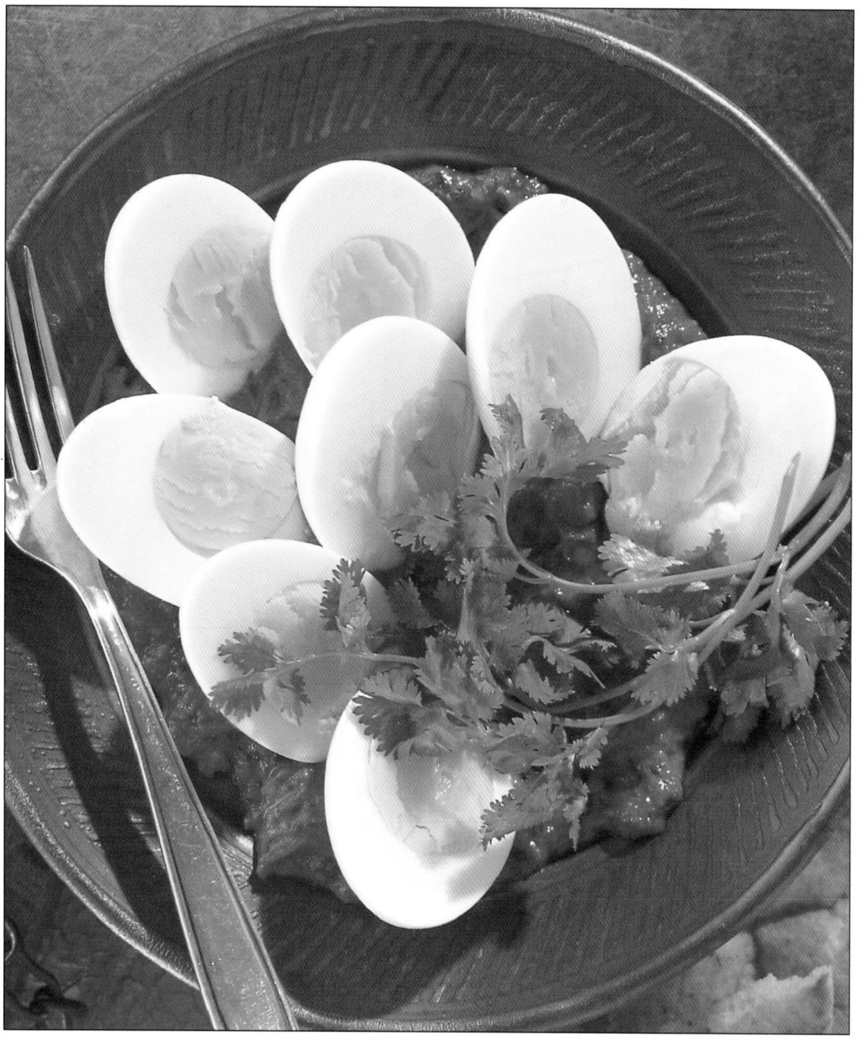

Roquefort Tartlets

These can be made in shallow muffin pans to serve hot as a first course. You could also make them in tiny tart pans, to serve warm as appetizing bite-size snacks with a drink before a meal.

INGREDIENTS

Makes 12

1½ cups all-purpose flour
large pinch of salt
8 tablespoons (1 stick) butter
1 egg yolk
2 tablespoons cold water

For the filling

1 tablespoon butter
2 tablespoons flour
⅔ cup milk
4 ounces Roquefort cheese, crumbled
⅔ cup heavy cream
½ teaspoon dried mixed herbs, such as tarragon, thyme and savory
3 egg yolks
salt and freshly ground black pepper

1 To make the pastry, sift the flour and salt into a bowl and rub the butter into the flour until it resembles bread crumbs. Mix the egg yolk with the water and stir into the flour to make a soft dough. Knead until smooth, wrap in plastic wrap and chill for 30 minutes. (You can also make the dough in a food processor.)

2 In a saucepan, melt the butter and stir in the flour and then the milk. Boil to thicken, stirring constantly. Off the heat, beat in the cheese and season with salt and pepper. Let cool. In another saucepan, bring the cream and herbs to a boil and cook until the liquid has reduced to 2 tablespoons. Beat into the cheese sauce with the eggs.

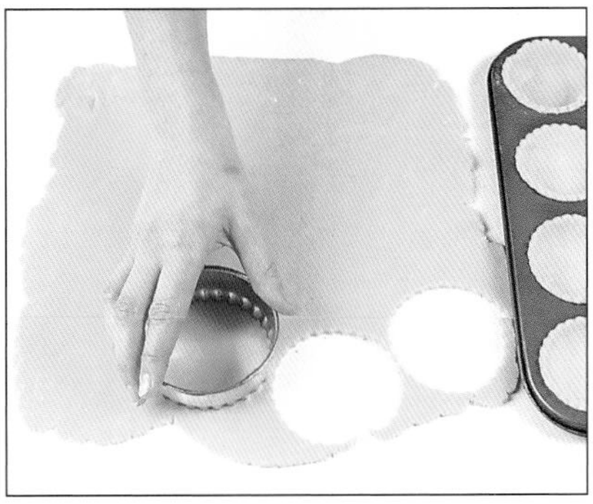

3 Preheat the oven to 375°F. On a lightly floured work surface, roll out the pastry to ⅛ inch thick. Stamp out rounds with a fluted cutter and use to line your chosen pans.

4 Divide the filling among the tartlets; they should be filled or two-thirds full. Stamp out smaller fluted rounds or star shapes for the tops and lay on top of each tartlet. Bake for 20–25 minutes, or until golden brown.

SALADS

Parmesan and Poached Egg Salad

Soft poached eggs, hot garlic croutons and cool, crisp salad greens make an unforgettable combination.

INGREDIENTS

Serves 2

½ small loaf sandwich bread
5 tablespoons olive oil
2 eggs
4 ounces mixed salad greens
2 garlic cloves, crushed
½ tablespoon white wine vinegar
1 ounce Parmesan cheese
freshly ground black pepper (optional)

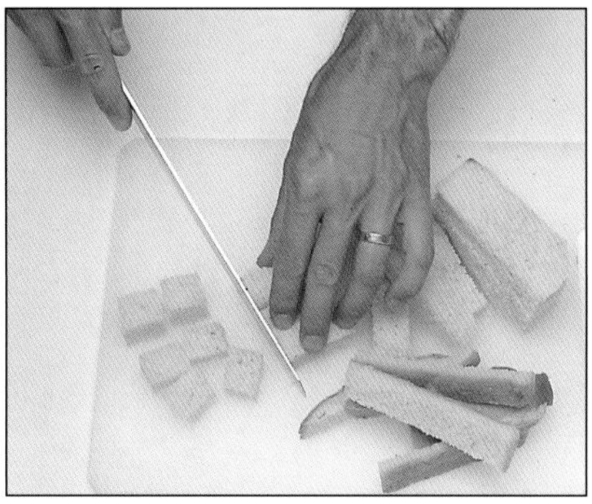

1 Remove the crusts from the bread. Cut the bread into 1-inch cubes.

2 Heat 2 tablespoons of the olive oil in a frying pan. Sauté the bread for about 5 minutes, tossing the cubes occasionally, until they are golden brown.

3 Meanwhile, bring a pan of water to a boil. Carefully slide in the shelled eggs, one at a time. Gently poach the eggs for 4 minutes, until lightly cooked.

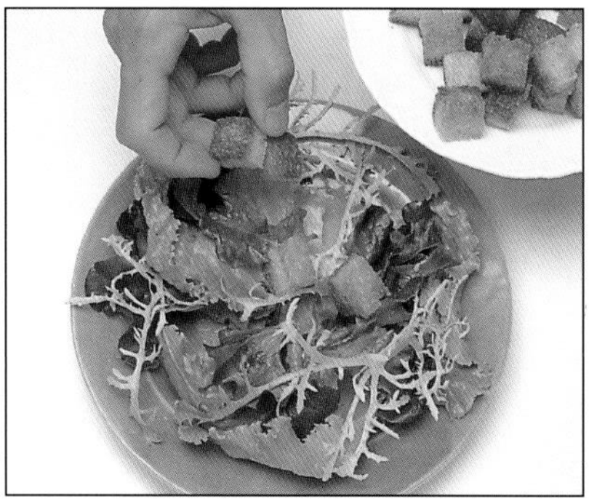

4 Divide the salad greens between two plates. Remove the croutons from the pan and arrange them over the leaves. Wipe the pan clean with paper towels.

5 Heat the remaining oil in the pan, add the garlic and vinegar and cook over high heat for 1 minute. Pour the warm dressing over each salad.

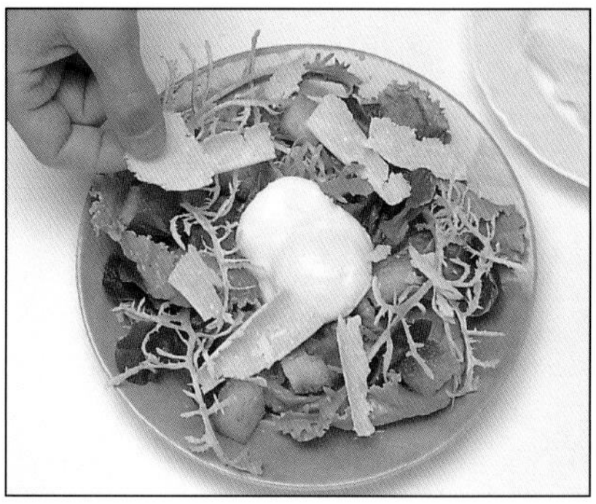

6 Place a poached egg on each salad. Sprinkle with shavings of Parmesan and freshly ground black pepper, if using.

VARIATION

As an alternative to the poached eggs, you could add 1½ ounces / 1½ cups of Greek black olives.

COOK'S TIP

Add a dash of vinegar to the water before poaching the eggs. This helps to keep the whites together. To make sure that a poached egg has a good shape, swirl the water with a spoon, whirlpool-fashion, before sliding in the egg.

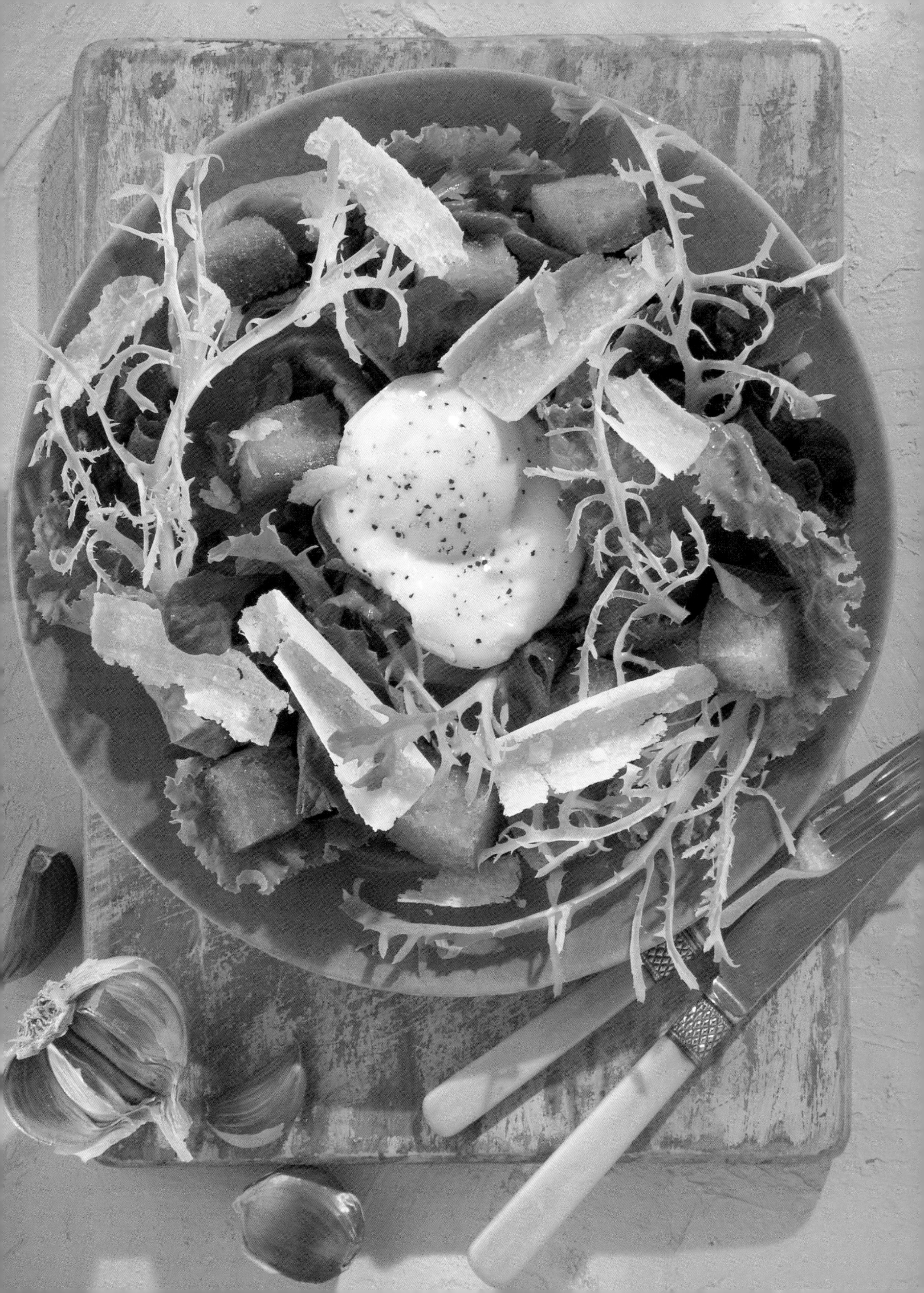

Pear and Pecan Salad with Blue Cheese

Toasted pecans have a special affinity for crisp white pears. Their robust flavors combine especially well with a rich blue cheese dressing and make this a salad to remember.

INGREDIENTS

Serves 4

½ cup shelled pecan halves
3 crisp pears
6 ounces young spinach, stems removed
1 head escarole or Boston lettuce
1 head radicchio
2 tablespoons blue cheese dressing
salt and freshly ground black pepper
crusty bread, to serve

1 Toast the pecans under a moderate broiler, to bring out their flavor.

2 Cut the pears into even slices, leaving the skin intact and discarding the cores.

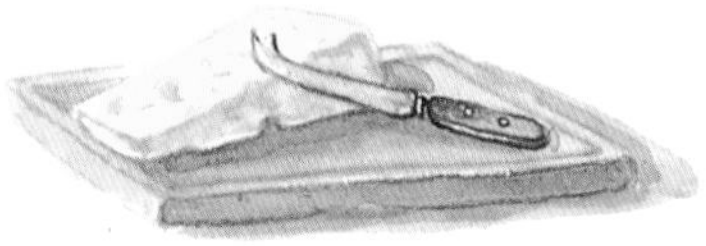

3 Wash the salad greens and spin dry. Add the pears together with the toasted pecans, then toss with the dressing. Distribute among four large plates and season with salt and pepper. Serve with warm crusty bread.

VARIATION

If you want a lighter dressing, without cheese, combine 1 teaspoon of whole-grain mustard, ½ teaspoon of sugar, ¼ teaspoon of dried tarragon, 2 teaspoons of lemon juice and ¼ cup of olive oil in a jar and shake vigorously.

New Spring Vegetable Salad

This chunky salad makes a satisfying meal. Use other spring vegetables, if you like.

INGREDIENTS

Serves 4

1½ pounds small new potatoes, halved
14-ounce can fava beans, drained
4 ounces cherry tomatoes
½ cup walnut halves
2 tablespoons white wine vinegar
1 tablespoon whole-grain mustard
¼ cup olive oil
pinch of sugar
8 ounces young asparagus spears, trimmed
6 scallions, trimmed
salt and freshly ground black pepper
baby spinach leaves, to serve

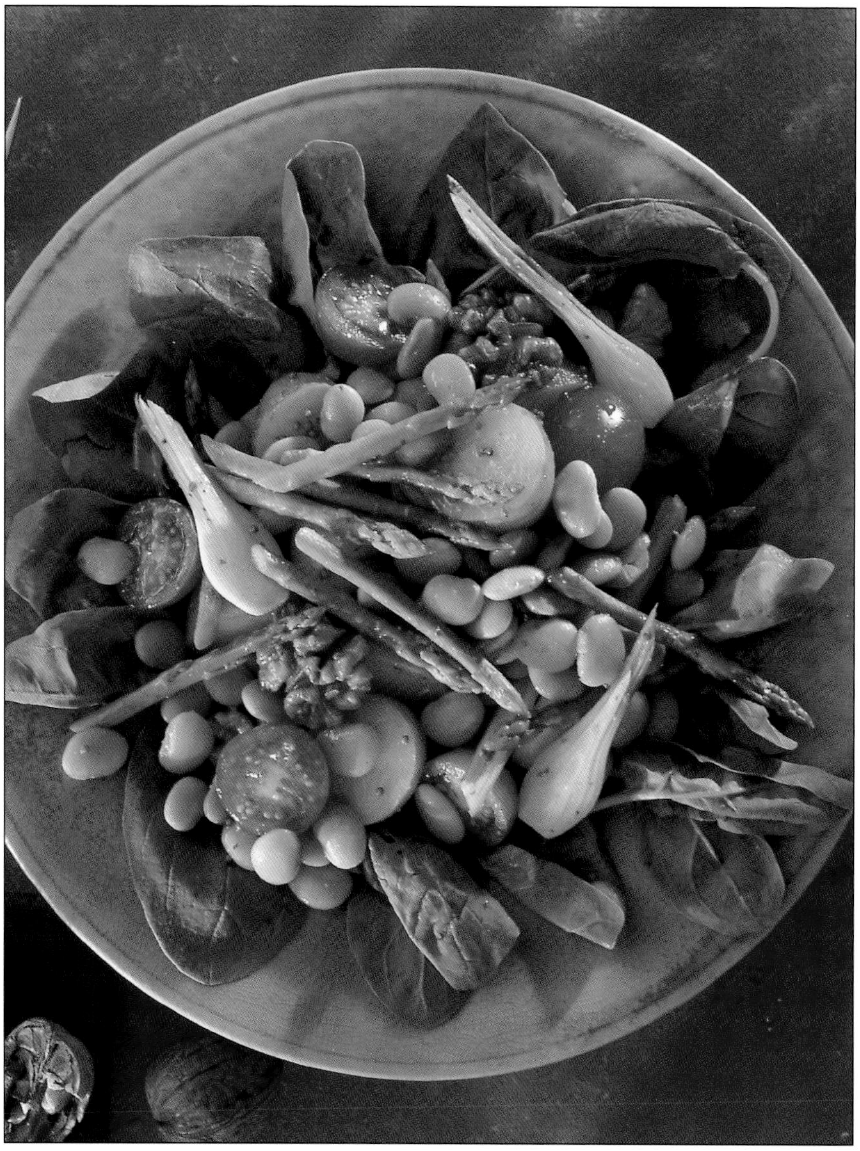

1 Put the potatoes in a saucepan. Cover with cold water and bring to a boil. Cook for 10–12 minutes, until tender. Meanwhile, put the fava beans in a bowl. Cut the tomatoes in half and add them to the bowl with the walnuts.

2 Put the white wine vinegar, mustard, olive oil and sugar into a screw-top jar. Season with salt and pepper. Close the jar tightly and shake well.

3 Add the asparagus to the potatoes and cook for 3 minutes more. Drain the cooked vegetables well. Cool under cold running water and drain again. Thickly slice the potatoes and cut the scallions in half.

4 Add the asparagus, potatoes and scallions to the bowl containing the fava bean mixture. Pour the dressing over the salad and toss well. Serve on a bed of baby spinach leaves.

Couscous Salad

This is a spicy variation on a classic lemon-flavored tabbouleh, which is traditionally made with bulgur rather than couscous.

INGREDIENTS

Serves 4

3 tablespoons olive oil
5 scallions, chopped
1 garlic clove, crushed
1 teaspoon ground cumin
1½ cups vegetable stock
1 cup couscous
2 tomatoes, peeled and chopped
¼ cup chopped fresh parsley
¼ cup chopped fresh mint
1 fresh green chile, seeded and finely chopped
2 tablespoons lemon juice
salt and freshly ground black pepper
toasted pine nuts and grated lemon zest, to garnish
crisp lettuce leaves, to serve

1 Heat the oil in a saucepan. Add the scallions and garlic. Stir in the cumin and cook for 1 minute. Add the stock and bring to a boil.

2 Remove the pan from the heat, stir in the couscous, cover the pan and let it stand for 10 minutes, until the couscous has swelled and all the liquid has been absorbed. If you are using instant couscous, follow the package instructions.

3 Scrape the couscous into a bowl. Stir in the tomatoes, parsley, mint, chile and lemon juice. Season with salt and pepper. If possible, set aside for up to an hour, to allow the flavors to develop fully.

4 To serve, line a bowl with lettuce leaves and spoon the couscous salad over the top. Sprinkle the toasted pine nuts and grated lemon rind over the top, to garnish.

Brown Bean Salad

Brown beans are a smaller variety of the fava bean, sometimes called "ful." They are used in a classic Egyptian dish called "ful madames" and are occasionally seen in health food stores. Dried fava beans, black or kidney beans make a good substitute.

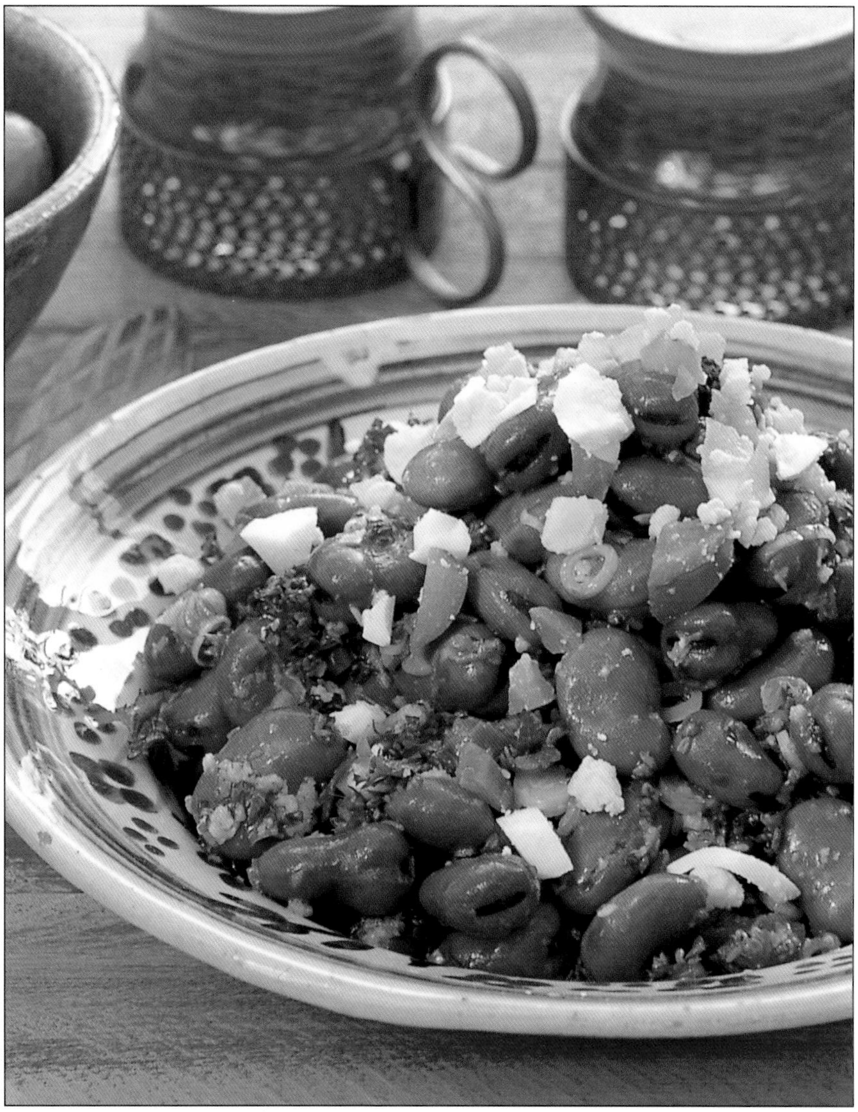

INGREDIENTS

Serves 6

12 ounces (1½ cups) dried brown beans
2 sprigs of fresh thyme
2 bay leaves
1 onion, halved
4 garlic cloves, crushed
1½ teaspoons cumin seeds, crushed
3 scallions, finely chopped
6 tablespoons chopped fresh parsley
4 teaspoons lemon juice
6 tablespoons olive oil
3 hard-boiled eggs, shelled and roughly chopped
1 pickled cucumber, roughly chopped
salt and freshly ground black pepper

1 Put the beans in a bowl with plenty of cold water and let soak overnight. Drain, transfer to a saucepan and cover with fresh water. Bring to a boil and boil rapidly for 10 minutes.

2 Reduce the heat and add the thyme, bay leaves and onion. Simmer very gently for about 1 hour, until tender. Drain and discard the herbs and onion.

3 Mix together the garlic, cumin, scallions, parsley, lemon juice and oil. Season with salt and pepper. Pour over the beans and toss lightly together. Gently stir in the eggs and cucumber and serve at once.

COOK'S TIP

The cooking time for dried beans can vary considerably. They may need only 45 minutes, or a lot longer.

Pepper and Wild Mushroom Pasta Salad

A combination of broiled peppers and wild mushrooms makes this pasta salad colorful as well as nutritious.

INGREDIENTS

Serves 6

1 red bell pepper, halved
1 yellow bell pepper, halved
1 green bell pepper, halved
12 ounces whole-wheat pasta shells or twists
2 tablespoons olive oil
3 tablespoons balsamic vinegar
5 tablespoons tomato juice
2 tablespoons chopped fresh basil
1 tablespoon chopped fresh thyme
6 ounces shiitake mushrooms, sliced
6 ounces oyster mushrooms, sliced
14-ounce can black-eyed peas, rinsed and drained
⅔ cup golden raisins
2 bunches scallions, finely chopped
salt and freshly ground black pepper

1 Preheat the broiler. Put the peppers cut side down on a broiler pan rack and place under the hot broiler for 10–15 minutes, until the skins are charred. Cover the peppers with a clean, damp dish towel and set aside to cool.

2 Meanwhile, cook the pasta in lightly salted boiling water for 10–12 minutes, until tender, then drain thoroughly.

3 Mix together the oil, vinegar, tomato juice, fresh basil and thyme. Add to the warm pasta and toss together.

4 Remove and discard the skins from the bell peppers. Seed and slice the peppers and add to the pasta with the mushrooms, black-eyed peas, golden raisins and scallions. Season with salt and pepper. Toss to mix and serve immediately or cover and chill in the refrigerator before serving.

Whole-Wheat Pasta Salad

This substantial salad is easily assembled from any combination of seasonal vegetables.

INGREDIENTS

Serves 8

1 pound short whole-wheat pasta, such as fusilli or penne
3 tablespoons olive oil
2 medium carrots
1 small head broccoli
1 cup shelled peas, fresh or frozen
1 red or yellow bell pepper, seeded
2 celery ribs
4 scallions
1 large tomato
½ cup pitted olives

For the dressing

3 tablespoons wine or balsamic vinegar
¼ cup olive oil
1 tablespoon Dijon mustard
1 tablespoon sesame seeds
2 teaspoons chopped mixed fresh herbs such as parsley, thyme and basil
4 ounces (⅔ cup diced) Cheddar or mozzarella, or a combination of both
salt and freshly ground black pepper
cilantro, to garnish

1 Cook the pasta in a large pan of rapidly boiling salted water until it is tender. Drain and rinse under cold water to stop the cooking.

2 Drain well and turn into a large bowl. Toss with the 3 tablespoons of olive oil and set aside. Allow to cool completely before mixing with the other ingredients.

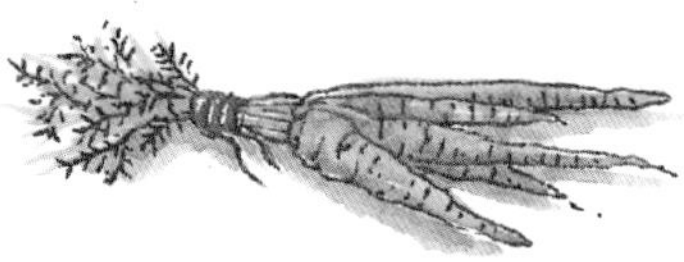

3 Lightly blanch the carrots, broccoli and peas in a large pan of boiling water. Refresh under cold water. Drain well.

4 Chop the carrots and broccoli into bite-size pieces and add to the pasta with the peas. Slice the pepper, celery, scallions and tomato into small pieces. Add them to the salad with the olives.

5 Make the dressing in a small bowl by combining the vinegar with the oil and mustard. Stir in the sesame seeds and herbs. Mix the dressing into the salad. Taste for seasoning; add salt and pepper or more oil and vinegar as necessary. Stir in the cheese. Allow the salad to stand for 15 minutes before serving. Garnish with cilantro.

Fruity Rice Salad

An appetizing and colorful rice salad combining many different flavors, ideal for a packed lunch.

INGREDIENTS

Serves 4–6

1 cup mixed brown and wild rice
1 yellow bell pepper, seeded and diced
1 bunch scallions, chopped
3 celery ribs, chopped
1 large beefsteak tomato, chopped
2 green-skinned eating apples, chopped
6 ounces (¾ cup) chopped dried apricots
4 ounces (⅔ cup) raisins
2 tablespoons unsweetened apple juice
2 tablespoons dry sherry
2 tablespoons light soy sauce
dash of Tabasco sauce
2 tablespoons chopped fresh parsley
1 tablespoon chopped fresh rosemary
salt and freshly ground black pepper

1 Cook the rice in a large saucepan of lightly salted boiling water for about 30 minutes (or according to the package instructions), until tender. Rinse the cooked rice under cold running water to cool quickly, and drain thoroughly.

2 Place the pepper, scallions, celery, tomato, apples, apricots, raisins and the cooked rice in a serving bowl and mix well.

3 In a small bowl, mix together the apple juice, sherry, soy sauce, Tabasco sauce and herbs. Season with salt and pepper.

4 Pour the dressing over the rice mixture and toss the ingredients together to mix. Serve immediately or cover and chill in the refrigerator before serving.

Marinated Cucumber Salad

Sprinkling the cucumber with salt draws out some of the liquid.

INGREDIENTS

Serves 4–6

2 medium cucumbers
1 tablespoon salt
½ cup sugar
¾ cup dry cider
1 tablespoon cider vinegar
3 tablespoons chopped fresh dill
pinch of freshly ground black pepper
sprig of dill, to garnish

1 Slice the cucumbers thinly and place them in a colander, sprinkling salt between each layer. Set the colander over a bowl and let drain for 1 hour.

2 Thoroughly rinse the cucumber slices under cold running water to remove excess salt, then pat dry on absorbent paper towels.

3 Gently heat the sugar, cider and vinegar in a saucepan until the sugar has dissolved. Remove from the heat and let cool. Put the cucumber slices in a bowl, pour the cider mixture over them and let marinate for 2 hours.

4 Drain the cucumber and sprinkle with the dill and pepper to taste. Mix well and transfer to a serving dish. Garnish with a sprig of dill. Chill until ready to serve.

Classic Greek Salad

If you have ever visited Greece, you'll know that a Greek salad with a chunk of bread makes a delicious, filling meal.

INGREDIENTS

Serves 4

1 head romaine lettuce
½ cucumber, halved lengthwise
4 tomatoes
8 scallions
⅓ cup Greek black olives
4 ounces feta cheese
6 tablespoons white wine vinegar
½ cup olive oil
salt and freshly ground black pepper
olives and bread, to serve (optional)

1 Tear the lettuce into pieces and place them in a large mixing bowl. Slice the cucumber and add to the bowl.

2 Cut the tomatoes into wedges and put them in the bowl.

COOK'S TIP

The salad can be assembled in advance and chilled, but add the lettuce and dressing just before serving. Keep the dressing at room temperature, as chilling deadens its flavor.

3 Slice the scallions. Add them to the bowl with the olives and toss well.

4 Cut the feta cheese into cubes and add to the salad.

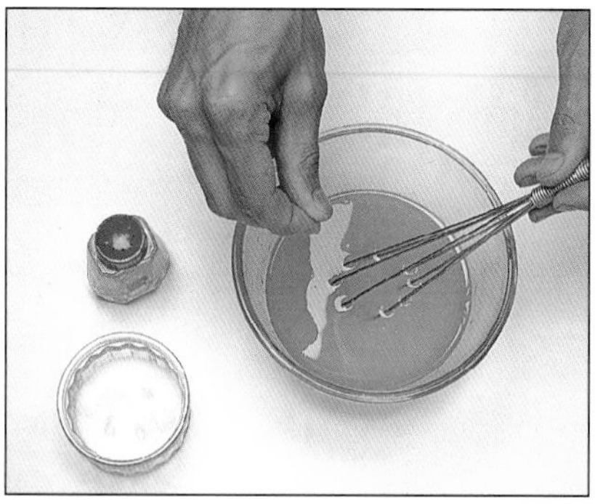

5 Put the vinegar, olive oil and salt and pepper into a small bowl and whisk well. Pour the dressing over the salad and toss to combine. Serve at once, with olives and chunks of bread, if desired.

Fresh Spinach and Avocado Salad

Young, tender spinach leaves are delicious served with avocado, cherry tomatoes and radishes in a tofu sauce.

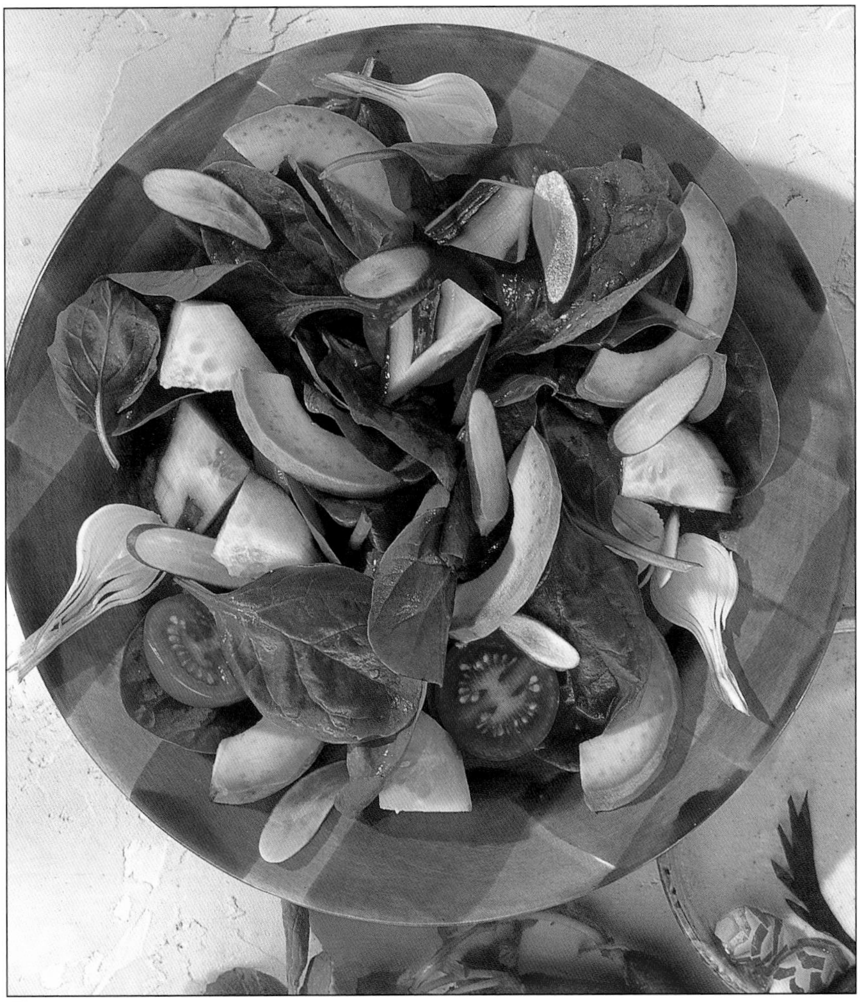

INGREDIENTS

Serves 2–3

1 large avocado
juice of 1 lime
8 ounces fresh baby spinach leaves
4 ounces cherry tomatoes
4 scallions, sliced
½ cucumber
2 ounces radishes, sliced
radish roses and herb sprigs, to garnish

For the dressing

4 ounces soft, silken tofu
3 tablespoons milk
2 teaspoons prepared mustard
½ teaspoon white wine vinegar
pinch of cayenne, plus extra to serve
salt and freshly ground black pepper

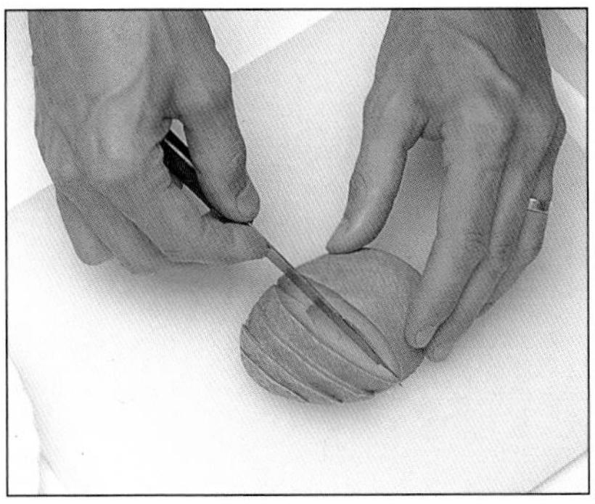

1 Cut the avocado in half, remove the pit, and strip off the skin. Cut the flesh into slices. Transfer to a plate, drizzle with the lime juice and set aside.

COOK'S TIP

Soft, silken tofu can be found in most supermarkets in long-life cartons.

2 Wash and dry the spinach leaves. Put them in a mixing bowl.

3 Cut the larger cherry tomatoes in half and add all the tomatoes to the mixing bowl, with the scallions. Cut the cucumber into chunks and add to the bowl with the sliced radishes.

4 Make the dressing. Put the tofu, milk, mustard, wine vinegar and cayenne in a food processor or blender. Add salt and pepper to taste. Process for 30 seconds, until smooth. Scrape the dressing into a bowl and add a little extra milk if you like a thinner dressing. Sprinkle with a little extra cayenne and garnish with radish roses and herb sprigs.

Sweet and Sour Peppers with Pasta Bows

A zesty dressing makes this simple pasta salad really special.

INGREDIENTS

Serves 4–6

1 each red, yellow and orange bell pepper
1 garlic clove, crushed
2 tablespoons capers
2 tablespoons raisins
1 teaspoon whole-grain mustard
grated zest and juice of 1 lime
1 teaspoon honey
2 tablespoons chopped cilantro
8 ounces pasta bows
salt and freshly ground black pepper
shavings of Parmesan cheese, to serve (optional)

1 Quarter the peppers and remove the stalks and seeds. Place in boiling water and cook for 10–15 minutes, until tender. Drain and rinse under cold water. Peel away the skins and seeds and cut the flesh lengthwise into strips.

2 Put the garlic, capers, raisins, mustard, lime zest and juice, honey and cilantro into a bowl. Season with salt and pepper and whisk together.

3 Cook the pasta in a large pan of boiling salted water for 10–12 minutes, until tender. Drain thoroughly.

4 Return the pasta to the pan and add the peppers and dressing. Heat gently and toss to mix. Transfer to a warm serving bowl. Serve with a few shavings of Parmesan cheese, if you like.

Bulgur and Fava Bean Salad

This appetizing salad is ideal served with fresh crusty whole-wheat bread and homemade chutney or relish.

INGREDIENTS

Serves 6

2 cups bulgur
8 ounces frozen fava or lima beans
1 cup frozen petit pois (tiny peas)
8 ounces cherry tomatoes, halved
1 Spanish onion, chopped
1 red bell pepper, seeded and chopped
2 ounces snow peas, chopped
2 ounces watercress
1 tablespoon chopped fresh parsley
1 tablespoon chopped fresh basil
1 tablespoon chopped fresh thyme
French dressing
salt and freshly ground black pepper

1 Soak and cook the bulgur according to the package instructions. Drain thoroughly and put into a serving bowl.

2 Meanwhile, cook the beans and petit pois in boiling water for 3 minutes. Drain and add to the prepared bulgur.

3 Add the cherry tomatoes, onion, pepper, snow peas and watercress to the bulgur mixture. Toss together in the bowl until all the ingredients are well combined.

4 Add the chopped fresh parsley, basil, thyme and French dressing to taste. Season with salt and pepper and toss the ingredients together. Serve immediately or cover and chill in the refrigerator before serving.

COOK'S TIP

Use cooked couscous, boiled brown rice or whole-wheat pasta in place of the bulgur.

Sweet and Sour Artichoke Salad

Agrodolce is a sweet and sour sauce that works perfectly in this salad.

INGREDIENTS

Serves 4

6 small globe artichokes
juice of 1 lemon
2 tablespoons olive oil
2 medium onions, roughly chopped
6 ounces fresh or frozen fava beans, about 1 cup
6 ounces fresh or frozen peas, about 1½ cup
salt and freshly ground black pepper
fresh mint leaves, to garnish

For the salsa agrodolce

½ cup white wine vinegar
1 tablespoon sugar
handful of fresh mint leaves, roughly torn

1 Peel the outer leaves from the artichokes and cut into quarters. Place them in a bowl of water with the lemon juice.

2 Heat the oil in a large saucepan and cook the onions until golden. Add the beans and stir.

3 Drain the artichokes and add them to the pan. Pour in about 1¼ cups of water and cover. Simmer gently for 10–15 minutes.

4 Add the peas, season with salt and pepper and cook for another 5 minutes, stirring from time to time, until the vegetables are tender.

5 Drain the vegetables in a sieve and place them in a bowl. Let cool, then cover and chill in the refrigerator.

6 To make the salsa, mix all the ingredients in a pan. Heat gently until the sugar has dissolved. Simmer for 5 minutes. Let cool. Drizzle over the salad. Garnish with mint leaves.

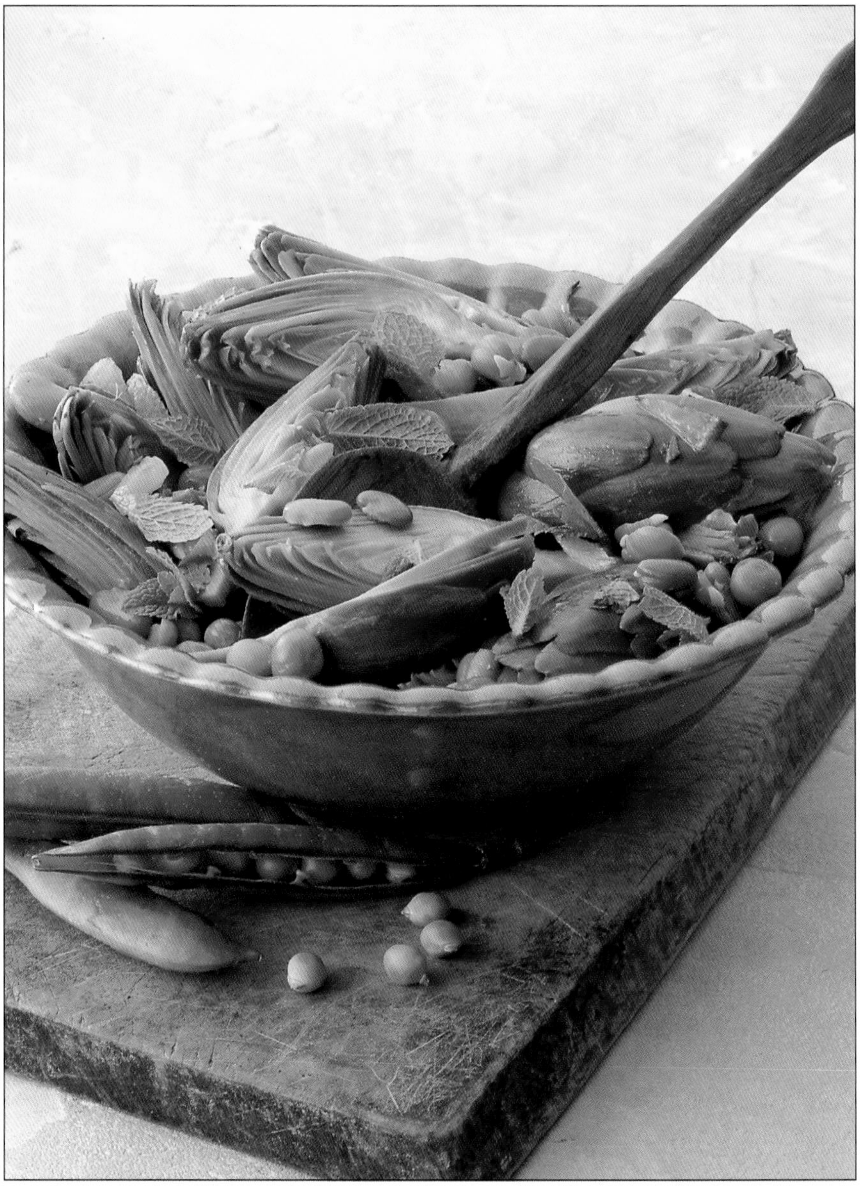

Spanish Asparagus and Orange Salad

Complicated salad dressings are rarely found in Spain—they simply rely on the wonderful flavor of a good quality olive oil.

INGREDIENTS

Serves 4

8 ounces asparagus, trimmed and cut into 2-inch pieces
2 large oranges
2 tomatoes, cut into eighths
3–4 romaine lettuce leaves, shredded (2 ounces)
2 tablespoons olive oil
½ teaspoon sherry vinegar
salt and freshly ground black pepper

1 Cook the asparagus in boiling salted water for 3–4 minutes, until just tender. Drain and refresh under cold water.

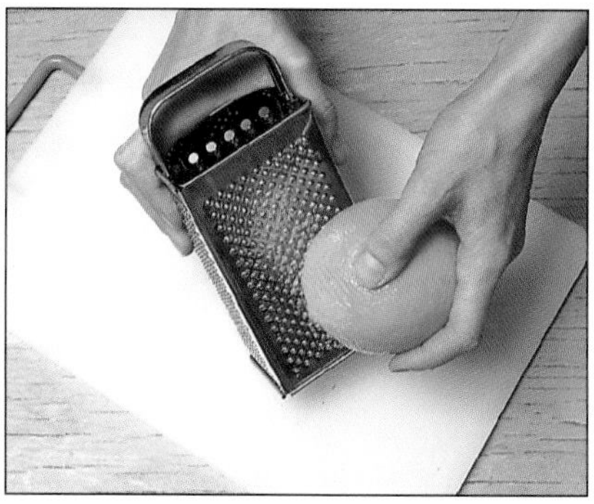

2 Grate the zest from half an orange and reserve. Peel both the oranges and cut into segments. Squeeze out the juice from the membrane and reserve the juice.

3 Put the asparagus, orange segments, tomatoes and lettuce into a salad bowl. Mix together the oil and vinegar and add 1 tablespoon of the reserved orange juice and 1 teaspoon of the zest. Season the dressing with salt and pepper. Just before serving, pour the dressing over the salad and mix gently to coat.

COOK'S TIP

Bibb lettuce can be used in place of romaine.

Grilled Goat Cheese Salad

Here is the salad and cheese course on one plate—or serve it as a quick and satisfying appetizer or light lunch. The fresh tangy flavor of goat cheese contrasts with the mild salad greens.

INGREDIENTS

Serves 4

2 firm round whole goat cheeses, such as Crottin de Chavignol (2½–4 ounces each)
4 slices French bread
olive oil, for drizzling
6 ounces mixed salad greens, including soft and bitter varieties
snipped fresh chives, to garnish

For the dressing

½ clove garlic
1 teaspoon Dijon mustard
1 teaspoon white wine vinegar
1 teaspoon dry white wine
3 tablespoons olive oil
salt and freshly ground black pepper

1 To make the dressing, rub a large salad bowl with the cut side of the garlic clove. Combine the mustard, vinegar, wine, salt and pepper in a bowl. Whisk in the oil, 1 tablespoon at a time, to form a thick vinaigrette.

2 Cut the goat cheeses in half crosswise using a sharp knife.

3 Preheat the broiler to hot. Arrange the bread slices on a baking sheet and toast on one side. Turn over and place a piece of cheese, cut side up, on each slice. Drizzle with oil and broil until the cheese is lightly browned.

4 Place the greens and the dressing in the salad bowl and toss to coat the greens thoroughly. Divide the salad among four plates, top each with a goat cheese crouton and serve, garnished with chives.

Tomato and Feta Cheese Salad

Sweet sun-ripened tomatoes are rarely more delicious than when served with feta cheese and olive oil. This salad, popular in Greece and Turkey, is enjoyed as a light meal with pieces of crisp bread.

INGREDIENTS

Serves 4

2 pounds tomatoes
7 ounces feta cheese
½ cup olive oil, preferably Greek
12 black olives
4 sprigs of fresh basil
freshly ground black pepper

1 Remove the tough cores from the tomatoes with a small, sharp knife.

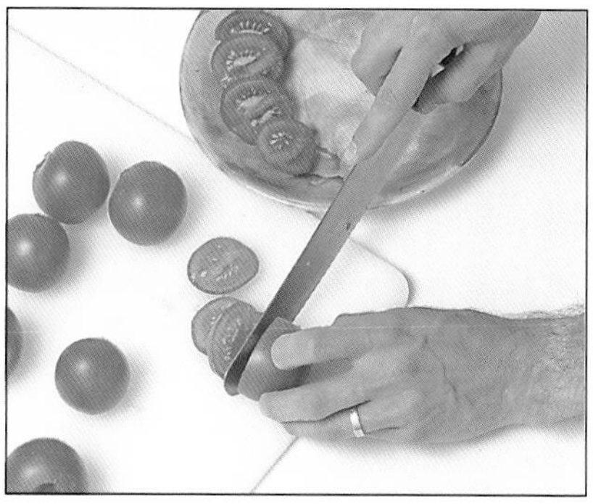

2 Slice the tomatoes thickly and arrange in a shallow dish.

3 Crumble the cheese over the tomatoes, drizzle with olive oil, then sprinkle with olives and fresh basil. Season with black pepper and serve at room temperature.

COOK'S TIP

Feta cheese has a strong flavor and can be salty. The least salty varieties are imported from Greece and Turkey and are available at good delicatessens.

Fennel, Orange and Arugula Salad

This light and refreshing salad is the ideal companion for spicy or rich foods.

INGREDIENTS

Serves 4

2 oranges
1 fennel bulb
4 ounces arugula leaves
⅓ cup black olives

For the dressing

2 tablespoons olive oil
1 tablespoon balsamic vinegar
1 small garlic clove, crushed
salt and freshly ground black pepper

1 With a vegetable peeler, cut strips of zest from the oranges, leaving the pith behind.

2 Cut the strips into thin julienne strips. Cook in boiling water for a few minutes. Drain.

3 Peel the oranges, removing all the white pith. Cut the orange flesh crosswise into thin rounds and discard any seeds.

4 Cut the fennel bulb in half lengthwise and slice across the bulb as thinly as possible. It is easier to do this with a food processor fitted with a slicing disk or using a mandoline.

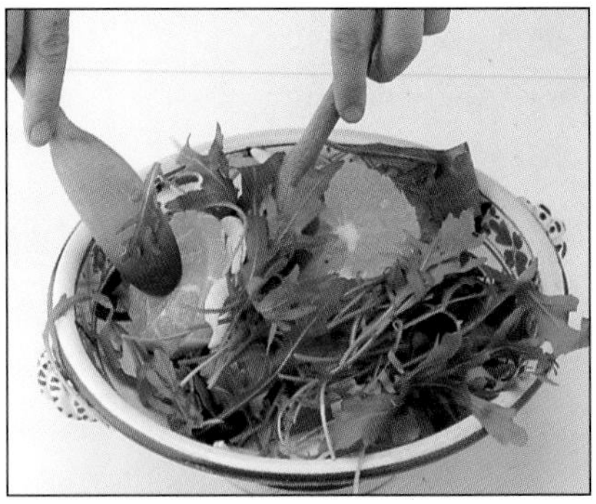

5 Combine the oranges and fennel in a serving bowl and toss with the arugula leaves.

6 Mix together the oil, vinegar, garlic and seasoning and pour over the salad. Toss well and let stand for a few minutes. Sprinkle with the black olives and julienne strips of orange zest.

Eggplant, Lemon and Caper Salad

This cooked vegetable relish is delicious served with pasta or simply on its own with crusty bread.

INGREDIENTS

Serves 4

1 large eggplant, about 1½ pounds
1 teaspoon salt
4 tablespoons olive oil
grated zest and juice of 1 lemon
2 tablespoons capers, rinsed
12 pitted green olives
1 small garlic clove, chopped
2 tablespoons chopped fresh flat-leaf parsley
salt and freshly ground black pepper

1 Cut the eggplant into 1-inch cubes. Place the cubes in a colander and sprinkle with the salt. Set aside for 30 minutes, then rinse thoroughly under cold running water. Pat dry with paper towels.

2 Heat the olive oil in a large frying pan. Cook the eggplant cubes over medium heat for about 10 minutes, tossing regularly, until golden and softened. You may need to do this in two batches to ensure that all the eggplant cubes brown well. Drain on paper towels and season with a little salt.

COOK'S TIP

This will taste even better when made the day before. It will keep, covered, in the refrigerator for up to 4 days. To enrich this dish to serve on its own as a main course, add toasted pine nuts and shavings of Parmesan cheese. Serve with crusty bread.

3 Place the eggplant cubes in a large serving bowl and toss with the lemon zest and juice, capers, olives, garlic and chopped parsley.

4 Season with salt and pepper. Serve at room temperature.

Arugula, Pear and Parmesan Salad

For a sophisticated start to an elaborate meal, try this simple salad of honey-rich pears, fresh Parmesan and aromatic leaves of arugula.

INGREDIENTS

Serves 4

3 ripe pears, Bartlett or Comice
2 teaspoons lemon juice
3 tablespoons hazelnut or walnut oil
4 ounces arugula
3 ounces Parmesan cheese
freshly ground black pepper
open-textured bread, to serve

1 Peel and core the pears and slice thickly. Moisten with lemon juice to keep the flesh white.

2 Combine the nut oil with the pears. Add the arugula leaves and toss.

3 Turn the salad out onto four small plates and top with shavings of Parmesan cheese. Season with freshly ground black pepper and serve with open-textured bread.

COOK'S TIP

If you are unable to buy arugula easily, you can grow your own from early spring to late summer.

Tomato, Scallion and Cilantro Salad

Known as "cachumbar," this salad relish is most commonly served with Indian curries. There are many versions; this one will leave your mouth feeling cool and fresh after a spicy meal.

INGREDIENTS

Serves 4

3 ripe tomatoes
2 scallions, chopped
¼ teaspoon sugar
3 tablespoons chopped cilantro
salt

1 Remove the tough cores from the tomatoes with a small, sharp knife.

2 Halve the tomatoes, remove the seeds and dice the flesh.

3 Combine the tomatoes with the scallions, sugar, chopped cilantro and salt. Serve at room temperature.

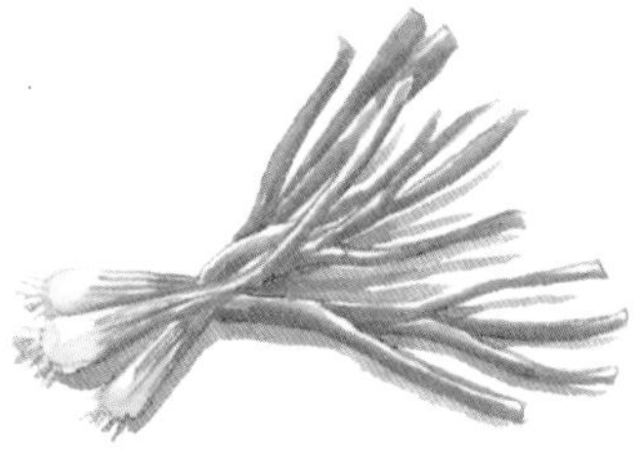

COOK'S TIP

This refreshing salad also makes a fine filler for pita bread with hummus.

SIDE DISHES

Sautéed Potatoes

These rosemary-scented, crisp golden potatoes are a favorite in French households.

INGREDIENTS

Serves 6

3 pounds baking potatoes
4–6 tablespoons oil or clarified butter
2 or 3 sprigs of fresh rosemary, leaves removed and chopped
salt and freshly ground black pepper

1 Peel the potatoes and cut them into 1-inch pieces. Place them in a bowl, cover with cold water and let soak for 10–15 minutes. Drain, rinse and drain again, then dry thoroughly in a dish towel.

2 Heat about 4 tablespoons of the oil or butter over medium-high heat until very hot but not smoking. Add the potatoes and cook for 2 minutes without stirring, so that they seal completely and brown on one side.

3 Shake the pan and toss the potatoes to brown on another side. Season with salt and pepper.

4 Add a little more oil or butter and continue cooking the potatoes over medium-low to low heat, stirring and shaking the pan frequently, for 20–25 minutes, until tender when pierced with a knife. About 5 minutes before the end of cooking, sprinkle the potatoes with the chopped rosemary.

Straw Potato Cake

These fried grated potatoes resemble straw, hence the name of the dish. You could make several small cakes instead of a large one, if you prefer—simply adjust the cooking time accordingly.

INGREDIENTS

Serves 4

1 pound baking potatoes
$1\frac{1}{2}$ tablespoons melted butter
1 tablespoon vegetable oil, plus more if needed
salt and freshly ground black pepper

1 Peel the potatoes and grate them coarsely, then immediately toss them with melted butter and season with salt and pepper.

2 Heat the oil in a large nonstick frying pan. Add the potato mixture and press down to form an even layer that covers the pan. Cook over medium heat for 7–10 minutes, until the bottom is well browned.

3 Loosen the potato cake by shaking the pan or running a thin spatula under it.

4 To turn the potato cake over, invert a large baking sheet over the frying pan and, holding it tightly against the pan, turn them both over together. Lift off the frying pan, return it to the heat and add a little oil if it looks dry. Slide the potato cake into the frying pan and continue cooking until crisp and browned on both sides. Serve hot.

Salines de Guérande
LE SEL DE LA VIE

Puffy Creamed Potatoes

This accompaniment consists of creamed potatoes incorporated into mini Yorkshire puddings. Serve them with a vegetable casserole or, for a meal on its own, serve two or three per person and accompany with salads.

INGREDIENTS

Makes 6

10 ounces potatoes
creamy milk and butter for mashing
1 teaspoon chopped fresh parsley
1 teaspoon chopped fresh tarragon
⅔ cup all-purpose flour
1 egg
about ½ cup milk
oil or sunflower margarine, for baking
salt and freshly ground black pepper

1 Boil the potatoes until tender and mash with a little milk and butter. Stir in the chopped parsley and tarragon and season with salt and pepper. Preheat the oven to 400°F.

2 Process the flour, egg, milk and a pinch of salt in a food processor or blender to make a smooth batter.

3 Place about ½ teaspoon oil or a small pat of sunflower margarine in each of six ramekins and place in the oven on a baking sheet for 2–3 minutes, until the oil is very hot.

4 Working quickly, pour a small amount of batter (about 4 teaspoons) into each ramekin. Add a heaping tablespoon of mashed potatoes and then pour an equal amount of the remaining batter into each dish. Place in the oven and bake for 15–20 minutes, until the puddings are puffy and golden brown.

5 Using a thin spatula, carefully ease the puddings out of the ramekins and arrange on a large, warm serving dish. Serve at once.

Potatoes Dauphinois

Rich, creamy and satisfying, this is a comforting dish to serve when it's cold outside.

INGREDIENTS

Serves 4

1½ pounds potatoes, peeled and thinly sliced
1 garlic clove
2 tablespoons butter
1¼ cups light cream
¼ cup milk
salt and white pepper

1 Preheat the oven to 300°F. Place the potato slices in a bowl of cold water to remove the excess starch. Drain and pat dry with paper towels.

2 Cut the garlic in half and rub the cut side around the inside of a wide, shallow ovenproof dish. Butter the dish generously. Blend the cream and milk in a bowl.

3 Cover the bottom of the dish with a layer of potatoes. Dot a little butter over the potato layer, season with salt and pepper and then pour a little of the cream and milk mixture over the potatoes.

4 Continue making layers until all the ingredients have been used up, ending with a layer of cream. Bake for about 1¼ hours. If the dish browns too quickly, cover with a lid or with a piece of foil. The potatoes are ready when they are very soft and the top is golden brown.

Spicy Potatoes and Cauliflower

This dish is simplicity itself to make and can be eaten as a main course with Indian breads or rice, a raita such as cucumber and yogurt, and a fresh mint relish.

INGREDIENTS

Serves 2

8 ounces potatoes
5 tablespoons peanut oil
1 teaspoon ground cumin
1 teaspoon ground coriander
¼ teaspoon ground turmeric
¼ teaspoon cayenne pepper
1 fresh green chile, seeded and finely chopped
1 medium cauliflower, broken up into small florets
1 teaspoon cumin seeds
2 garlic cloves, cut into shreds
1–2 tablespoons cilantro, finely chopped
salt

1 Cook the potatoes in their skins in boiling salted water for about 20 minutes, until just tender. Drain and let cool. When cool enough to handle, peel and cut into 1-inch cubes.

2 Heat 3 tablespoons of the oil in a frying pan or wok. When hot, add the ground cumin, coriander, turmeric, cayenne pepper and chile. Let the spices sizzle for a few seconds.

3 Add the cauliflower and about ¼ cup water. Cook over medium heat, stirring constantly, for 6–8 minutes. Add the potatoes and stir-fry for 2–3 minutes. Season with salt, then remove from the heat.

4 Heat the remaining oil in a small frying pan. When hot, add the cumin seeds and garlic and cook until lightly browned. Pour the mixture over the vegetables. Sprinkle with the chopped cilantro and serve at once.

Garlic Mashed Potatoes

These creamy mashed potatoes have a wonderful aroma. Although two bulbs seems like a lot of garlic, the flavor is sweet and subtle when garlic is cooked in this way.

INGREDIENTS

Serves 6–8

2 garlic bulbs, separated into cloves, unpeeled
8 tablespoons (1 stick) unsalted butter
3 pounds baking potatoes
½–¾ cup milk
salt and white pepper

1 Bring a small saucepan of water to a boil over high heat. Add the garlic cloves and boil for 2 minutes, then drain and peel.

2 In a heavy frying pan, melt half of the butter over low heat. Add the blanched garlic cloves, then cover and cook gently for 20–25 minutes, until very tender and just golden, shaking the pan and stirring occasionally. Do not allow the garlic to scorch or brown.

3 Remove the pan from the heat and cool slightly. Spoon the garlic and any butter from the pan into a blender or food processor fitted with a metal blade and process until smooth. Transfer to a small bowl, press plastic wrap onto the surface to prevent a skin from forming and set aside.

4 Peel and quarter the potatoes, place in a large saucepan and add enough cold water to just cover them. Salt the water generously and bring to a boil over high heat.

5 Cook the potatoes until tender, then drain and work through a food mill or press through a sieve back into the saucepan. Return the pan to medium heat and, using a wooden spoon, stir the potatoes for 1–2 minutes to dry them out completely. Remove from the heat.

6 Warm the milk over medium-high heat until bubbles form around the edge. Gradually beat the milk, remaining butter and reserved garlic purée into the potatoes, then season with salt, if needed, and white pepper.

Roasted Potatoes, Peppers and Shallots

This popular dish from the Deep South is often served in elegant New Orleans restaurants.

INGREDIENTS

Serves 4

1¼ pounds waxy potatoes
2 yellow bell peppers
12 shallots
olive oil
2 sprigs of fresh rosemary
salt and freshly ground black pepper

1 Preheat the oven to 400°F. Wash the potatoes and blanch for 5 minutes in boiling water. Drain.

2 When the potatoes are cool enough to handle, peel them and halve lengthwise. Cut each pepper lengthwise into 8 strips, dicarding the seeds and pith.

3 Peel the shallots, allowing them to fall into their natural segments.

4 Oil a shallow ovenproof dish thoroughly with olive oil.

5 Arrange the potatoes and peppers in alternating rows and stud with the shallots.

6 Cut the rosemary sprigs into 2-inch lengths and tuck among the vegetables. Season the dish generously with olive oil, salt and pepper and bake, uncovered, for 30–40 minutes, until all the vegetables are tender.

Baked Sweet Potatoes

Give sweet potatoes a Cajun flavor with salt, three different kinds of pepper and lavish quantities of butter. Serve half a potato per person as an accompaniment, or a whole one as a supper dish with a green salad peppered with watercress.

INGREDIENTS

Serves 3–6

3 pink-skinned sweet potatoes, about 1 pound each
6 tablespoons butter, sliced
black, white and cayenne peppers
salt

1 Wash the potatoes and leave the skins wet. Rub salt into the skins, prick them all over with a fork and place on the middle shelf of the oven. Turn on the oven to 400°F and bake for about an hour, until the flesh yields and feels soft when pressed.

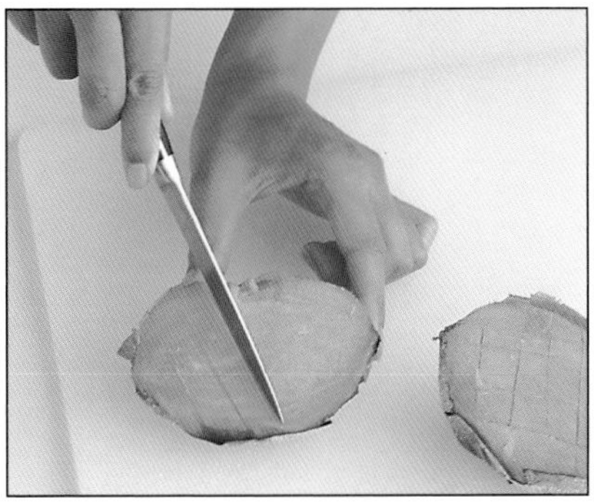

2 The potatoes can either be served in halves or whole. For halves, split each one lengthwise and make close crisscross cuts in the flesh of each half. Then spread with slices of butter and work the butter and seasonings roughly into the cuts with a knife point.

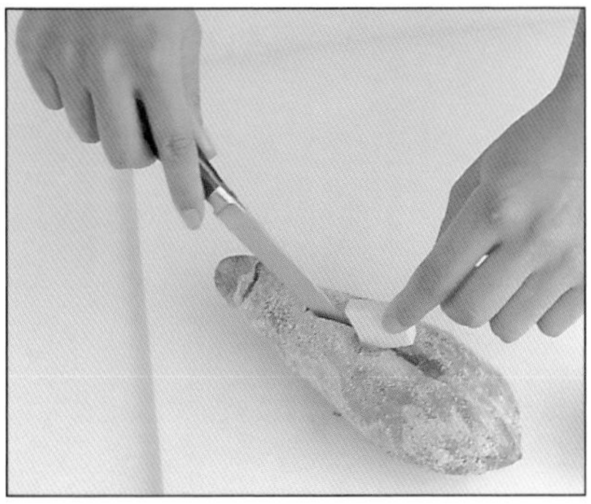

3 Alternatively, make an incision along the length of each potato if they are to be served whole. Open them slightly and put in butter slices along the length, seasoning with the peppers and a pinch of salt.

COOK'S TIP

Sweet potatoes cook more quickly than ordinary ones, so there is no need to preheat the oven.

Thai Fragrant Rice

This lovely, soft, fluffy rice dish, perfumed with fresh lemongrass, is a classic Thai accompaniment to red and green curries.

INGREDIENTS

Serves 4

1 stalk of lemongrass
2 limes
1 cup brown basmati rice
1 tablespoon olive oil
1 onion, chopped
1-inch piece of fresh ginger root, peeled and finely chopped
1½ teaspoons coriander seeds
1½ teaspoons cumin seeds
3 cups vegetable stock
¼ cup chopped cilantro
lime wedges, to serve

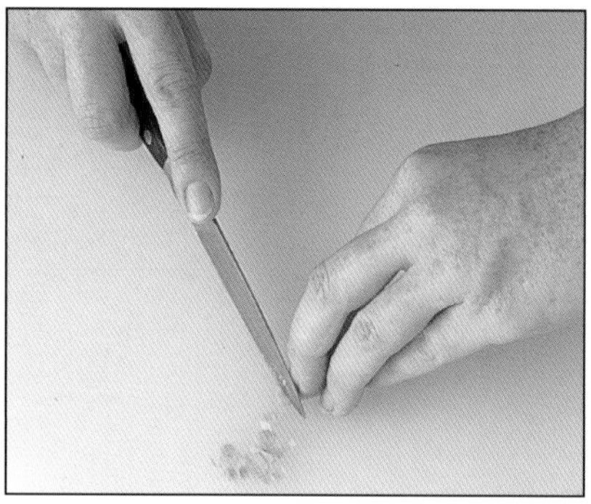

1 Finely chop the lemongrass using a sharp knife.

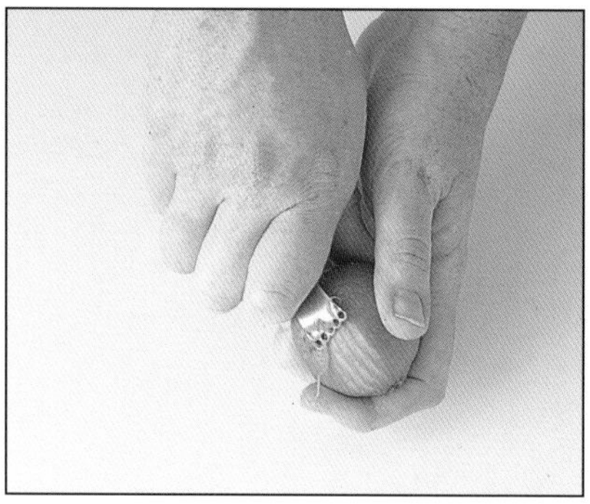

2 Remove the zest from the limes using a zester or fine grater. Avoid removing the pith with the zest.

3 Rinse the rice in plenty of cold water until the water runs clear. Drain through a sieve.

4 Heat the oil in a large pan and add the onion, ginger, spices, lemongrass and lime zest and cook gently for 2–3 minutes.

COOK'S TIP

Other varieties of rice, such as white basmati or long-grain, can be used for this dish, but you will need to adjust the cooking times accordingly.

5 Add the rice and cook for another minute, then add the stock and bring to a boil. Reduce the heat to very low and cover the pan. Cook gently for 30 minutes, then check the rice. If it is still crunchy, cover the pan again and cook for 3–5 minutes more. Remove from the heat.

6 Stir in the chopped cilantro, fluff up the rice, cover and let sit for 10 minutes. Serve with lime wedges.

Rice with Seeds and Spices

A change from plain rice and a colorful accompaniment to spicy curries. Basmati rice gives the best texture and flavor, but you can use ordinary long-grain rice, if you prefer.

INGREDIENTS

Serves 4

1 teaspoon sunflower oil
½ teaspoon ground turmeric
6 cardamom pods, lightly crushed
1 teaspoon coriander seeds, lightly crushed
1 garlic clove, crushed
1 cup basmati rice
1⅔ cups vegetable stock
½ cup plain yogurt
1 tablespoon toasted sunflower seeds
1 tablespoon toasted sesame seeds
salt and freshly ground black pepper
cilantro leaves, to garnish

1 Heat the oil in a nonstick frying pan and sauté the spices and garlic for about 1 minute, stirring all the time.

2 Add the rice and stock, bring to a boil, then cover and simmer for 15 minutes, or until just tender.

3 Stir in the yogurt and the toasted sunflower and sesame seeds. Season with salt and pepper and serve hot, garnished with cilantro leaves.

COOK'S TIP

Seeds are particularly rich in minerals, so they are a good addition to all kinds of dishes. Light toasting will improve their flavor.

Red Fried Rice

This vibrant rice dish owes its appeal as much to the bright colors of red onion, red bell pepper and tomatoes as it does to their flavors.

INGREDIENTS

Serves 2

¾ cup basmati rice
2 tablespoons peanut oil
1 small red onion, chopped
1 red bell pepper, seeded and chopped
8 ounces cherry tomatoes, halved
2 eggs, beaten
salt and freshly ground black pepper

1 Wash the rice several times under cold running water. Drain well. Bring a large pan of water to a boil. Add the rice and cook for 10–12 minutes.

2 Meanwhile, heat the oil in a wok until very hot. Add the onion and pepper and stir-fry for 2–3 minutes. Add the cherry tomatoes and continue stir-frying for 2 minutes more.

3 Pour in the beaten eggs all at once. Cook for 30 seconds without stirring, then stir to break up the egg as it sets.

4 Drain the cooked rice thoroughly. Add to the wok and toss it over the heat with the vegetable and egg mixture for 3 minutes. Season with salt and pepper and serve immediately.

Herbed Rice Pilaf

A quick and easy dish to make, this simple pilaf is delicious to eat. Serve with a selection of fresh seasonal vegetables, such as broccoli florets and carrots.

INGREDIENTS

Serves 4

8 ounces mixed brown basmati and wild rice
1 tablespoon olive oil
1 onion, chopped
1 garlic clove, crushed
1 teaspoon ground cumin
1 teaspoon ground turmeric
½ cup golden raisins
3 cups vegetable stock
2–3 tablespoons chopped fresh mixed herbs
salt and freshly ground black pepper
sprigs of fresh herbs and ¼ cup pistachio nuts, chopped, to garnish

1 Wash the rice under cold running water, then drain well. Heat the oil, add the onion and garlic and cook gently for 5 minutes, stirring occasionally.

2 Add the spices and rice and cook gently for 1 minute, stirring. Stir in the raisins and stock, bring to a boil, cover and simmer gently for 20–25 minutes, stirring occasionally.

3 Stir in the chopped mixed herbs and season with salt and pepper. Spoon the pilaf into a warmed serving dish and garnish with fresh herb sprigs and a sprinkling of chopped pistachio nuts. Serve immediately.

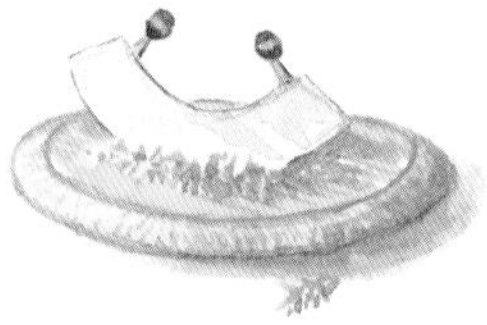

Cheese-Topped Roast Baby Vegetables

This is a simple way to bring out the flavor of baby vegetables.

INGREDIENTS

Serves 6

2¼ pounds mixed baby vegetables, such as eggplant, onions or shallots, zucchini, corn, button mushrooms
1 red bell pepper, seeded and cut into large chunks
1–2 garlic cloves, finely chopped
1–2 tablespoons olive oil
2 tablespoons chopped fresh mixed herbs
8 ounces cherry tomatoes
4 ounces mozzarella cheese, coarsely grated
salt and freshly ground black pepper
black olives, to garnish (optional)

1 Preheat the oven to 425°F. Cut the eggplant and onions or shallots in half lengthwise.

2 Place the baby vegetables, pepper and garlic in a shallow ovenproof dish. Season with salt and pepper, drizzle with the oil and toss the vegetables to coat. Bake for 20 minutes, until tinged brown at the edges, stirring once.

3 Stir in the herbs, scatter the tomatoes over the top and sprinkle with the mozzarella cheese. Bake for another 5–10 minutes, until the cheese has melted and is bubbling. Serve at once, garnished with black olives, if you like.

Chinese Brussels Sprouts

If you are bored with plain boiled Brussels sprouts, try pepping them up Chinese-style with this unusual stir-fried method.

INGREDIENTS

Serves 4

1 pound Brussels sprouts
1 teaspoon sesame or sunflower oil
2 scallions, sliced
½ teaspoon Chinese five-spice powder
1 tablespoon light soy sauce

1 Trim the Brussels sprouts, then shred them finely using a large, sharp knife or a food processor.

2 Heat the oil and add the sprouts and scallions. Stir-fry for about 2 minutes, without allowing the mixture to brown.

3 Stir in the five-spice powder and soy sauce, then cook, stirring, for another 2–3 minutes, until just tender. Serve hot with other Chinese dishes.

Festive Brussels Sprouts

This recipe originated in France, where it is a popular side dish at Christmastime.

INGREDIENTS

Serves 4–6

8 ounces chestnuts
½ cup milk
1¼ pounds (4 cups) small, tender Brussels sprouts
2 tablespoons butter
1 shallot, finely chopped
2–3 tablespoons dry white wine or water

1 Using a small knife, score a cross in the bottom of each chestnut. Bring a saucepan of water to a boil over medium-high heat, then drop in the chestnuts and boil for 6–8 minutes. Remove pan from the heat.

2 Using a slotted spoon, remove a few chestnuts from the pan, leaving the others immersed in the water until ready to peel. Before the chestnuts cool, remove the outer shell with a knife and then peel off the inner skin.

3 Rinse the pan, return the peeled chestnuts to it and add the milk. Add enough water to completely cover the chestnuts. Simmer over medium heat for 12–15 minutes, until the chestnuts are just tender. Drain and set aside.

4 Remove any wilted or yellow leaves from the Brussels sprouts. Trim the root ends but leave intact, or the leaves will separate. Using a small knife, score a cross in the bottom of each sprout so they cook evenly.

5 In a large, heavy frying pan, melt the butter over medium heat. Stir in the chopped shallot and cook for 1–2 minutes, until just softened, then add the Brussels sprouts and wine or water. Cook, covered, over medium heat for 6–8 minutes, shaking the pan and stirring occasionally, adding a little more water if necessary.

6 Add the poached chestnuts and toss gently to combine, then cover and cook for 3–5 minutes more, until the chestnuts and Brussels sprouts are tender.

Szechuan Eggplant

This medium-hot dish is also known as "fish fragrant eggplant" in China, because the eggplant is cooked with flavorings that are often used with fish.

INGREDIENTS

Serves 4

2 small eggplants
1 teaspoon salt
3 dried red chiles
peanut oil, for deep-frying
3–4 garlic cloves, finely chopped
½-inch piece of fresh ginger root, finely chopped
4 scallions, cut into 1-inch lengths (white and green parts separated)
1 tablespoon Chinese rice wine or medium-dry sherry
1 tablespoon light soy sauce
1 teaspoon sugar
¼ teaspoon ground roasted Szechuan peppercorns
1 tablespoon Chinese rice vinegar
1 teaspoon sesame oil

1 Trim the eggplant and cut into strips about 1½ inches wide and 3 inches long. Place the eggplant strips in a colander and sprinkle with the salt. Set aside for 30 minutes, then rinse thoroughly under cold running water. Pat dry with paper towels.

2 Meanwhile, soak the chiles in warm water for 15 minutes. Drain, then cut each chile into four pieces, discarding the seeds.

3 Half-fill a wok with oil and heat to 350°F. Deep-fry the eggplant until golden brown. Drain on paper towels. Pour off most of the oil from the wok. Reheat the oil and add the garlic, ginger and white scallion parts.

4 Stir-fry for 30 seconds. Add the eggplant and toss, then add the rice wine or sherry, soy sauce, sugar, ground peppercorns and rice vinegar. Stir-fry for 1–2 minutes. Sprinkle with the sesame oil and green scallion parts and serve immediately.

Bok Choy with Soy Sauce

In this recipe, Chinese greens are prepared in a very simple way—stir-fried and served with soy sauce. The combination makes a very simple, quickly prepared, tasty accompaniment.

INGREDIENTS

Serves 3-4

1 pound bok choy

2 tablespoons peanut oil

1–2 tablespoons plum sauce

1 Trim the bok choy, removing any discolored leaves and damaged stems. Tear into manageable pieces.

2 Heat a wok until hot, add the oil and swirl it around.

3 Add the bok choy and stir-fry for 2–3 minutes, until the greens have wilted a little.

4 Add the plum sauce and continue to stir-fry for a few seconds more, until the greens are cooked but still slightly crisp. Serve immediately.

VARIATION

You can replace the Chinese greens with Chinese flowering cabbage, which is also known by its Cantonese name, choy sam. It has green leaves and tiny yellow flowers, which are also eaten along with the leaves and stalks. It is available at Asian markets.

Sweet and Sour Onions

Cooked in this way, sweet pearl onions make an unusual and tasty side dish. This recipe originated in the Provence region of France.

INGREDIENTS

Serves 6

1 pound pearl onions, peeled
¼ cup wine vinegar
3 tablespoons olive oil
3 tablespoons sugar
3 tablespoons tomato paste
1 bay leaf
2 sprigs of fresh parsley
½ cup raisins
salt and freshly ground black pepper

1 Put all the ingredients in a saucepan with 1¼ cups water. Bring to a boil and simmer gently, uncovered, for 45 minutes, or until the onions are tender and most of the liquid has evaporated.

2 Remove the bay leaf and parsley, check the seasoning and transfer to a serving dish. Serve at room temperature.

Spinach with Raisins and Pine Nuts

Raisins and pine nuts are perfect partners. Here, tossed with wilted spinach and croutons, their contrasting textures make a delicious main-dish accompaniment.

INGREDIENTS

Serves 4

⅓ cup raisins
1 thick slice crusty white bread
3 tablespoons olive oil
⅓ cup pine nuts
1¼ pounds young spinach, stalks removed
2 garlic cloves, crushed
salt and freshly ground black pepper

1 Put the raisins in a small bowl with boiling water and let soak for 10 minutes. Drain.

2 Cut the bread into cubes and discard the crusts. Heat 2 tablespoons of the oil and sauté the bread until golden. Drain.

3 Heat the remaining oil in the pan. Sauté the pine nuts until they are beginning to color. Add the spinach and garlic and cook quickly, turning the spinach until it has just wilted.

4 Toss in the raisins and season with salt and pepper. Transfer to a warmed serving dish. Sprinkle with croutons and serve hot.

VARIATION

Use Swiss chard or beet greens instead of the spinach, and cook them a little longer.

Hot Parsnip Fritters on Baby Spinach

Deep-frying brings out the luscious sweetness of parsnips, and their flavor is perfectly complemented by walnut-dressed baby spinach leaves.

INGREDIENTS

Serves 4

2 large parsnips
1 cup all-purpose flour
1 egg, separated
½ cup milk
4 ounces baby spinach leaves, washed and dried
2 tablespoons olive oil
1 tablespoon walnut oil
1 tablespoon sherry vinegar
oil for deep-frying
1 tablespoon coarsely chopped walnuts
salt, freshly ground black pepper, and cayenne pepper

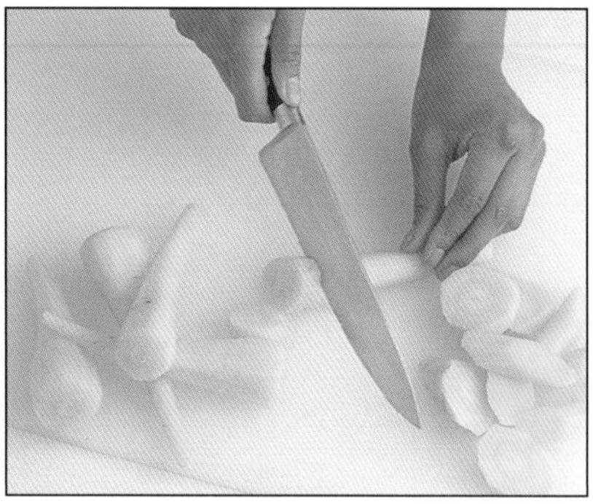

1 Peel the parsnips, bring to a boil in a pan of salted water and simmer for 10–15 minutes, until tender but not at all mushy. Drain, cool and cut diagonally into slices about 2 inches long and ¼–½ inch thick.

2 Put the flour in a bowl and make a well in the center. Put the egg yolk in the well and mix in with a fork. Add the milk while continuing to mix in the flour. Season with salt and black and cayenne peppers, and beat with a whisk until the batter is smooth.

3 Put the spinach leaves in a bowl. Mix the oils and vinegar. Season with salt and pepper.

4 When you are ready to serve, beat the egg white to soft peaks, fold in a little of the yolk batter, then fold the white into the batter. Heat the oil for frying.

5 Shake the dressing vigorously and toss with the salad. Arrange the salad on four plates and sprinkle with walnuts.

6 Dip the parsnip slices in batter and fry until puffy and golden. Drain on paper towels and keep warm. Arrange the fritters on top of the salad.

Parsnip and Chestnut Croquettes

The distinctive sweet, nutty taste of chestnuts blends perfectly with the sweet but earthy flavor of parsnips. Fresh chestnuts need to be peeled, but canned unsweetened chestnuts are nearly as good for this recipe.

INGREDIENTS

Makes 10–12

1 pound parsnips, cut roughly into small pieces
4 ounces shelled fresh or canned whole chestnuts
2 tablespoons butter
1 garlic clove, crushed
1 tablespoon chopped cilantro
1 egg, beaten
1½–2 ounces fresh white bread crumbs
vegetable oil, for frying
salt and freshly ground black pepper
sprig of cilantro, to garnish

1 Place the parsnips in a saucepan with enough water to cover. Bring to a boil, cover and simmer for 15–20 minutes.

2 Place the chestnuts in a pan of water, bring to a boil and simmer for 8–10 minutes. Drain, place in a bowl and mash roughly into a pulp.

3 Melt the butter in a saucepan and cook the garlic for 30 seconds. Drain the parsnips and mash with the garlic butter. Stir in the chestnuts and chopped cilantro. Season with salt and pepper.

4 Take about 1 tablespoon of the mixture at a time and form into small croquettes, about 3 inches long. Dip each croquette into the beaten egg and then roll in the bread crumbs.

5 Heat a little oil in a frying pan and fry each of the croquettes for 3–4 minutes, until crisp and golden, turning frequently so they brown evenly.

6 Drain the croquettes on sheets of paper towel, wiping away any excess oil, and serve at once, garnished with sprigs of cilantro.

Balti Baby Vegetables

There is a wide and wonderful selection of baby vegetables available in supermarkets these days, and this simple recipe does full justice to their delicate flavor and attractive appearance. Serve as part of a main meal or even as a light appetizer.

INGREDIENTS

Serves 4–6

10 new potatoes, halved
12–14 baby carrots
12–14 baby zucchini
2 tablespoons corn oil
15 pearl onions
2 tablespoons chili sauce
1 teaspoon garlic pulp
1 teaspoon ginger pulp
1 teaspoon salt
14-ounce can chickpeas, drained
10 cherry tomatoes
1 teaspoon crushed red pepper and 2 tablespoons sesame seeds, to garnish

1 Bring a medium pan of salted water to a boil and add the new potatoes and baby carrots. After 12–15 minutes, add the zucchini and boil for another 5 minutes, or until all the vegetables are just tender.

2 Drain the vegetables well and set aside.

3 Heat the oil in a deep, round-bottomed frying pan or wok and add the onions. Cook until the onions turn golden brown. Lower the heat and add the chili sauce, garlic, ginger and salt, taking care not to burn the mixture.

4 Add the chickpeas and stir-fry over medium heat until the moisture has been absorbed.

5 Add the cooked vegetables and cherry tomatoes and continue cooking over medium heat, stirring with a slotted spoon, for about 2 minutes.

6 Garnish with crushed red pepper and sesame seeds and serve.

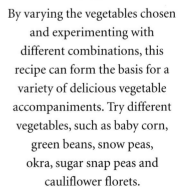

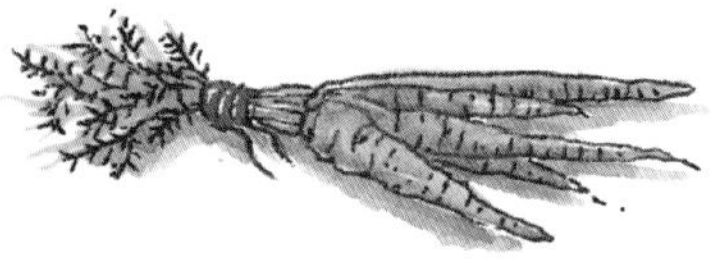

VARIATION

By varying the vegetables chosen and experimenting with different combinations, this recipe can form the basis for a variety of delicious vegetable accompaniments. Try different vegetables, such as baby corn, green beans, snow peas, okra, sugar snap peas and cauliflower florets.

Spring Vegetable Stir-Fry

A colorful, dazzling medley of fresh and sweet young vegetables.

INGREDIENTS

Serves 4

1 tablespoon peanut oil
1 garlic clove, sliced
1-inch piece of fresh ginger root, finely chopped
4 ounces baby carrots
4 ounces pattypan squash
4 ounces baby corn
4 ounces green beans, trimmed
4 ounces sugar snap peas, trimmed
4 ounces young asparagus, cut into 3-inch pieces
8 scallions, trimmed and cut into 2-inch pieces
4 ounces cherry tomatoes

For the dressing

juice of 2 limes
1 tablespoon honey
1 tablespoon soy sauce
1 teaspoon sesame oil

1 Heat the peanut oil in a wok or large frying pan.

2 Add the garlic and ginger and stir-fry over high heat for 1 minute.

3 Add the carrots, pattypan squash, baby corn and beans and stir-fry for another 3–4 minutes.

4 Add the sugar snap peas, asparagus, scallions and cherry tomatoes and stir-fry for another 1–2 minutes.

5 Mix the dressing ingredients together and add to the pan.

6 Stir well and then cover the pan. Cook for 2–3 minutes more, until the vegetables are just tender but still crisp.

COOK'S TIP

Stir-fries take only moments to cook, so prepare this dish at the last minute.

Fried Noodles, Bean Sprouts and Asparagus

Soft fried noodles contrast beautifully with crisp bean sprouts and asparagus in this superquick recipe.

INGREDIENTS

Serves 2

4 ounces dried Chinese egg noodles
4 tablespoons vegetable oil
1 small onion, chopped
1-inch piece of fresh ginger root, peeled and grated
2 garlic cloves, crushed
6 ounces young asparagus spears, trimmed
4 ounces bean sprouts
4 scallions, sliced
3 tablespoons soy sauce
salt and freshly ground black pepper

1 Bring a pan of salted water to a boil. Add the noodles and cook for 2–3 minutes, until just tender. Drain and toss with 2 tablespoons of the oil.

2 Heat the remaining oil in a wok or frying pan until very hot. Add the onion, ginger and garlic and stir-fry for 2–3 minutes. Add the asparagus and stir-fry for 2–3 minutes more.

3 Add the egg noodles and bean sprouts and stir-fry for 2 minutes.

4 Stir in the scallions and soy sauce. Season with salt and pepper, adding salt sparingly, as the soy sauce will probably supply enough salt in itself. Stir-fry for 1 minute, then serve at once.

Deep-Fried Root Vegetables with Spiced Salt

All kinds of root vegetables may be finely sliced and deep-fried to make chips. Serve as an accompaniment to an Asian-style meal or simply by themselves as a snack.

INGREDIENTS

Serves 4–6

1 carrot

2 parsnips

2 raw beets

1 sweet potato

peanut oil, for deep-frying

¼ teaspoon cayenne pepper

1 teaspoon sea salt flakes

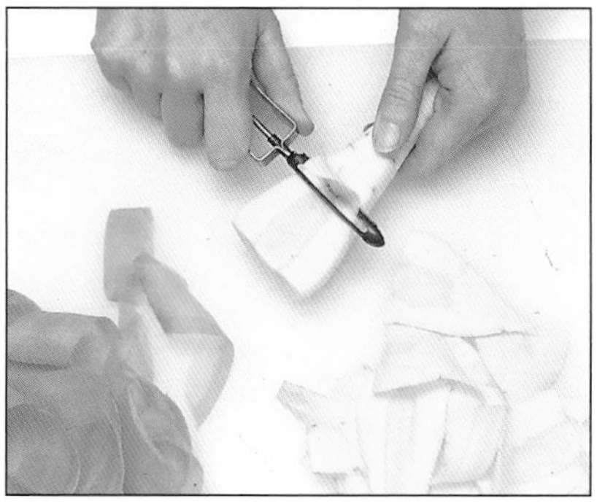

1 Peel all the vegetables, then slice the carrot and parsnips into long, thin ribbons and the beets and sweet potato into thin rounds. Pat dry all the vegetables on paper towels.

2 Half-fill a wok with oil and heat to 350°F. Add the vegetable slices in batches and deep-fry for 2–3 minutes, until golden and crisp. Remove and drain on paper towels.

3 Place the cayenne pepper and sea salt in a mortar and grind together to a coarse powder.

4 Pile up the vegetable chips on a serving plate and sprinkle with the spiced salt.

COOK'S TIP

To save time, you can slice the vegetables using a mandoline or a blender or food processor with a thin slicing disk attached.

Vegetables Provençal

The flavors of the Mediterranean shine through in this delicious side dish.

INGREDIENTS

Serves 6

1 onion, sliced
2 leeks, sliced
2 garlic cloves, crushed
1 red bell pepper, seeded and sliced
1 green bell pepper, seeded and sliced
1 yellow bell pepper, seeded and sliced
12 ounces zucchini, sliced
8 ounces mushrooms, sliced
14-ounce can chopped tomatoes
2 tablespoons ruby port
2 tablespoons tomato paste
1 tablespoon ketchup
14-ounce can chickpeas
1 cup pitted black olives
3 tablespoons chopped fresh mixed herbs
salt and freshly ground black pepper
chopped fresh mixed herbs, to garnish

1 Put the onion, leeks, garlic, peppers, zucchini and mushrooms in a large saucepan.

2 Add the tomatoes, port, tomato paste and ketchup and mix well.

3 Rinse and drain the chickpeas and add to the pan.

4 Cover, bring to a boil and simmer gently for 20–30 minutes, stirring occasionally, until the vegetables are cooked and tender but not overcooked.

5 Remove the lid and increase the heat slightly for the last 10 minutes of the cooking time, to thicken the sauce, if you like.

6 Stir in the olives and herbs and season with salt and pepper. Serve immediately, garnished with chopped mixed herbs.

COOK'S TIP

This dish is also delicious served cold. It can be prepared in advance for a picnic, stored in the refrigerator, and served with plain yogurt or a refreshing tzatziki.

HABITAT
JAPAN

Spicy Chickpeas

Chickpeas are used and cooked in a variety of ways all over the Indian subcontinent. Tamarind gives this spicy dish a deliciously sharp, tangy flavor.

INGREDIENTS

Serves 4

- 1¼ cups dried chickpeas
- 2 ounces tamarind pulp
- ½ cup boiling water
- 3 tablespoons corn oil
- ½ teaspoon cumin seeds
- 1 onion, finely chopped
- 2 garlic cloves, crushed
- 1-inch piece of fresh ginger root, peeled and grated
- 1 fresh green chile, finely chopped
- 1 teaspoon ground cumin
- 1 teaspoon ground coriander
- ¼ teaspoon ground turmeric
- ½ teaspoon salt
- 8 ounces tomatoes, peeled and finely chopped
- ½ teaspoon garam masala
- chopped fresh chiles and chopped onion, to garnish

1 Put the chickpeas in a large bowl and cover with plenty of cold water. Let soak overnight.

2 Drain the chickpeas and place in a large saucepan with double the volume of cold water. Bring to a boil and boil vigorously for 10 minutes. Skim off any scum. Cover and simmer for 1½–2 hours, or until the chickpeas are soft.

3 Meanwhile, break up the tamarind and soak in the boiling water for about 15 minutes. Rub the tamarind through a sieve into a bowl, discarding any seeds and fiber.

COOK'S TIP

To save time, make double the quantity of tamarind pulp and freeze in ice-cube trays. It will keep for up to 2 months.

4 Heat the oil in a large saucepan and sauté the cumin seeds for 2 minutes, until they splutter. Add the onion, garlic, ginger and chile and sauté for 5 minutes.

5 Add the cumin, coriander, turmeric and salt and sauté for 3–4 minutes. Add the tomatoes and tamarind pulp. Bring to a boil and simmer for 5 minutes.

6 Add the chickpeas and garam masala. Cover and simmer for about 45 minutes. Garnish with chopped chiles and onion.

Frijoles

A traditional Mexican bean dish that tastes great with tortillas and vegetable chili.

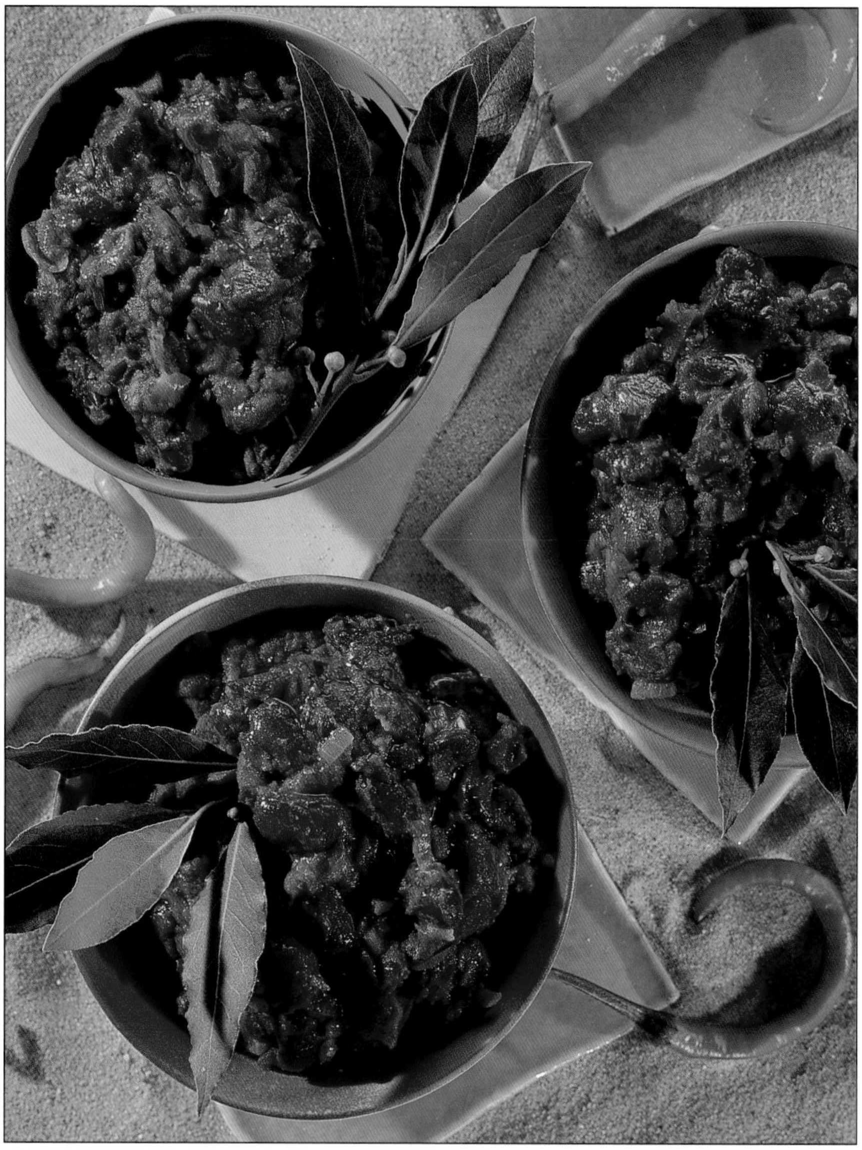

INGREDIENTS

Serves 6–8

1¼–1½ cups dried red kidney, pinto or black beans, picked over and rinsed
2 onions, finely chopped
2 garlic cloves, chopped
1 bay leaf
1 or more small fresh green chiles
2 tablespoons corn oil
2 tomatoes, peeled, seeded and chopped
salt
sprigs of fresh bay leaves, to garnish

1 Put the beans in a pan and add cold water to cover by 1 inch.

2 Add half the onion, half the garlic, the bay leaf and the chile or chiles. Bring to a boil and boil vigorously for about 10 minutes. Put the beans and liquid into an earthenware pot or large saucepan, cover and cook over low heat for 30 minutes. Add boiling water if the mixture starts to become dry.

3 When the beans begin to wrinkle, add 1 tablespoon of the corn oil and cook for another 30 minutes, or until the beans are tender. Add salt to taste and cook for 30 minutes more, but try to avoid adding any more water.

4 Remove the beans from the heat. Heat the remaining oil in a small frying pan and sauté the remaining onion and garlic together until the onion is soft. Add the tomatoes and cook for a few minutes more.

5 Spoon 3 tablespoons of the beans out of the pot or pan and add them to the tomato mixture. Mash to a paste. Stir into the beans to thicken the liquid. Cook for just long enough to heat through, if necessary. Serve the beans in small bowls and garnish with fresh bay leaves.

Peas with Pearl Onions and Cream

Ideally, use fresh peas and fresh pearl onions. Frozen peas are an acceptable substitute if fresh ones aren't available, but frozen onions tend to be insipid and are not worth using. Alternatively, use the white parts of scallions.

INGREDIENTS

Serves 4

6 ounces pearl onions
1 tablespoon butter
2 pounds fresh peas (about 12 ounces shelled or frozen)
⅔ cup heavy cream
2 tablespoons all-purpose flour
2 teaspoons chopped fresh parsley
1–2 tablespoons lemon juice (optional)
salt and freshly ground black pepper

1 Peel the onions and halve them if necessary. Melt the butter in a flameproof casserole and cook the onions for 5–6 minutes over moderate heat, until they begin to be flecked with brown.

2 Add the peas and stir-fry for a few minutes. Add ½ cup water and bring to a boil. Partially cover and simmer for about 10 minutes, until the peas and onions are tender. There should be a thin layer of water on the bottom of the pan—add a little more water if necessary or, if there is too much liquid, remove the lid and increase the heat until the liquid is reduced.

3 Using a small whisk, blend the cream with the flour. Remove the pan from the heat and stir in the combined cream and flour and the chopped parsley. Season with salt and pepper.

4 Cook over gentle heat for 3–4 minutes, until the sauce is thick. Taste and adjust the seasoning; add a little lemon juice to sharpen, if desired.

Red Cabbage in Port and Red Wine

A sweet and sour, spicy red cabbage dish, with the added crunch of pears and walnuts.

INGREDIENTS

Serves 6

1 tablespoon walnut oil
1 onion, sliced
2 whole star anise
1 teaspoon ground cinnamon
pinch of ground cloves
1 pound red cabbage, finely shredded
2 tablespoons dark brown sugar
3 tablespoons red wine vinegar
1¼ cups red wine
⅔ cup port
2 pears, cut into ½-inch cubes
½ cup raisins
½ cup walnut halves
salt and freshly ground black pepper

1 Heat the oil in a large pan. Add the onion and cook gently for about 5 minutes, until softened.

2 Add the star anise, cinnamon, cloves and cabbage and cook for about 3 minutes more.

COOK'S TIP

You can braise this dish in a low oven for up to 1½ hours.

3 Stir in the brown sugar, vinegar, red wine and port. Cover the pan; simmer gently for 10 minutes, stirring occasionally.

4 Stir in the cubed pears and raisins and cook for another 10 minutes, or until the cabbage is tender. Season with salt and pepper. Mix in the walnut halves and serve.

Beet and Celeriac Casserole

Beautiful ruby-red slices of beets and celeriac make a stunning light accompaniment to any main-course dish.

INGREDIENTS

Serves 6

12 ounces raw beets
12 ounces raw celeriac
4 sprigs of fresh thyme, chopped
6 juniper berries, crushed
½ cup fresh orange juice
½ cup vegetable stock
salt and freshly ground black pepper

1 Preheat the oven to 375°F. Peel and slice the beets very finely. Quarter and peel the celeriac and slice very finely.

2 Fill a 10-inch cast-iron ovenproof or flameproof frying pan with alternate layers of beet and celeriac slices, sprinkling with thyme, juniper and salt and pepper between each layer.

3 Mix the orange juice and stock together and pour over the gratin. Place over medium heat and bring to a boil. Boil for 2 minutes.

4 Cover with foil and place in the oven for 15–20 minutes. Remove the foil and raise the oven temperature to 400°F. Cook for another 10 minutes.

Runner Beans with Garlic

Delicate and fresh-tasting flageolet beans and sautéed garlic add a distinctly French flavor to this simple side dish.

INGREDIENTS

Serves 4

1¼ cups flageolet beans
1 tablespoon olive oil
2 tablespoons butter
1 onion, finely chopped
1–2 garlic cloves, crushed
3–4 tomatoes, peeled and chopped
12 ounces runner beans, prepared and sliced
⅔ cup white wine
⅔ cup vegetable stock
2 tablespoons chopped fresh parsley
salt and freshly ground black pepper

1 Place the flageolet beans in a large saucepan of water, bring to a boil and simmer for ¾–1 hour, until tender.

2 Heat the olive oil and butter in a large frying pan and sauté the onion and garlic for 3–4 minutes, until soft.

3 Add the chopped tomatoes to the onions in the pan and continue cooking over gentle heat until they are soft.

4 Stir the flageolet beans into the onion and tomato mixture, then add the runner beans, wine, stock and a little salt. Stir. Cover and simmer for 5–10 minutes.

5 Increase the heat to reduce the liquid, then stir in the parsley, more salt, if necessary, and pepper.

Lima Beans in Chili Sauce

Try this fabulous dish of lima beans with a tomato and chile sauce for warming up on winter evenings.

INGREDIENTS

Serves 4

1 pound lima or fava beans, thawed if frozen
2 tablespoons olive oil
1 onion, finely chopped
2 garlic cloves, chopped
12 ounces tomatoes, peeled, seeded and chopped
1 or 2 drained canned jalapeño chiles, seeded and chopped
salt
chopped cilantro, to garnish

1 Cook the beans in a saucepan of boiling water for 15–20 minutes, until tender. Drain and keep hot, to one side, in the covered saucepan.

2 Heat the olive oil in a frying pan and sauté the onion and garlic until the onion is soft but not brown. Add the tomatoes and cook until the mixture thickens.

3 Add the jalapeños and cook for 1–2 minutes. Season with salt.

4 Pour the mixture over the reserved beans and check that they are hot. If not, return everything to the frying pan and cook over low heat for just long enough to heat through. Place in a warmed serving dish, garnish with cilantro and serve.

Zucchini with Sun-Dried Tomatoes

Sun-dried tomatoes have a concentrated, sweet flavor that goes well with zucchini.

INGREDIENTS

Serves 6

10 sun-dried tomatoes, dry or preserved in oil and drained
¾ cup warm water
5 tablespoons olive oil
1 large onion, finely sliced
2 garlic cloves, finely chopped
2¼ pounds zucchini, cut into thin strips
salt and freshly ground black pepper

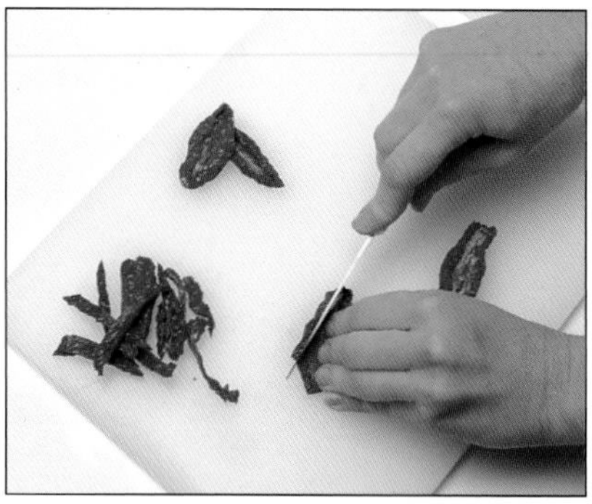

1 Slice the sun-dried tomatoes into thin strips. Place in a bowl with the warm water. Let stand for 20 minutes.

2 In a large frying pan or saucepan, heat the oil and stir in the onion. Cook over low to moderate heat until the onion softens but does not brown.

3 Stir in the garlic and zucchini strips. Cook for about 5 minutes, continuing to stir the mixture.

4 Stir in the tomatoes and their soaking liquid. Season with salt and pepper. Raise the heat slightly and cook until the zucchini are just tender. Adjust seasoning and serve hot or cold.

Tomato and Okra Stew

Okra is an unusual and delicious vegetable. It releases a sticky sap when cooked, which helps to thicken the stew.

INGREDIENTS

Serves 6

1 tablespoon olive oil
1 onion, chopped
12-ounce jar pimientos, drained
2 x 14-ounce cans chopped tomatoes
10 ounces okra
2 tablespoons chopped fresh parsley
salt and freshly ground black pepper

1 Heat the oil in a heavy pan. Add the onion and cook for 2–3 minutes.

2 Coarsely chop the pimientos and add to the onion. Add the chopped tomatoes and mix well.

3 Cut the tops off the okra and cut into halves or quarters if large. Add to the tomato sauce in the pan. Season with plenty of salt and pepper.

4 Bring the stew to a boil. Lower the heat, cover the pan and simmer for 12 minutes, until the vegetables are tender and the sauce has thickened. Stir in the chopped parsley and serve at once.

Glazed Carrots with Cider

This dish is extremely simple to make. The carrots are cooked in the minimum of liquid to bring out the best of their flavor, and the cider adds a pleasant sharpness.

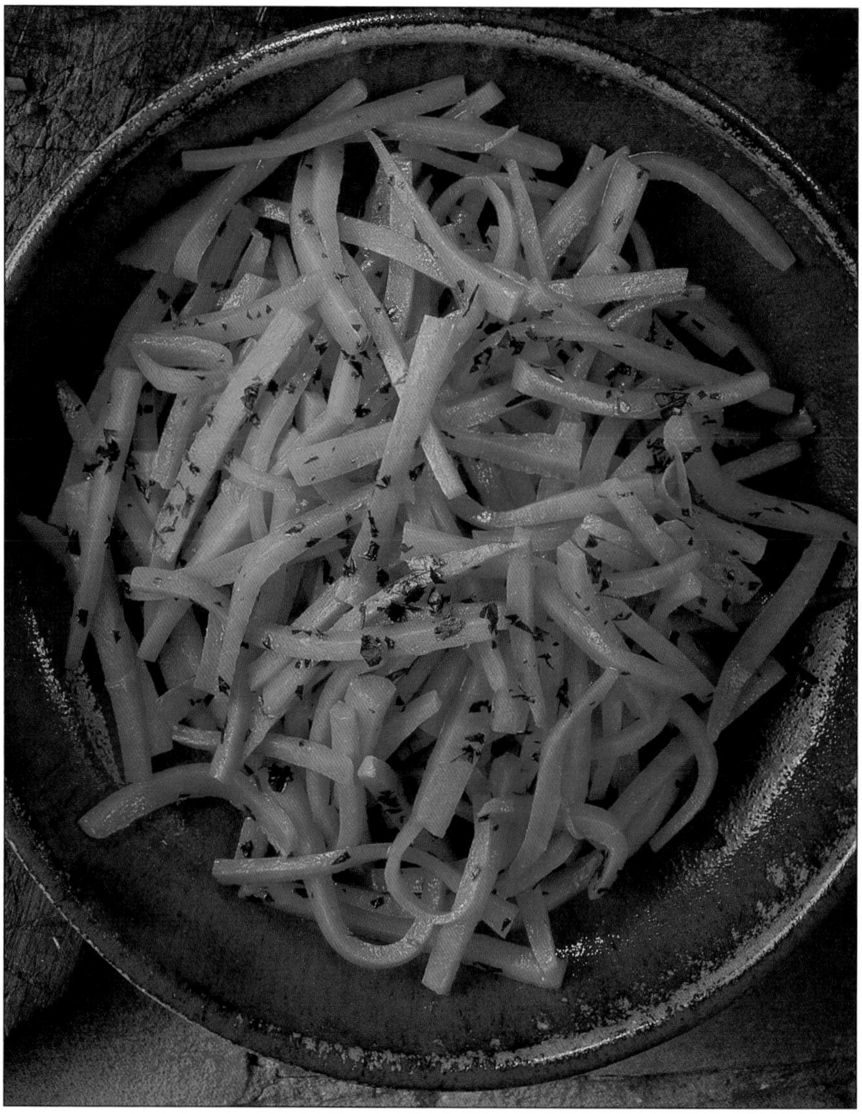

INGREDIENTS

Serves 4

1 pound young carrots
2 tablespoons butter
1 tablespoon brown sugar
½ cup cider
4 tablespoons vegetable stock or water
1 teaspoon Dijon mustard
1 tablespoon finely chopped fresh parsley

1 Trim the tops and bottoms of the carrots and peel them. Using a sharp knife, cut them into julienne strips.

2 Melt the butter in a frying pan, add the carrots and sauté for 4–5 minutes, stirring frequently. Sprinkle the brown sugar over the carrots and cook, stirring, for 1 minute, or until the sugar has dissolved.

3 Add the cider and stock or water, bring to a boil and stir in the mustard. Partially cover the pan and simmer for 10–12 minutes, until the carrots are just tender. Remove the lid and continue cooking until the liquid has reduced to a thick sauce.

4 Remove the saucepan from the heat, stir in the chopped fresh parsley and then spoon into a warmed serving dish.

COOK'S TIP

If the carrots are cooked before the liquid in the saucepan has reduced, transfer the carrots to a serving dish and rapidly boil the liquid until thick. Pour over the carrots and sprinkle with parsley.

Broccoli and Cauliflower Gratin

Broccoli and cauliflower make an attractive combination, and a yogurt and cheese sauce gives them extra piquant flavor.

INGREDIENTS

Serves 4

1 small cauliflower (about 9 ounces)
1 small head broccoli (about 9 ounces)
½ cup plain yogurt
1 cup grated Cheddar cheese
1 teaspoon whole-grain mustard
2 tablespoons whole-wheat bread crumbs
salt and freshly ground black pepper

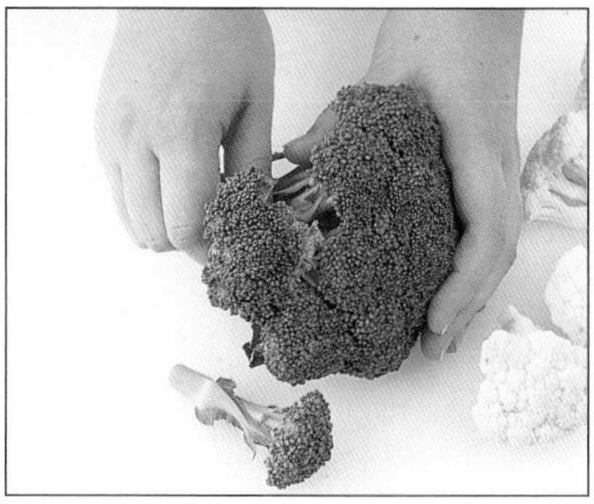

1 Break the cauliflower and broccoli into florets and cook in lightly salted boiling water for 8–10 minutes, until just tender. Drain well and transfer to a flameproof dish.

COOK'S TIP

When preparing the cauliflower and broccoli, discard the tougher parts of the stalk, then break the florets into same-size pieces so they cook evenly.

2 Mix together the yogurt, grated cheese and mustard, then season the mixture with salt and pepper and spoon over the cauliflower and broccoli.

3 Preheat the broiler to moderately hot. Sprinkle the bread crumbs over the vegetables and broil until golden brown. Serve hot.

LIGHT LUNCHES

Summer Tomato Pasta

This is a deliciously light pasta dish, full of fresh flavors. Use buffalo-milk mozzarella if you can—the flavor is noticeably better.

INGREDIENTS

Serves 4

- 2¼ cups dried penne
- 1 pound plum tomatoes
- 10 ounces mozzarella, drained
- ¼ cup olive oil
- 1 tablespoon balsamic vinegar
- grated zest and juice of 1 lemon
- 15 fresh basil leaves, shredded
- salt and freshly ground black pepper
- fresh basil leaves, to garnish

1 Cook the pasta in boiling salted water, according to the package instructions, until just tender.

2 Quarter the tomatoes and remove the seeds, then chop the flesh into small cubes. Slice the mozzarella into similar-size pieces.

3 Mix together the olive oil, balsamic vinegar, grated lemon zest, 1 tablespoon of the lemon juice and the basil. Season with salt and pepper. Add the tomatoes and mozzarella and let stand until the pasta is cooked.

4 Drain the pasta and toss with the tomato mixture. Serve immediately, garnished with fresh basil leaves.

Pappardelle and Provençal Sauce

A classic French sauce of tomatoes and fresh vegetables adds color and robust flavor to pasta.

INGREDIENTS

Serves 4

2 small purple onions, peeled, root left intact
⅔ cup vegetable stock
1–2 garlic cloves, crushed
4 tablespoons red wine
2 zucchini, cut into short lengths
1 yellow bell pepper, seeded and sliced
14-ounce can whole peeled tomatoes
2 teaspoons chopped fresh thyme
1 teaspoon sugar
12 ounces pappardelle
salt and freshly ground black pepper
fresh thyme and 6 black olives, pitted and roughly chopped, to garnish

1 Cut each onion into eight wedges through the root end, to hold them together during cooking. Place in a saucepan with the stock and garlic. Bring to a boil, cover and simmer for 5 minutes, until tender.

2 Add the red wine, zucchini, pepper, tomatoes, thyme and sugar. Season with salt and pepper. Bring to a boil and cook gently for 5–7 minutes, shaking the pan occasionally to coat the vegetables with the sauce. (Do not overcook the vegetables, as they are much better if they are slightly crunchy.)

3 Cook the pasta in a large pan of boiling salted water, according to the instructions on the package, until tender. Drain the pasta thoroughly.

4 Transfer to a warmed serving dish and top with the vegetables. Garnish with fresh thyme and chopped black olives.

Fusilli with Peppers and Onions

Broiling the peppers for this simple pasta dish intensifies their natural sweetness and gives them a delicious smoky flavor.

INGREDIENTS

Serves 4

1 pound red and yellow bell peppers (about 2 large ones)
6 tablespoons olive oil
1 large red onion, thinly sliced
2 cloves garlic, crushed
14 ounces (4 cups) fusilli or other short pasta
3 tablespoons finely chopped fresh parsley
salt and freshly ground black pepper
freshly grated Parmesan cheese, to serve

1 Place the peppers under a hot broiler and turn occasionally until they are black and blistered on all sides. Remove, place in a paper bag and let sit for 5 minutes.

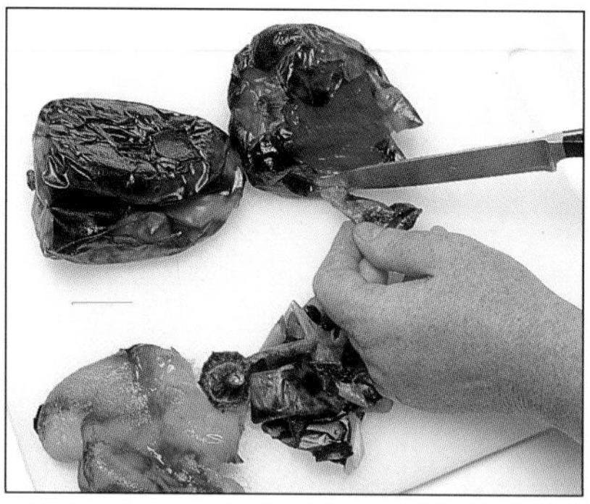

2 Peel the peppers. Cut them into quarters, remove the stems and seeds and slice the flesh into thin strips. Bring a large pan of water to a boil.

3 Heat the olive oil in a large frying pan. Add the onion and cook over moderate heat until it is translucent, 5–8 minutes. Stir in the garlic and cook for 2 minutes more.

4 Add salt and the pasta to the boiling water and cook until the pasta is tender.

5 Meanwhile, add the peppers to the onions and mix together gently. Stir in about 3 tablespoons of the pasta cooking water. Season with salt and pepper. Stir in the chopped parsley.

6 Drain the pasta. Transfer it to the pan with the vegetables and cook over moderate heat for 3–4 minutes, stirring constantly to mix the pasta into the sauce. Serve with the Parmesan passed separately.

COOK'S TIP

Bell peppers were brought to Europe by Christopher Columbus, who discovered them in Haiti. The large red, yellow and orange peppers are ripe and therefore usually sweeter than green peppers, and have a fuller flavor.

Pasta Primavera

There's no better way to showcase the best of the spring season's young vegetables than in this delightful pasta dish.

INGREDIENTS

Serves 4

8 ounces thin asparagus spears, cut in half
4 ounces snow peas, topped and tailed
4 ounces whole baby corn
8 ounces whole baby carrots
1 small red bell pepper, seeded and chopped
8 scallions, sliced
8 ounces torchietti or other pasta cuts
⅔ cup cottage cheese
⅔ cup low-fat yogurt
1 tablespoon lemon juice
1 tablespoon chopped fresh parsley
milk (optional)
1 tablespoon snipped chives
salt and freshly ground black pepper
sun-dried tomato bread, to serve

1 Cook the asparagus spears in a pan of boiling salted water for 3–4 minutes. Add the snow peas halfway through the cooking time. Drain and rinse both under cold water.

2 Cook the baby corn, carrots, pepper and scallions in the same way until tender. Drain and rinse.

3 Cook the pasta in a large pan of boiling salted water until tender. Drain thoroughly. Put the cottage cheese, yogurt, lemon juice and parsley into a food processor or blender. Season with salt and pepper, then process until smooth. Thin the sauce with a little milk, if necessary.

4 Put the sauce in a large pan with the pasta and vegetables, heat gently and toss carefully. Transfer to a warmed serving plate, sprinkle the chives over the top and serve with sun-dried tomato bread.

Penne with Fennel, Tomato and Blue Cheese

The anise flavor of the fennel makes it the perfect partner for tomato, especially when topped with blue cheese.

INGREDIENTS

Serves 2

1 fennel bulb
8 ounces penne or other dried pasta shapes (about 2 cups)
2 tablespoons olive oil
1 shallot, finely chopped
$1\frac{1}{4}$ cups passata or tomato sauce
pinch of sugar
1 teaspoon chopped fresh oregano
4 ounces blue cheese
salt and freshly ground black pepper

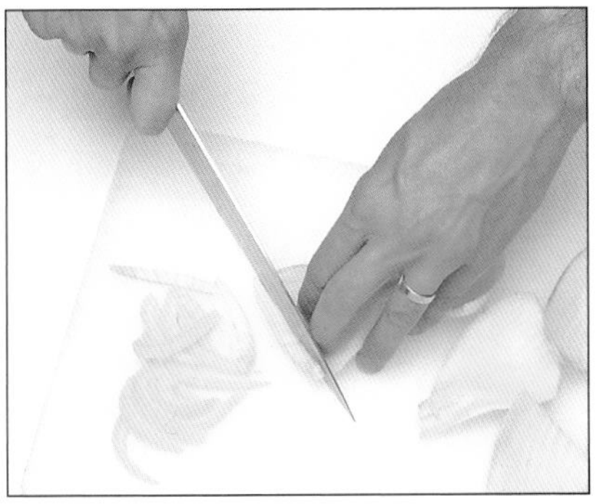

1 Cut the fennel bulb in half. Cut away the hard core and root. Slice the fennel thinly, then cut the slices into strips.

2 Bring a large pan of salted water to a boil. Add the pasta and cook for 10–12 minutes, until just tender.

3 Meanwhile, heat the oil in a small saucepan. Add the fennel and shallot and cook for 2–3 minutes over high heat, stirring occasionally.

4 Add the passata, sugar and oregano. Cover the pan and simmer gently for 10–12 minutes, until the fennel is tender. Season with salt and pepper. Drain the pasta and return it to the pan. Toss with the sauce. Serve with blue cheese crumbled over the top.

Peanut Noodles

Add any of your favorite vegetables to this quick lunch recipe—and increase the quantity of chile, if you can take the heat!

INGREDIENTS

Serves 4

7 ounces medium Chinese egg noodles
2 tablespoons olive oil
2 garlic cloves, crushed
1 large onion, roughly chopped
1 red bell pepper, seeded and roughly chopped
1 yellow bell pepper, seeded and roughly chopped
12 ounces zucchini, roughly chopped
generous ¾ cup roasted unsalted peanuts, roughly chopped

For the dressing

¼ cup olive oil
grated zest and juice of 1 lemon
1 fresh red chile, seeded and finely chopped
3 tablespoons snipped fresh chives
1–2 tablespoons balsamic vinegar
salt and freshly ground black pepper
snipped fresh chives, to garnish

1 Cook the noodles according to the package instructions and drain well.

2 Meanwhile, heat the oil in a very large frying pan or wok and cook the garlic and onion for 3 minutes, or until beginning to soften. Add the peppers and zucchini and cook for another 15 minutes over medium heat, until beginning to soften and brown. Add the peanuts and cook for 1 minute more.

3 Whisk together the olive oil, grated lemon zest and 3 tablespoons of the lemon juice, the chile, chives and balsamic vinegar to taste. Season with salt and pepper.

4 Toss the noodles into the vegetables and stir-fry to heat through. Add the dressing, stir to coat and serve immediately, garnished with fresh chives.

Stir-Fried Vegetables with Cashew Nuts

Stir-frying is the perfect way to make a delicious, colorful and very speedy meal.

INGREDIENTS

Serves 4

2 pounds mixed vegetables (see Cook's Tip)
2–4 tablespoons sunflower or olive oil
2 garlic cloves, crushed
1 tablespoon grated fresh ginger root
½ cup cashew nuts or 4 tablespoons sunflower seeds, pumpkin seeds or sesame seeds
soy sauce
salt and freshly ground black pepper

1 Prepare the vegetables according to type. Carrots and cucumber should be cut into very fine matchsticks.

2 Heat a frying pan, then trickle the oil around the rim so that it runs down to coat the surface. When the oil is hot, add the garlic and ginger and cook for 2–3 minutes, stirring. Add the harder vegetables and toss over the heat for another 5 minutes, until they start to soften.

3 Add the softer vegetables and stir-fry everything over high heat for 3–4 minutes.

4 Stir in the cashew nuts or seeds. Season with soy sauce, salt and pepper. Serve at once.

COOK'S TIP

Use a package of stir-fry vegetables or make up your own mixture. Choose from carrots, snow peas, baby corn, bok choy, cucumber, bean sprouts, mushrooms, bell peppers and scallions. Drained canned bamboo shoots and water chestnuts are delicious additions.

Rice Noodles with Vegetable Chile Sauce

Fresh chile and cilantro combine to give this recipe quite a strong flavor kick.

INGREDIENTS

Serves 4

1 tablespoon sunflower oil
1 onion, chopped
2 garlic cloves, crushed
1 fresh red chile, seeded and finely chopped
1 red bell pepper, seeded and diced
2 carrots, finely chopped
6 ounces baby corn, halved
8-ounce can sliced bamboo shoots, rinsed and drained
14-ounce can red kidney beans, rinsed and drained
1¼ cups passata or tomato sauce
1 tablespoon soy sauce
1 teaspoon ground coriander
9 ounces rice noodles
2 tablespoons chopped cilantro
salt and freshly ground black pepper
fresh parsley sprigs, to garnish

1 Heat the oil in a saucepan, add the onion, garlic, chile and pepper and cook gently for 5 minutes, stirring. Add the carrots, corn, bamboo shoots, kidney beans, passata, soy sauce and ground coriander and stir to mix.

2 Bring to a boil, then cover and simmer gently for 30 minutes, stirring occasionally, until the vegetables are tender. Season with salt and pepper.

3 Meanwhile, place the noodles in a bowl and cover with boiling water. Stir with a fork and let stand for 3–4 minutes, or according to the package instructions. Rinse and drain.

4 Stir the chopped cilantro into the sauce. Spoon the noodles onto warmed serving plates, top with the sauce, garnish with parsley and serve.

Frittata with Sun-Dried Tomatoes

Adding just a few sun-dried tomatoes gives this frittata a distinctly Mediterranean flavor.

INGREDIENTS

Serves 3–4

6 sun-dried tomatoes, dry or packed in oil and drained
¼ cup olive oil
1 small onion, finely chopped
pinch of fresh thyme leaves
6 eggs
½ cup freshly grated Parmesan cheese
salt and freshly ground black pepper

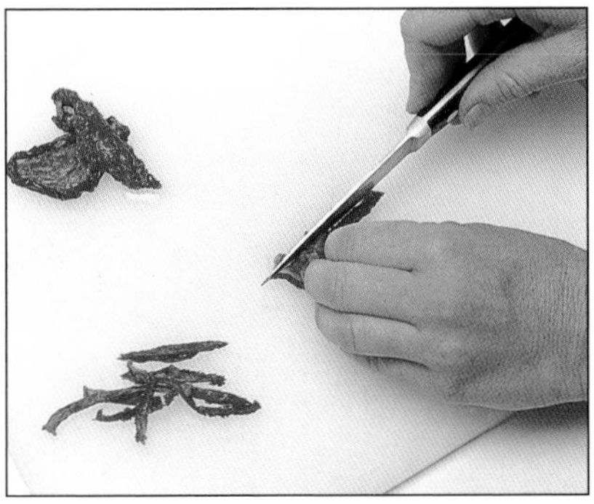

1 Place the tomatoes in a small bowl and pour on enough hot water to just cover them. Soak for about 15 minutes. Lift the tomatoes out of the water and slice them into thin strips. Reserve the soaking water.

2 Heat the oil in a large nonstick or heavy frying pan. Stir in the onion and cook for 5–6 minutes, or until soft and golden. Add the tomatoes and thyme and continue to stir over moderate heat for 2–3 minutes. Season with salt and pepper.

3 Break the eggs into a bowl and beat lightly with a fork. Stir in 3–4 tablespoons of the tomato soaking water and the grated Parmesan cheese.

4 Raise the heat under the pan. When the oil is sizzling, pour in the eggs. Mix them quickly into the other ingredients and stop stirring. Lower the heat to moderate and cook for 4–5 minutes on the first side, or until the frittata is puffed and golden brown underneath.

5 Take a large plate, place it upside down over the pan and, holding it firmly with oven mitts, turn the pan and the frittata over onto it. Slide the frittata back into the pan and continue cooking until golden brown on the second side, 3–4 minutes more. Remove from the heat. The frittata can be served hot, at room temperature or cold. Cut it into wedges to serve.

Potato Gnocchi

Gnocchi are little dumplings made either with mashed potato and flour, as here, or with semolina. They should be light in texture, and must not be overworked while being made.

INGREDIENTS

Serves 4–6

- 2¼ pounds waxy potatoes, scrubbed
- 1 tablespoon salt
- 2–2½ cups all-purpose flour
- 1 egg
- pinch of grated nutmeg
- 2 tablespoons butter
- freshly grated Parmesan cheese, to serve

1 Place the unpeeled potatoes in a large pan of salted water. Bring to a boil and cook until the potatoes are tender but not falling apart. Drain. Peel as soon as possible, while the potatoes are still hot but cool enough to handle.

VARIATION

Green gnocchi are made in exactly the same way as potato gnocchi, with the addition of fresh or frozen spinach. Use 1½ pounds fresh spinach or 14 ounces frozen leaf spinach. Mix with the potato and the flour in Step 2.

Almost any pasta sauce is suitable for serving with gnocchi; they are particularly good with a creamy Gorgonzola sauce, or simply drizzled with olive oil. Gnocchi can also be served in clear soup.

2 On a work surface, spread out a layer of flour. Mash the hot potatoes with a food mill, dropping them directly onto the flour. Sprinkle with about half of the remaining flour and mix very lightly into the potatoes.

3 Break the egg into the mixture, add the nutmeg and knead lightly, drawing in more flour as necessary. When the dough is light to the touch and no longer moist or sticky, it is ready to be rolled. Do not overwork, or the gnocchi will be heavy.

4 Divide the dough into four parts. On a lightly floured board form each part into a roll about ¾ inch in diameter, taking care not to overhandle the dough. Cut the rolls crosswise into pieces about ¾ inch long.

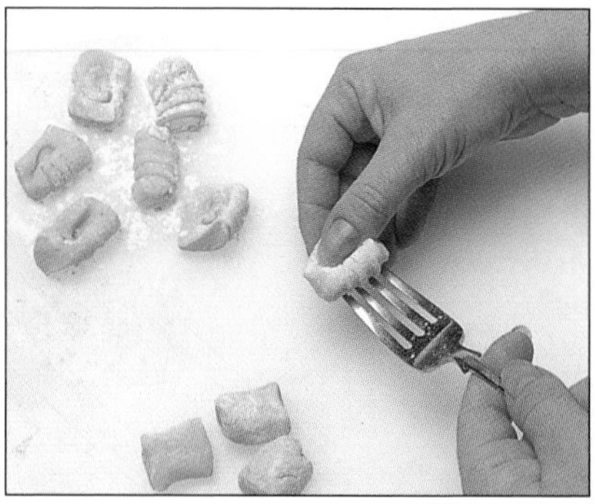

5 Hold an ordinary table fork with long tines sideways, leaning on the board. One by one, press and roll the gnocchi lightly along the tines of the fork toward the points, making ridges on one side and a depression with your thumb on the other.

6 Bring a large pan of water to a hard boil. Add salt and drop in about half the gnocchi.

7 When the gnocchi rise to the surface, after 3–4 minutes, they are done. Scoop them out, let drain and place in a warmed serving bowl. Dot with butter. Keep warm while the remaining gnocchi are boiling. As soon as they are cooked, toss the gnocchi with the butter or a heated sauce, sprinkle with grated Parmesan and serve.

Vegetable Fajitas

A colorful medley of mushrooms and bell peppers in a spicy sauce, wrapped in tortillas and served with creamy guacamole.

INGREDIENTS

Serves 2
1 onion
1 red bell pepper
1 green bell pepper
1 yellow bell pepper
1 garlic clove, crushed
8 ounces mushrooms
6 tablespoons vegetable oil
2 tablespoons medium chili powder
salt and freshly ground black pepper

For the guacamole
1 ripe avocado
1 shallot, coarsely chopped
1 fresh green chile, seeded and coarsely chopped
juice of 1 lime

To serve
4–6 flour tortillas, warmed
1 lime, cut into wedges
sprigs of cilantro

1 Slice the onion. Cut the peppers in half, remove the seeds and cut the flesh into strips. Combine the onion and peppers in a bowl. Add the crushed garlic and mix lightly.

2 Remove the mushroom stalks. Save for making stock, or discard. Slice the mushroom caps and add to the pepper mixture in the bowl. Mix the oil and chili powder in a cup, pour over the vegetable mixture and stir well. Set aside.

3 Make the guacamole. Cut the avocado in half and remove the pit and the peel. Put the flesh into a food processor or blender with the shallot, green chile and lime juice.

4 Process for 1 minute, until smooth. Scrape into a small bowl, cover tightly and put in the refrigerator to chill until required.

5 Heat a frying pan or wok until very hot. Add the marinated vegetables and stir-fry over high heat for 5–6 minutes, until the mushrooms and peppers are just tender. Season with salt and pepper. Spoon the filling onto each tortilla and roll up. Garnish with cilantro and serve with the guacamole and lime wedges.

Baked Eggs with Creamy Leeks

This is a traditional French way of enjoying eggs. You can vary the dish quite easily by experimenting with other vegetables, such as puréed spinach or ratatouille, as a base.

INGREDIENTS

Serves 4

1 tablespoon butter, plus extra for greasing
8 ounces small leeks, thinly sliced
5–6 tablespoons whipping cream
freshly grated nutmeg
4 eggs
salt and freshly ground black pepper

1 Preheat the oven to 375°F. Generously butter the bottoms and sides of four ramekins or individual soufflé dishes.

2 Melt the butter in a small frying pan and cook the leeks over medium heat, stirring frequently, until softened but not browned.

3 Add 3 tablespoons of the cream and cook gently for about 5 minutes, until the leeks are very soft and the cream has thickened a little. Season with salt, pepper and nutmeg.

4 Arrange the ramekins in a small roasting pan and divide the leeks among them. Break an egg into each, spoon 1–2 teaspoons of the remaining cream over each egg and season lightly.

5 Pour boiling water into the roasting pan to come halfway up the side of the ramekins or soufflé dishes. Bake for about 10 minutes, until the whites are set and the yolks are still soft, or a little longer if you prefer them more well done.

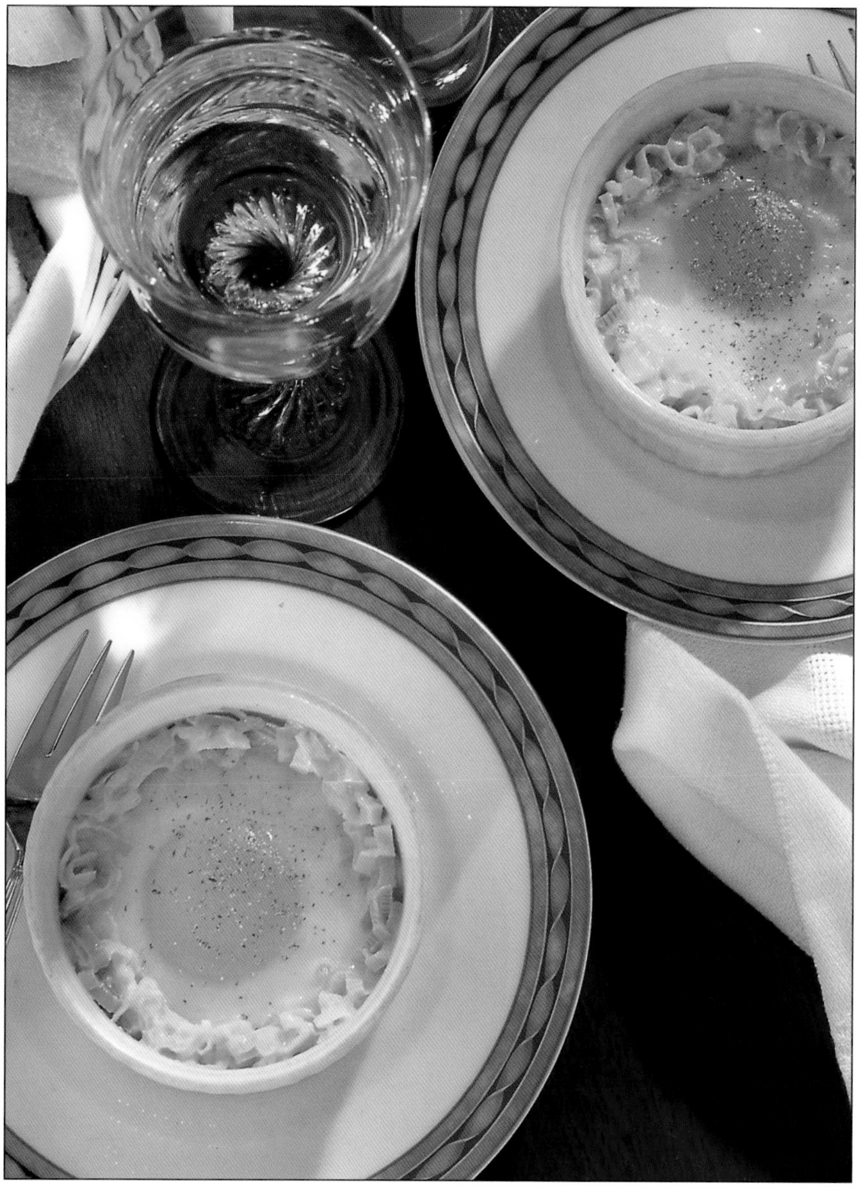

VARIATION

Put 1 tablespoon of cream in each dish with some chopped herbs. Break in the eggs, add 1 tablespoon cream and a little grated cheese, then bake.

Chinese Garlic Mushrooms

High in protein and very low in fat, tofu is useful to keep handy for quick meals and snacks like this one.

INGREDIENTS

Serves 4

8 large portobello mushrooms
3 scallions, sliced
1 garlic clove, crushed
2 tablespoons mushroom sauce (a substitute for oyster sauce}
10-ounce package marinated tofu (bean curd), cut into small dice
7-ounce can corn, drained
2 teaspoons sesame oil
salt and freshly ground black pepper

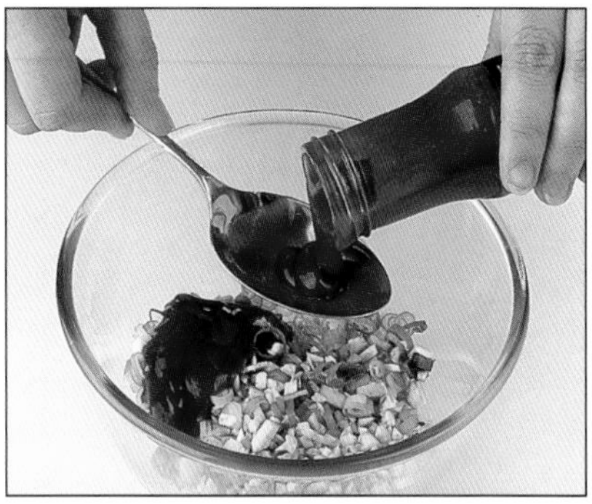

1 Preheat the oven to 400°F. Finely chop the mushroom stalks and mix with the scallions, garlic and mushroom sauce.

2 Stir in the diced marinated tofu and corn, season with salt and pepper, then spoon the filling into the mushrooms.

3 Brush the edges of the mushrooms with the sesame oil. Arrange the stuffed mushrooms in a baking dish and bake for 12–15 minutes, until just tender. Serve at once.

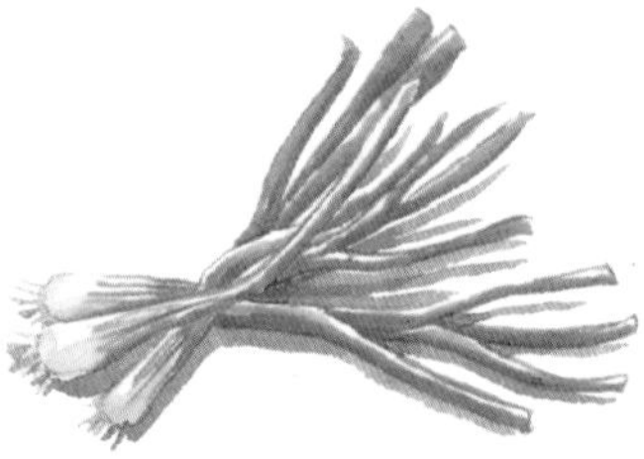

COOK'S TIP

If you prefer, omit the mushroom sauce and use light soy sauce instead.

Savory Nut Loaf

This delicious nut loaf makes perfect picnic food.

INGREDIENTS

Serves 4

1 tablespoon olive oil, plus extra for greasing
1 onion, chopped
1 leek, chopped
2 celery ribs, finely chopped
8 ounces mushrooms, chopped
2 garlic cloves, crushed
15-ounce can lentils, rinsed and drained
1 cup mixed nuts, such as hazelnuts, cashews and almonds, finely chopped
½ cup all-purpose flour
½ cup grated aged Cheddar cheese
1 medium egg, beaten
3–4 tablespoons chopped fresh mixed herbs
salt and freshly ground black pepper
chives and sprigs of flat-leaf parsley, to garnish

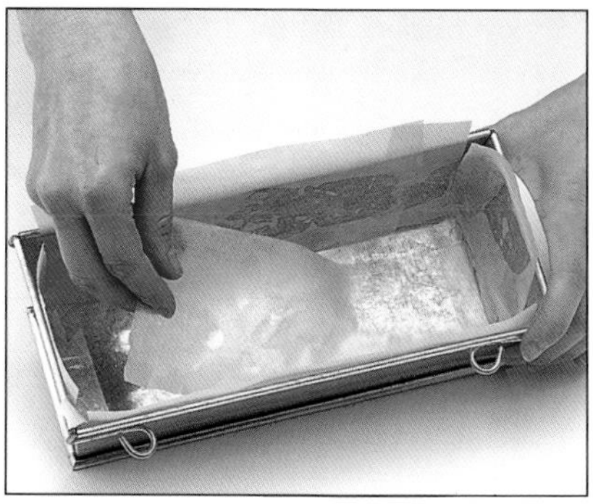

1 Preheat the oven to 375°F. Lightly grease the bottom and sides of a 9 x 5 x 3-inch (8-cup) loaf pan and line with waxed paper.

2 Heat the oil in a large saucepan, add the chopped onion, leek, celery ribs and mushrooms and the crushed garlic, then cook gently for 10 minutes, until the vegetables have softened, stirring occasionally.

3 Add the lentils, mixed nuts, flour, grated cheese, egg and herbs. Season with salt and pepper and mix thoroughly.

4 Spoon the nut, vegetable and lentil mixture into the prepared loaf pan, making sure that it is pressed into the corners, and level the surface. Bake, uncovered, for 50–60 minutes, or until the nut loaf is lightly browned on top and firm to the touch.

5 Cool the loaf slightly in the pan, then turn out onto a serving plate. Serve hot or cold, cut into slices and garnished with chives and flat-leaf parsley.

Spicy Bean and Lentil Loaf

An appetizing, high-fiber savory loaf, ideal for brown-bag lunches.

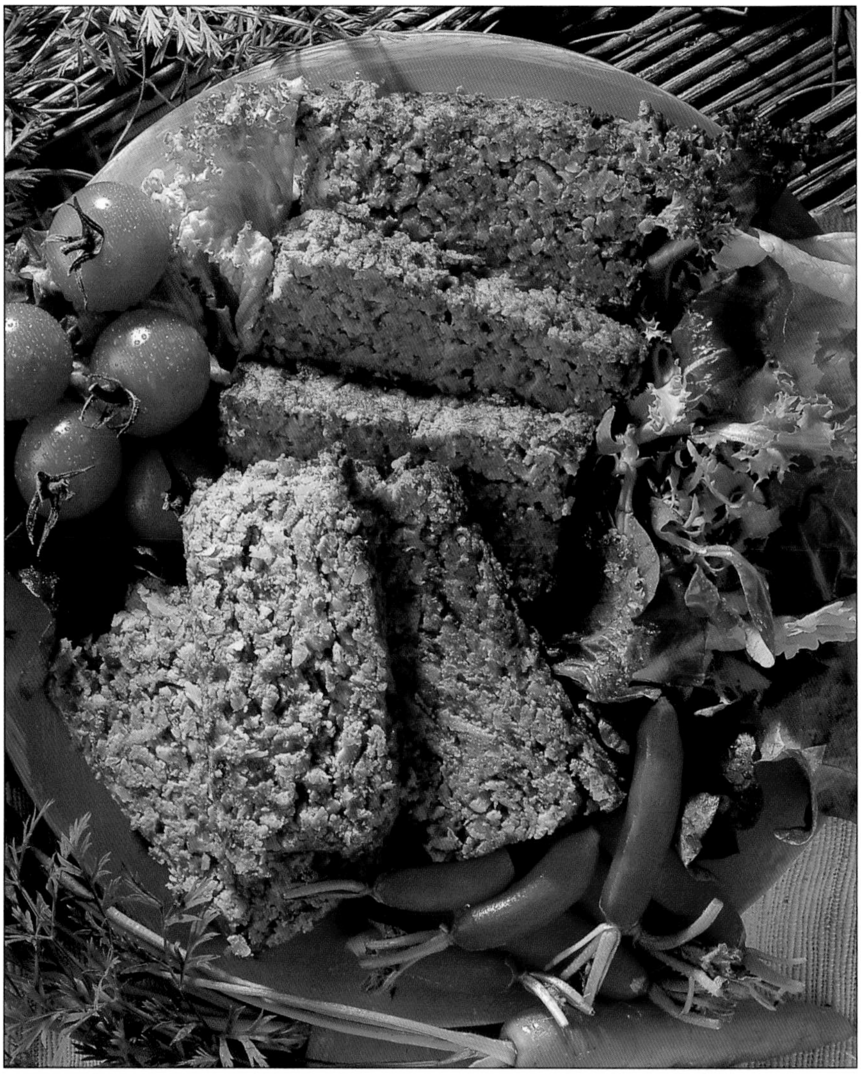

INGREDIENTS

Serves 12

2 teaspoons olive oil
1 onion, finely chopped
1 garlic clove, crushed
2 celery ribs, finely chopped
14-ounce can red kidney beans
14-ounce can lentils
1 egg
1 carrot, coarsely grated
½ cup finely grated aged Cheddar cheese
1 cup fresh whole-wheat bread crumbs
1 tablespoon tomato paste
1 tablespoon ketchup
1 teaspoon each ground cumin, ground coriander and hot chili powder
salt and freshly ground black pepper
salad, to serve

1 Preheat the oven to 350°F. Lightly grease a 9 x 5 x 3-inch (8-cup) loaf pan.

2 Heat the oil in a saucepan, add the onion, garlic and celery and cook gently for 5 minutes, stirring occasionally. Remove the pan from the heat and cool slightly.

3 Rinse and drain the beans and lentils. Place in a blender or food processor with the onion mixture and egg and process until smooth.

4 Transfer the mixture to a bowl, add all the remaining ingredients and mix well. Season with salt and pepper.

5 Spoon the mixture into the prepared pan and level the surface. Bake for about 1 hour, then remove from the pan and serve hot or cold in slices, accompanied by a salad.

Stuffed Mushrooms

This is a classic mushroom dish, strongly flavored with garlic. Use portobello mushrooms or cremini mushrooms, which are sometimes available at farmers' markets.

INGREDIENTS

Serves 4

- 1 pound portobello or cremini mushrooms
- butter, for greasing
- about 5 tablespoons olive oil
- 2 garlic cloves, crushed
- 3 tablespoons finely chopped parsley
- ¾–1 cup fresh white bread crumbs
- salt and freshly ground black pepper
- sprig of flat-leaf parsley, to garnish

1 Preheat the oven to 350°F. Cut off the mushroom stalks and reserve.

2 Arrange the mushroom caps in a buttered shallow dish, gill side up.

3 Heat 1 tablespoon of the oil in a frying pan and sauté the garlic briefly. Finely chop the mushroom stalks and mix with the parsley and bread crumbs. Add the garlic and 1 tablespoon of the oil. Season with salt and pepper. Pile a little of the mixture into each mushroom.

4 Add the remaining oil to the dish and cover the mushrooms with buttered waxed paper. Bake for 15–20 minutes, removing the paper for the last 5 minutes to brown the tops. Garnish with a sprig of flat-leaf parsley.

Baked Onions Stuffed with Feta

Serve these cheesy, nutty onions with warm olive bread for a fabulous lunch.

INGREDIENTS

Serves 4

4 large red onions
1 tablespoon olive oil
¼ cup pine nuts
4 ounces feta cheese, crumbled
½ cup fresh white bread crumbs
1 tablespoon chopped cilantro
salt and freshly ground black pepper

1 Preheat the oven to 350°F. Lightly grease a shallow ovenproof dish. Peel the onions and cut a thin slice from the top and bottom of each. Place the onions in a large saucepan of boiling water and cook for 10–12 minutes.

2 Remove the onions with a slotted spoon. Lay them out to drain on a sheet of paper towels and let cool slightly.

3 Using a small knife or your fingers, remove the inner sections of the onions, leaving about two or three outer rings. Finely chop the inner sections and place the outer shells in an ovenproof dish.

4 Heat the oil in a medium-size frying pan and sauté the chopped onions for 4–5 minutes, until golden, then add the pine nuts and stir-fry for a few minutes.

5 Place the feta cheese in a small bowl and stir in the onions, pine nuts, bread crumbs and cilantro. Season with a little salt and pepper.

6 Spoon the mixture into the onion shells. Cover loosely with foil and bake for about 30 minutes, removing the foil for the last 10 minutes to allow them to brown slightly. Serve hot.

Onion Tarts with Goat Cheese

A variation of the classic French Tarte à l'Oignon, this recipe uses young goat cheese as well as cream. The goat cheese is mild and creamy and complements the flavor of the onions.

INGREDIENTS

Serves 8

1½ cups all-purpose flour
5 tablespoons butter
1 ounce goat cheese or Cheddar cheese, grated

For the filling

1–1½ tablespoons olive or sunflower oil
3 onions, finely sliced
6 ounces young goat cheese
2 eggs, beaten
1 tablespoon light cream
2 ounces firm goat cheese or Cheddar cheese, grated
1 tablespoon chopped fresh tarragon
salt and freshly ground black pepper

1 To make the pastry, sift the flour into a bowl and rub in the butter until the mixture resembles fine bread crumbs. Stir in the cheese and enough cold water to make a dough. Knead lightly, put in a plastic bag and chill. Preheat the oven to 375°F.

2 Roll out the dough on a lightly floured surface, then cut into eight rounds using a 4½-inch pastry cutter, and line eight 4-inch tart pans. Prick the bottoms with a fork and bake for 10–15 minutes. Reduce the heat to 350°F.

3 Heat the oil in a large frying pan and cook the onions over low heat for 20–25 minutes, until they are a deep golden brown. Stir to prevent them from burning.

4 Beat the goat cheese with the eggs, cream, firm goat or Cheddar and tarragon. Season with salt and pepper and then stir in the onions.

5 Pour the mixture into the partially baked pastry shells and bake for 20–25 minutes, until golden. Serve warm or cold with a green salad.

Corn and Cheese Beggar's Purses

These tasty pastries are simple to make. Why not make double? They'll go like hotcakes.

INGREDIENTS

Makes 18–20

2 medium ears corn, or 9 ounces canned corn
4 ounces feta cheese
1 egg, beaten
2 tablespoons whipping cream
2 tablespoons freshly grated Parmesan
3 scallions, chopped
8–10 small sheets phyllo pastry
8 tablespoons butter, melted
freshly ground black pepper

1 Preheat the oven to 375°F. Butter two muffin pans.

2 If using fresh corn, strip the kernels from the cob using a large sharp knife, cutting downward from top to bottom of the cob. Simmer in a little salted water for 3–5 minutes, until tender. For canned corn, drain and rinse well under cold running water.

3 Crumble the feta cheese into a bowl and stir in the corn. Add the egg, cream, Parmesan cheese, scallions and ground black pepper and stir well.

4 Take one sheet of pastry and cut it in half to make a square. (Keep the remaining pastry covered with a damp cloth to prevent it from drying out.) Brush with melted butter and then fold in four to make a smaller square (about 3 inches).

5 Place a heaping teaspoon of filling in the center of each pastry square and then squeeze the pastry around the filling to make a "beggar's purse."

6 Continue making beggar's purses until all the filling is used up. Brush the outside of each purse with any remaining butter, put them in the prepared pans, and bake for about 15 minutes, until golden brown. Serve hot.

Cheese and Spinach Tart

This tart freezes well and can be reheated. It makes an excellent addition to a festive buffet.

INGREDIENTS

Serves 8

8 tablespoons butter
2 cups all-purpose flour
½ teaspoon English mustard powder
½ teaspoon paprika
large pinch of salt
4 ounces Cheddar cheese, finely grated
1 egg, beaten, to glaze

For the filling

1 pound frozen spinach
1 onion, chopped
pinch of grated nutmeg
8 ounces (1 cup) cottage cheese
2 large eggs, beaten
½ cup freshly grated Parmesan cheese
⅔ cup light cream
salt and freshly ground black pepper

1 Rub the butter into the flour until it resembles fine bread crumbs. Stir in the mustard powder, paprika, salt and cheese. Blend to a dough with 3–4 tablespoons cold water. Knead until smooth, wrap and chill in the refrigerator for 30 minutes.

2 Put the spinach and onion in a pan, cover and cook slowly. Season with salt, pepper and nutmeg. Turn the spinach out into a bowl and cool slightly. Add the remaining filling ingredients.

3 Roll out two-thirds of the pastry on a lightly floured surface and use it to line a 9-inch tart pan. Press it well into the edges, removing excess pastry with a rolling pin. Spoon the filling into the pastry shell.

4 Preheat the oven to 400°F. Put a baking sheet in the oven to preheat.

5 Roll out the remaining pastry and cut it with a lattice pastry cutter. With the help of a rolling pin, lay it over the tart. Brush the seams with egg glaze. Press the edges together and trim off the excess pastry. Brush the pastry lattice with egg glaze and bake on the hot baking sheet for 35–40 minutes, or until golden brown. Serve hot or cold.

Gado Gado

The peanut sauce on this traditional Indonesian vegetable dish owes its flavor to galangal, an aromatic rhizome that resembles ginger.

INGREDIENTS

Serves 4

9 ounces white cabbage, shredded
4 carrots, cut into matchsticks
4 celery ribs, cut into matchsticks
9 ounces (4 cups) bean sprouts
½ cucumber, cut into matchsticks
fried onion, salted peanuts and sliced fresh chile, to garnish

For the peanut sauce

1 tablespoon oil
1 small onion, finely chopped
1 garlic clove, crushed
1 small piece galangal, peeled and grated
1 teaspoon ground cumin
¼ teaspoon chili powder
1 teaspoon tamarind paste or lime juice
4 tablespoons crunchy peanut butter
1 teaspoon light brown sugar

1 Steam the cabbage, carrots and celery for 3–4 minutes, until just tender. Let cool. Spread out the bean sprouts on a large serving dish. Arrange the cabbage, carrots, celery and cucumber on top.

2 To make the sauce, heat the oil in a saucepan, add the onion and garlic and cook gently for 5 minutes, until soft.

3 Stir in the galangal and spices and cook for 1 minute. Add the tamarind paste or lime juice, peanut butter and sugar. Mix well.

4 Heat the sauce gently, stirring occasionally and adding a little hot water if necessary, to make the sauce runny enough to coat the vegetables when poured.

5 Spoon a little of the sauce over the vegetables and toss lightly together. Garnish with fried onion, peanuts and sliced chile. Serve the rest of the sauce separately in a bowl.

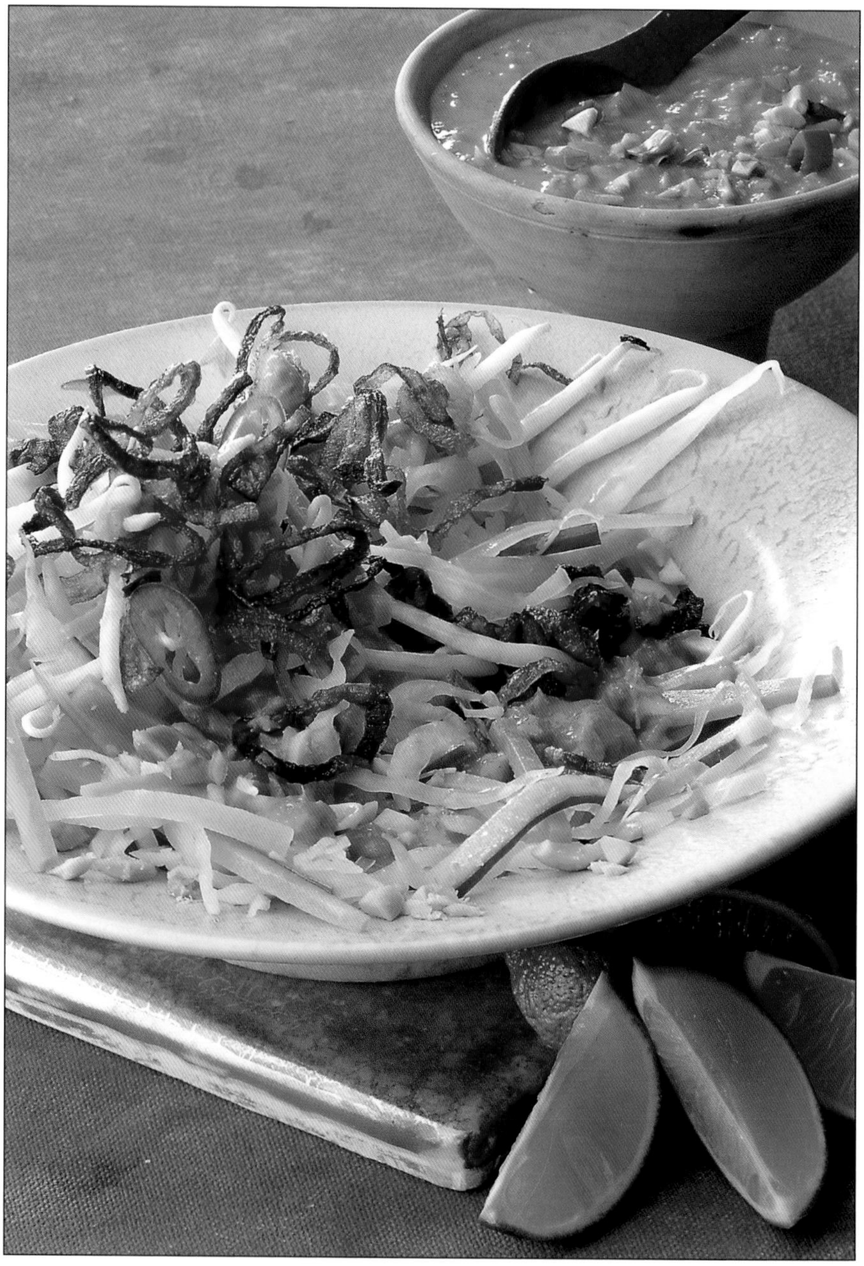

COOK'S TIP

As long as the sauce remains the same, the vegetables can be altered at the whim of the cook and to reflect the contents of the vegetable bin.

Sliced Frittata with Tomato Sauce

This dish—cold frittata with a tomato sauce—is ideal for a light summer lunch.

INGREDIENTS

Serves 3–4

6 eggs
2 tablespoons finely chopped fresh mixed herbs, such as basil, parsley, thyme and tarragon
¼ cup freshly grated Parmesan cheese
3 tablespoons olive oil
salt and freshly ground black pepper

For the tomato sauce

2 tablespoons olive oil
1 small onion, finely chopped
12 ounces fresh tomatoes, chopped, or 14-ounce can chopped tomatoes
1 garlic clove, chopped
salt and freshly ground black pepper

1 To make the frittata, break the eggs into a bowl and beat them lightly with a fork. Beat in the herbs and Parmesan. Season with salt and pepper. Heat the oil in a large nonstick or heavy frying pan until hot but not smoking.

2 Pour in the seasoned egg mixture. Cook, without stirring, until the frittata is puffed and golden brown underneath.

3 Take a large plate, place it upside down over the pan and, holding it firmly with oven mitts, turn the pan and the frittata over onto it. Slide the frittata back into the pan and continue cooking for 3–4 minutes more, until it is golden brown on the second side. Remove from the heat and let cool completely.

4 To make the tomato sauce, heat the oil in a medium-heavy saucepan. Add the onion and cook slowly until it is soft. Add the tomatoes, garlic and ¼ cup water and season with salt and pepper. Cover the pan and cook over moderate heat for about 15 minutes.

5 Remove from the heat and let cool slightly before pressing the sauce through a food mill or sieve. Let cool completely.

6 To assemble the salad, cut the frittata into thin slices. Place them in a serving bowl and toss lightly with the sauce. Serve at room temperature or chilled.

Ratatouille

A classic vegetable stew, packed full of fresh vegetables and herbs and absolutely bursting with wonderful flavor.

INGREDIENTS

Serves 4

2 large eggplant, roughly chopped
4 zucchini, roughly chopped
⅔ cup olive oil
2 onions, sliced
2 garlic cloves, chopped
1 large red bell pepper, seeded and roughly chopped
2 large yellow bell peppers, seeded and roughly chopped
sprig of fresh rosemary
sprig of fresh thyme
1 teaspoon coriander seeds, crushed
3 plum tomatoes, peeled, seeded and chopped
8 basil leaves, torn
salt and freshly ground black pepper
sprigs of fresh parsley or basil, to garnish

1 Sprinkle the eggplant and zucchini with salt, then put them in a colander with a plate and a weight on top to extract the bitter juices. Let sit for about 30 minutes.

2 Heat the olive oil in a large saucepan. Add the onions and cook gently for 6–7 minutes, until just softened. Add the garlic and cook for another 2 minutes.

3 Rinse the eggplant and zucchini and pat dry with a clean dish towel. Add to the pan with the peppers, increase the heat and sauté until the peppers are just turning brown.

4 Add the herbs and coriander seeds, then cover the pan and cook gently for about 40 minutes.

5 Add the tomatoes and season with salt and pepper. Cook gently for another 10 minutes, until the vegetables are soft but not too mushy. Remove the sprigs of herbs. Stir in the torn basil leaves and check the seasoning. Let cool slightly and serve warm or cold, garnished with sprigs of parsley or basil.

Corn Cakes with Grilled Tomatoes

Crisp corn fritters are simple to make and guaranteed to become a midday favorite.

INGREDIENTS

Serves 4

1 large ear of fresh corn
¾ cup all-purpose flour
1 egg
a little milk
2 large, firm tomatoes
1 garlic clove, crushed
1 teaspoon dried oregano
2–3 tablespoons olive oil, plus extra for shallow-frying
salt and freshly ground black pepper
8 cupped iceberg lettuce leaves, to serve
shredded fresh basil leaves, to garnish

1 Pull the husks and silk away from the corn, then hold the ear upright on a board and cut downward with a heavy knife to strip off the kernels. Put the kernels in a pan of boiling water and cook for 3 minutes after the water has returned to a boil, then drain and rinse under cold running water to cool quickly.

2 Put the flour in a bowl, make a well in the center and break the egg into it. Start stirring with a fork, adding a little milk to make a soft dropping consistency. Stir in the drained corn and season with salt and pepper.

3 Preheat the broiler. Halve the tomatoes horizontally and make two or three crisscross slashes across the cut side of each half. Rub in the crushed garlic and the oregano and season with salt and pepper. Drizzle with oil and broil until lightly browned.

4 While the tomatoes broil, heat some oil in a wide frying pan and drop a tablespoon of batter into the center. Cook the fritters one at a time over low heat, turning each one as soon as the top is set. Drain on paper towels and keep warm while cooking the remaining fritters. The mixture should make at least eight corn cakes.

5 For each serving, put two corn cakes on lettuce leaves, garnish with basil and serve with a broiled tomato half.

Fresh Cèpes with a Parsley Dressing

To capture the just-picked flavor of mushrooms, try this delicious salad enriched with an egg yolk and walnut oil dressing. Choose small cèpes or portobellos for a firm texture and a fine flavor.

INGREDIENTS

Serves 4

12 ounces fresh cèpes or portobellos
6 ounces mixed salad greens, such as young spinach and frisée
½ cup broken walnut pieces, toasted
2 ounces Parmesan cheese
salt and freshly ground black pepper

For the dressing

2 egg yolks
½ teaspoon Dijon mustard
5 tablespoons peanut oil
3 tablespoons walnut oil
2 tablespoons lemon juice
2 tablespoons chopped fresh parsley
pinch of sugar

1 For the dressing, place the egg yolks in a screw-top jar with the mustard, oils, lemon juice, parsley and sugar. Shake well.

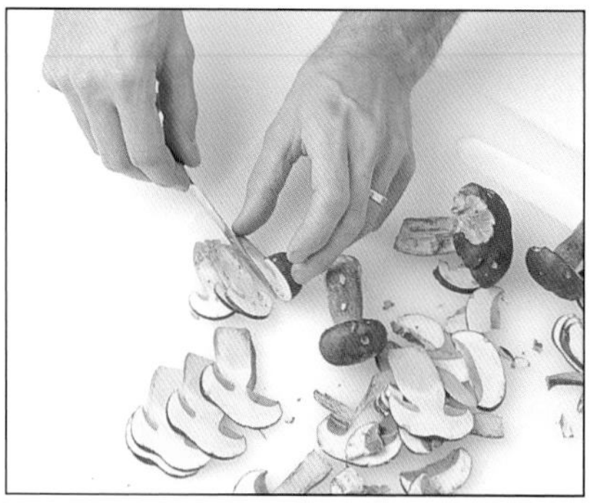

2 Slice the mushrooms thinly using a sharp knife.

3 Place the mushrooms in a large salad bowl and combine with the dressing. Let stand for 10–15 minutes for the flavors to mingle.

4 Wash and spin the salad greens, then toss with the mushrooms.

5 Turn out onto four large plates, season with salt and pepper, then sprinkle with toasted walnut pieces and shavings of Parmesan cheese.

COOK'S TIP

The dressing for this salad uses raw egg yolks. Be sure to use only the freshest eggs from a reputable supplier. Pregnant women, young children and the elderly are advised not to eat raw egg yolks. If this presents a problem, the dressing can be made without the egg yolks.

Sun-Dried Tomato and Parmesan Carbonara

The ingredients for this recipe can easily be doubled to serve four. Why not try it with plenty of garlic bread and a big green salad?

INGREDIENTS

Serves 2

6 ounces tagliatelle
10 sun-dried tomatoes in olive oil, drained
2 eggs, beaten
⅔ cup heavy cream
1 tablespoon whole-grain mustard
⅔ cup freshly grated Parmesan cheese
12 fresh basil leaves, shredded
salt and pepper
fresh basil leaves, to garnish
crusty bread, to serve

1 Cook the pasta in boiling salted water until it is just tender but still retains a little bite (al dente).

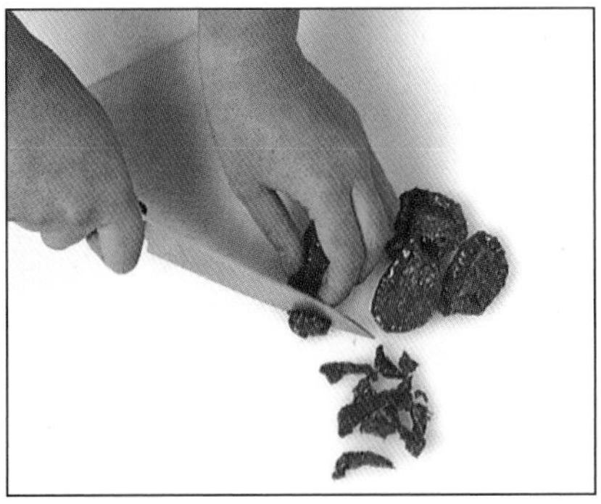

2 Meanwhile, cut the sun-dried tomatoes into small pieces.

3 Beat together the eggs, cream and mustard in a bowl, adding plenty of salt and pepper, until they are well combined and smooth. Do not allow the mixture to become frothy.

4 Drain the pasta and immediately return to the hot saucepan with the cream mixture, sun-dried tomatoes, Parmesan cheese and shredded fresh basil. Return to very low heat for 1 minute, stirring gently, until the mixture thickens slightly. Adjust the seasoning and serve immediately, garnished with basil leaves. Serve with plenty of crusty bread.

Omelet with Beans

Every good cook should have a few omelets in his or her repertoire. This version includes soft white beans and is finished with a layer of toasted sesame seeds.

INGREDIENTS

Serves 4

2 tablespoons olive oil
1 teaspoon sesame oil
1 Spanish onion, chopped
1 small red bell pepper, seeded and diced
2 celery ribs, chopped
14-ounce can soft white beans, such as cannellini, drained
8 eggs
3 tablespoons sesame seeds
salt and freshly ground black pepper
green salad, to serve

1 Heat the olive and sesame oils in a 12-inch flameproof frying pan. Add the onion, pepper and celery and cook to soften without coloring.

2 Add the beans and continue to cook for several minutes to heat through.

3 In a medium bowl, beat the eggs with a fork and season with salt and pepper, then pour over the ingredients in the pan.

4 Stir the egg mixture with a flat wooden spoon until it begins to stiffen, then allow to firm over low heat for 6–8 minutes.

5 Preheat the broiler to moderate. Sprinkle the omelet with sesame seeds and brown evenly under the broiler.

6 Cut the omelet into thick wedges and serve warm with a green salad.

VARIATION

You can also use sliced cooked potatoes, any seasonal vegetables, baby artichoke hearts and chickpeas in this omelet.

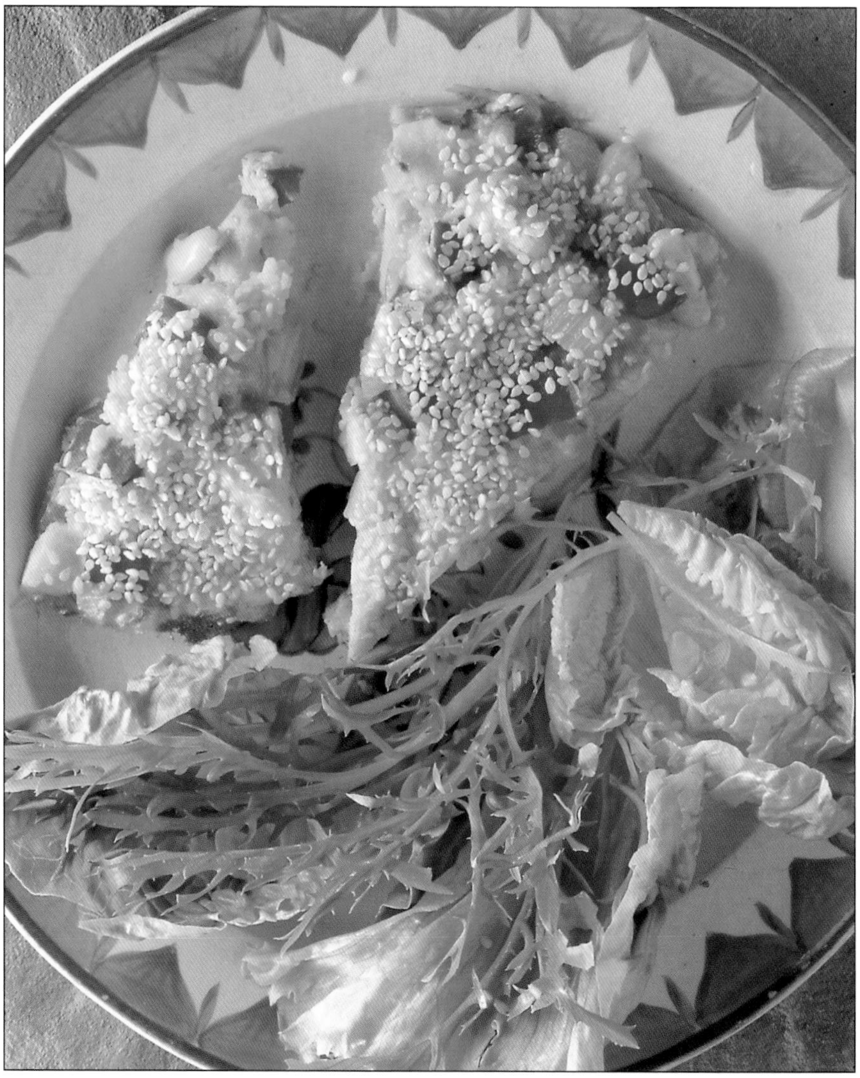

Mushroom Hunter's Omelet

Perfect for Sunday brunch, this omelet is simplicity itself to make.

INGREDIENTS

Serves 1

2 tablespoons unsalted butter, plus extra for cooking
4 ounces assorted wild and cultivated mushrooms such as young cèpes, chanterelles, cremini, portobellos, and oyster mushrooms, trimmed and sliced
3 eggs, at room temperature
salt and freshly ground black pepper

1 Melt the butter in a small omelet pan, add the mushrooms and cook until the juices run. Season with salt and pepper, remove from pan and set aside. Wipe the pan.

2 Break the eggs into a bowl, season and beat with a fork. Heat the pan over high heat, add a pat of butter and let it begin to brown. Pour in the beaten egg and stir briskly with the back of a fork.

3 When the eggs are two-thirds set, add the mushrooms and let the omelet finish cooking for 10–15 seconds.

4 Tap the handle of the omelet pan sharply with your fist to loosen the omelet from the pan, then fold and turn out onto a plate. Serve with warm crusty bread and a simple green salad.

SUPPERS

Vegetable Pilaf

A popular vegetable rice dish that makes a tasty light supper.

INGREDIENTS

Serves 4–6

1 cup basmati rice
2 tablespoons oil
½ teaspoon cumin seeds
2 bay leaves
4 green cardamom pods
4 cloves
1 onion, finely chopped
1 carrot, finely diced
⅓ cup thawed frozen peas
⅓ cup thawed frozen corn
¼ cup cashew nuts, lightly fried
¼ teaspoon ground cumin
salt

1 Wash the rice in several changes of cold water. Put in a bowl and cover with water. Let soak for about 30 minutes.

2 Heat the oil in a large frying pan and sauté the cumin seeds for 2 minutes. Add the bay leaves, cardamom and cloves and sauté for another 2 minutes.

3 Add the onion and cook for 5 minutes, until softened and lightly browned.

4 Stir in the carrot and cook for 3–4 minutes.

5 Drain the rice and add to the pan together with the peas, corn and cashew nuts. Cook for 4–5 minutes.

6 Add 2 cups water, ground cumin and salt. Bring to a boil, cover and simmer for 15 minutes over low heat, until all the water is absorbed. Let stand, covered, for 10 minutes before serving.

Red Pepper Risotto

The character of this delicious risotto depends on the type of rice you use. With arborio rice, the risotto should be moist and creamy. If you use brown rice, reduce the amount of liquid for a drier dish with a nutty flavor.

INGREDIENTS

Serves 6

3 large red bell peppers
2 tablespoons olive oil
3 large garlic cloves, thinly sliced
$1\frac{1}{2}$ x 14-ounce cans chopped tomatoes
2 bay leaves
5–$6\frac{1}{4}$ cups vegetable stock
$2\frac{1}{2}$ cups arborio rice or brown rice
6 fresh basil leaves, snipped
salt and freshly ground black pepper

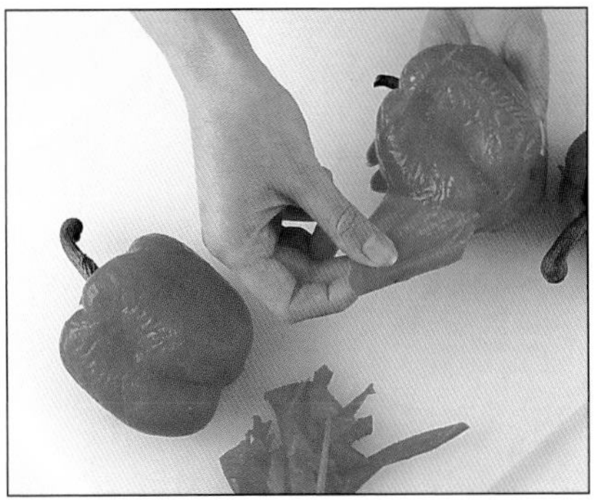

1 Preheat the broiler. Put the peppers in a broiler pan and broil until the skins are blackened and blistered all over. Put the peppers in a bowl, cover with several layers of damp paper towels and set aside for 10 minutes. Peel off the skins, then slice the peppers, discarding the cores and seeds.

2 Heat the oil in a wide, shallow pan. Add the garlic and tomatoes and cook over gentle heat for 5 minutes, then add the pepper slices and bay leaves. Stir well and cook for 15 minutes more, still over gentle heat.

3 Pour the stock into a large, heavy saucepan and heat it to simmering point. Stir the rice into the vegetable mixture and cook for about 2 minutes, then add two or three ladlefuls of the hot stock. Cook, stirring occasionally, until all the stock has been absorbed into the rice.

4 Continue to add stock in this way, making sure each addition has been absorbed before pouring in the next. When the rice is tender, season with salt and pepper. Remove the pan from the heat, cover and let stand for 10 minutes before stirring in the basil and serving.

Risotto with Mushrooms

The addition of wild mushrooms gives this risotto a wonderfully authentic woody flavor.

INGREDIENTS

Serves 3–4

- 1/3 cup dried wild mushrooms, preferably porcini
- 6 ounces fresh cultivated mushrooms
- juice of 1/2 lemon
- 6 tablespoons butter
- 2 tablespoons finely chopped parsley
- 3 3/4 cups vegetable stock
- 2 tablespoons olive oil
- 1 small onion, finely chopped
- 1 1/2 cups medium-grain risotto rice, such as arborio
- 1/2 cup dry white wine
- 3 tablespoons freshly grated Parmesan cheese
- salt and freshly ground black pepper
- sprig of flat-leaf parsley, to garnish

1 Place the dried mushrooms in a small bowl with about 1 1/2 cups warm water. Soak for at least 40 minutes. Rinse the mushrooms thoroughly. Filter the soaking water through a sieve lined with paper towels, and reserve.

2 Wipe the fresh mushrooms with a damp cloth and slice finely. Place in a bowl and toss with the lemon juice.

3 In a large, heavy frying pan or casserole, melt a third of the butter. Stir in the fresh sliced mushrooms and cook over moderate heat until they release their juices and begin to brown. Stir in the parsley, cook for 30 seconds more and remove to a side dish.

4 Place the stock in a saucepan and add the mushroom water. Heat broth to a simmer.

5 Heat another third of the butter with the olive oil in the same pan the mushrooms were cooked in. Stir in the onion and cook until it is soft and golden. Add the rice, stirring for 1–2 minutes to coat it with the oils in the pan. Add the soaked and sautéed mushrooms and mix well.

6 Pour in the wine, raise the heat slightly, and cook over moderate heat until it evaporates.

7 Add one small ladleful of the hot broth. Over moderate heat, cook until the broth is absorbed or evaporates, stirring the rice with a wooden spoon to prevent it from sticking to the pan. Add a little more broth and stir until the rice dries out again. Continue stirring and adding the liquid a little at a time. After about 20 minutes, taste the rice. Add salt and pepper.

8 Continue cooking, stirring and adding the liquid until the rice is al dente, or tender but still firm to the bite. The total cooking time of the risotto may be 20–35 minutes. If you run out of broth, use hot water.

9 Remove the risotto pan from the heat. Stir in the remaining butter and the Parmesan. Grind in a little black pepper and taste again for salt. Allow the risotto to rest for 3–4 minutes before serving, garnished with a sprig of flat-leaf parsley.

Parsnip, Eggplant and Cashew Biryani

Full of the flavors of India, this hearty supper dish is great for chilly winter evenings.

INGREDIENTS

Serves 4–6

1 small eggplant, sliced
10 ounces basmati rice
3 parsnips
3 onions
2 garlic cloves
1-inch piece of fresh ginger root, peeled
about 4 tablespoons vegetable oil
6 ounces (3/4 cup) unsalted cashew nuts
1/4 cup golden raisins
1 red bell pepper, seeded and sliced
1 teaspoon ground cumin
1 teaspoon ground coriander
1/2 teaspoon chili powder
1/2 cup plain yogurt
1 1/4 cups vegetable stock
2 tablespoons butter
salt and freshly ground black pepper
2 hard-boiled eggs, quartered, and sprigs of cilantro, to garnish

1 Sprinkle the eggplant with salt and set aside for 30 minutes. Rinse, pat dry and cut into bite-size pieces.

2 Soak the rice in a bowl of cold water for 40 minutes. Peel and core the parsnips. Cut into 1/2-inch pieces. Process 1 onion, the garlic and ginger in a food processor. Add 2–3 tablespoons water and process to a paste.

3 Finely slice the remaining onions. Heat 3 tablespoons of the oil in a large flameproof casserole and sauté the onions gently for 10–15 minutes, until they are soft and deep golden brown. Remove and drain.

4 Add 1/4 cup of the cashew nuts to the pan and stir-fry for 2 minutes, checking that they do not burn. Add the raisins and cook until they swell. Remove and drain on paper towels.

5 Add the eggplant and sliced pepper to the pan and stir-fry for 4–5 minutes. Drain on paper towels. Cook the parsnips for 4–5 minutes. Stir in the remaining cashew nuts and cook for 1 minute. Transfer to the plate with the eggplant and set aside.

6 Add the remaining 1 tablespoon of oil to the pan. Add the onion paste. Cook, stirring, over moderate heat for 4–5 minutes, until the mixture turns golden. Stir in the cumin, coriander and chili powder. Cook, stirring, for 1 minute, then reduce the heat and add the yogurt.

7 Bring the mixture slowly to a boil and stir in the stock, parsnips, eggplant and bell pepper. Season with salt and pepper, cover and simmer for 30–40 minutes, until the parsnips are tender. Transfer to an ovenproof casserole.

8 Preheat the oven to 300°F. Drain the rice and add to 1 1/4 cups salted boiling water. Cook gently for 5–6 minutes, until the rice is tender but slightly undercooked.

9 Drain the rice and pile it in a mound on top of the parsnip mixture. Make a hole from the top to the bottom using the handle of a wooden spoon. Sprinkle the reserved fried onions, cashew nuts and raisins over the rice and dot with butter. Cover with a double layer of foil and secure it in place with a lid.

10 Bake for 35–40 minutes. To serve, spoon the mixture onto a warmed serving dish and garnish with quartered eggs and sprigs of cilantro.

Leek, Mushroom and Lemon Risotto

A delicious risotto, packed full of flavor, this is a great recipe for an informal supper with friends.

INGREDIENTS

Serves 4

8 ounces trimmed leeks
8 ounces cremini mushrooms
2 tablespoons olive oil
3 garlic cloves, crushed
6 tablespoons butter
1 large onion, roughly chopped
scant 1¾ cups arborio rice
5 cups hot vegetable stock
grated zest and juice of 1 lemon
⅔ cup freshly grated Parmesan cheese
¼ cup mixed chopped fresh chives and flat-leaf parsley
salt and freshly ground black pepper
lemon wedges and sprigs of flat-leaf parsley, to serve

1 Wash the leeks well. Slice in half lengthwise and roughly chop. Wipe the mushrooms with paper towels and roughly chop.

2 Heat the oil in a large saucepan and cook the garlic for 1 minute. Add the leeks, mushrooms and plenty of seasoning and cook over medium heat for about 10 minutes, or until softened and browned. Remove from the pan and set aside.

3 Add 2 tablespoons of the butter to the pan and cook the onion over medium heat for about 5 minutes.

4 Stir in the rice and cook for 1 minute. Add a ladleful of stock to the pan and cook gently, stirring occasionally, until all the liquid is absorbed.

5 Stir in more liquid as each ladleful is absorbed; this should take 20–25 minutes. The risotto will turn thick and creamy, and the rice should be tender but not sticky.

6 Just before serving, stir in the leeks, mushrooms, remaining butter, grated lemon zest and 3 tablespoons of the juice, half the Parmesan and the herbs. Adjust the seasoning and serve, sprinkled with the remaining Parmesan and herbs. Serve with lemon wedges and sprigs of flat-leaf parsley.

VARIATION

For a tangier taste, you could substitute a lime for the lemon in this recipe.

Risotto alla Milanese

This traditional Italian risotto is rich and creamy, and deliciously flavored with garlic, shavings of Parmesan and fresh parsley.

INGREDIENTS

Serves 4

2 garlic cloves, crushed
4 tablespoons chopped fresh parsley
finely grated zest of 1 lemon

For the risotto

1 teaspoon saffron strands
2 tablespoons butter
1 large onion, finely chopped
1½ cups arborio rice
⅔ cup dry white wine
4 cups vegetable stock
Parmesan cheese shavings, to serve
salt and freshly ground black pepper

1 Mix together the garlic, parsley and lemon zest in a bowl. Reserve and set aside.

2 Put the saffron in a small bowl with 1 tablespoon boiling water and let stand while the saffron is infused. Melt the butter in a heavy frying pan and gently cook the onion for 5 minutes, until softened and golden.

3 Stir in the rice and cook for about 2 minutes, until it becomes translucent. Add the wine and saffron mixture and cook for several minutes, until all the wine is absorbed.

4 Add 2½ cups of the stock to pan and simmer gently until the stock is absorbed, stirring frequently.

5 Gradually add more stock, a ladleful at a time, until the rice is tender. (The rice might be tender and creamy before you've added all the stock, so add it slowly toward the end of the cooking time.)

6 Season the risotto with salt and pepper and transfer to a serving dish. Sprinkle lavishly with shavings of Parmesan cheese and the garlic and parsley mixture.

Vegetable Chili

This alternative to traditional chili con carne is delicious served with brown rice.

INGREDIENTS

Serves 4

2 onions, chopped
1 garlic clove, crushed
3 celery ribs, chopped
1 green bell pepper, seeded and diced
8 ounces mushrooms, sliced
2 zucchini, sliced
14-ounce can red kidney beans, rinsed and drained
14-ounce can chopped tomatoes
⅔ cup passata or tomato sauce
2 tablespoons tomato paste
1 tablespoon ketchup
1 teaspoon each hot chili powder, ground cumin and ground coriander
salt and freshly ground black pepper
plain yogurt and cayenne pepper, to serve
sprigs of cilantro, to garnish

1 Put the onions, garlic, celery, pepper, mushrooms and zucchini in a large saucepan and mix together.

2 Add the kidney beans, tomatoes, passata, tomato paste and ketchup.

3 Add the spices, season with salt and pepper and mix well.

4 Cover, bring to a boil and simmer for 20–30 minutes, stirring occasionally, until the vegetables are tender. Serve with plain yogurt, sprinkled with cayenne pepper. Garnish with cilantro sprigs.

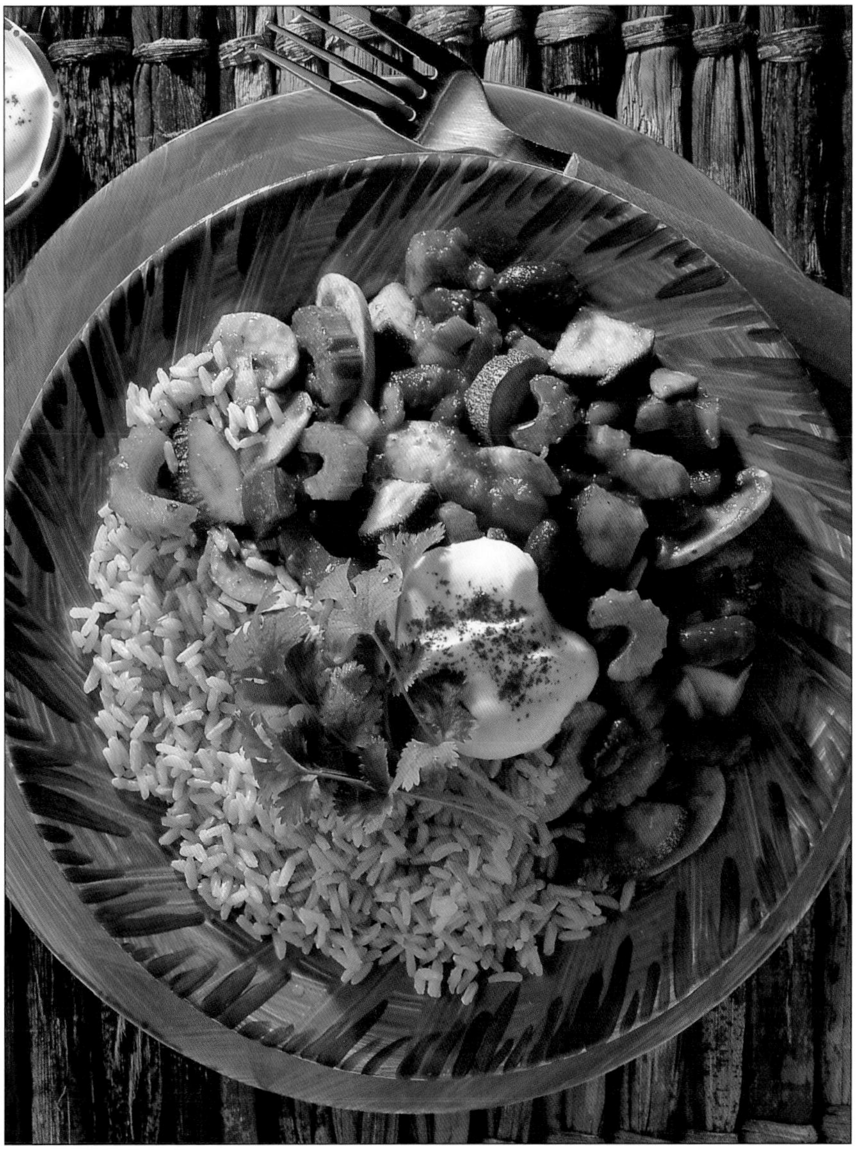

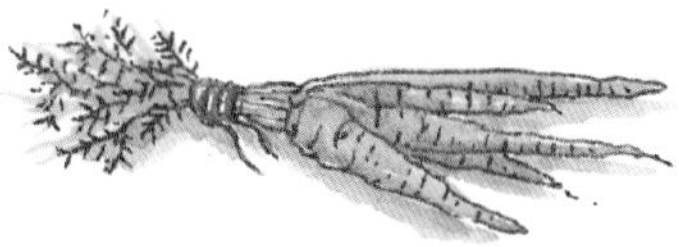

Whole-Wheat Pasta with Caraway Cabbage

Crunchy cabbage and Brussels sprouts are the perfect partners for pasta in this healthy dish.

INGREDIENTS

Serves 6

6 tablespoons olive oil or sunflower oil
3 onions, roughly chopped
12-ounce round white cabbage, roughly chopped
12 ounces Brussels sprouts, trimmed and halved
2 teaspoons caraway seeds
1 tablespoon chopped fresh dill
1⅔ cups vegetable stock
7 ounces (1¾ cups) fresh or dried whole-wheat pasta spirals
salt and freshly ground black pepper
fresh dill sprigs, to garnish

1 Heat the oil in a large saucepan and sauté the onions over low heat for 10 minutes, until softened.

2 Add the cabbage and Brussels sprouts and cook for 2–3 minutes, then stir in the caraway seeds and dill. Pour in the stock and season with salt and pepper. Cover and simmer for 5–10 minutes, until the cabbage and sprouts are crisp-tender.

3 Meanwhile, cook the pasta in a pan of lightly salted boiling water, following the package instructions, until just tender.

4 Drain the pasta, pour it into a bowl and add the cabbage mixture. Toss lightly, adjust the seasoning, garnish with dill and serve immediately.

Cauliflower and Broccoli with Tomato Sauce

The addition of broccoli to the cauliflower gives extra color and texture to this dish.

INGREDIENTS

Serves 6

1 onion, finely chopped
14-ounce can chopped tomatoes
3 tablespoons tomato paste
3 tablespoons whole-wheat flour
1¼ cups skim milk
1¼ cups water
2½ pounds (6 cups) mixed cauliflower and broccoli florets
salt and freshly ground black pepper

1 Mix the onion, tomatoes and tomato paste in a small saucepan. Bring to a boil, lower the heat and simmer gently for 15–20 minutes.

2 Mix the flour to a paste with a little of the milk. Stir the paste into the tomato mixture, then gradually add the remaining milk and water.

3 Stir the mixture constantly until it boils and thickens. Season with salt and pepper. Keep the sauce hot.

4 Steam the cauliflower and broccoli over boiling water for 5–7 minutes, or until the florets are just tender. Transfer the vegetables to a dish, pour the tomato sauce over them and serve with extra pepper sprinkled over the top, if you like.

Mushroom Bolognese

A quick—and exceedingly tasty—vegetarian version of the classic Italian dish. This dish is easy to prepare and makes a very satisfying meal.

INGREDIENTS

Serves 4

1 pound mushrooms
1 tablespoon olive oil
1 onion, chopped
1 garlic clove, crushed
1 tablespoon tomato paste
14-ounce can chopped tomatoes
3 tablespoons chopped fresh oregano
1 pound fresh pasta
salt and freshly ground black pepper
Parmesan cheese, to serve

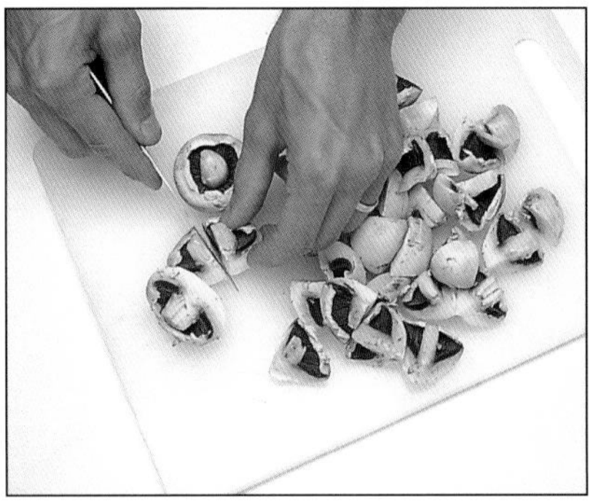

1 Trim the mushroom stems neatly, then cut each mushroom into quarters.

COOK'S TIP

If you prefer to use dried pasta, make this the first thing that you cook. It will take 10–12 minutes, during which time you can make the mushroom mixture. Use 12 ounces dried pasta.

2 Heat the oil in a large pan. Add the chopped onion and garlic and cook for 2–3 minutes.

3 Add the mushrooms to the pan and cook over high heat for 3–4 minutes, stirring occasionally.

4 Stir in the tomato paste, chopped tomatoes and 1 tablespoon of the oregano. Lower the heat, cover and cook for about 5 minutes.

5 Meanwhile, bring a large pan of salted water to a boil. Cook the pasta for 2–3 minutes, until just tender.

6 Season the bolognese sauce with salt and pepper. Drain the pasta, pour it into a bowl and add the mushroom mixture. Toss to mix well. Serve in individual bowls, topped with shavings of fresh Parmesan and the remaining chopped fresh oregano.

Broccoli and Ricotta Cannelloni

A fabulous pasta dish that looks very impressive but is actually quite quick and simple to prepare and tastes wonderful.

INGREDIENTS

Serves 4

2 teaspoons olive oil
12 dried cannelloni tubes, 3 inches long
4 cups broccoli florets
1½ cups fresh bread crumbs
⅔ cup milk
4 tablespoons olive oil, plus extra for brushing
1 cup ricotta cheese
pinch of grated nutmeg
6 tablespoons grated Parmesan or Pecorino cheese
2 tablespoons pine nuts
salt and freshly ground black pepper

For the tomato sauce

2 tablespoons olive oil
1 onion, finely chopped
1 garlic clove, crushed
2 x 14-ounce cans chopped tomatoes
1 tablespoon tomato paste
4 black olives, pitted and chopped
1 teaspoon dried thyme

1 Preheat the oven to 375°F. Lightly grease four ovenproof dishes with olive oil.

2 Bring a large saucepan of water to a boil, add the olive oil to the water to prevent the pasta from sticking together and simmer the cannelloni, uncovered, for 6–7 minutes, or until it is nearly cooked.

3 Meanwhile, steam or boil the broccoli for 10 minutes, until tender. Drain the pasta, rinse under cold water and set aside. Drain the broccoli and let it cool, then place in a food processor or blender and process until smooth. Set aside.

4 Place the bread crumbs in a bowl, add the milk and oil and stir until softened. Add the ricotta, broccoli purée, nutmeg and 4 tablespoons of the Parmesan or Pecorino cheese. Season with salt and pepper, then set aside.

5 To make the sauce, heat the oil in a frying pan and add the onions and garlic. Cook for 5–6 minutes, until softened, then stir in the tomatoes, tomato paste, black olives and thyme. Season with salt and pepper. Boil rapidly for 2–3 minutes, then pour into the four ovenproof dishes.

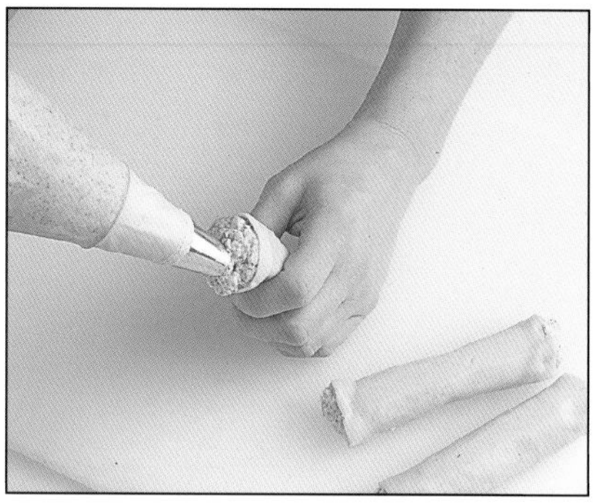

6 Spoon the cheese mixture into a pastry bag fitted with a ½-inch nozzle. Carefully open the cannelloni tubes. Standing each one upright on a board, pipe the filling into each tube. Divide the tubes equally among the four dishes and lay them in rows in the tomato sauce.

7 Brush the tops of the cannelloni with a little olive oil and sprinkle with the remaining Parmesan or Pecorino cheese and pine nuts. Bake for 25–30 minutes, until golden.

COOK'S TIP

If you don't have cannelloni tubes, you can cook lasagne sheets until al dente, spoon the mixture along one short edge of the sheet and roll it up to encase the filling.

Spiced Tofu Stir-Fry

The colors in this aromatic stir-fry are as pleasing to the eye as the flavors are to the palate. Serve with noodles or egg-fried rice.

INGREDIENTS

Serves 4

2 teaspoons ground cumin
1 tablespoon paprika
1 teaspoon ground ginger
good pinch of cayenne pepper
1 tablespoon sugar
10 ounces tofu (bean curd)
4 tablespoons oil
2 garlic cloves, crushed
1 bunch scallions, sliced
1 red bell pepper, seeded and sliced
1 yellow bell seeded and sliced
8 ounces (generous 3 cups) cremini mushrooms, halved or quartered if necessary
1 large zucchini, sliced
4 ounces haricots verts, halved
scant ½ cup pine nuts
1 tablespoon lime juice
1 tablespoon honey
salt and pepper

1 Mix together the cumin, paprika, ginger, cayenne and sugar with plenty of seasoning. Cut the tofu into cubes and coat them in the spice mixture.

2 Heat some of the oil in a wok or large frying pan. Cook the tofu over high heat for 3–4 minutes, turning occasionally (take care not to break up the tofu too much). Remove with a slotted spoon. Wipe out the pan with paper towels.

3 Add the remaining oil to the pan and cook the garlic and scallions for 3 minutes. Add the remaining vegetables and cook over medium heat for 6 minutes, or until beginning to soften and turn golden. Season well.

4 Return the tofu to the pan with the pine nuts, lime juice and honey. Heat through and serve immediately.

Butternut Squash and Sage Pizza

The combination of sweet butternut squash, sage and sharp goat cheese works wonderfully on this pizza.

INGREDIENTS

Serves 4

½ teaspoon active dry yeast
pinch of sugar
4 cups white bread flour
1 teaspoon salt
2 tablespoons olive oil
1 tablespoon butter
2 tablespoons olive oil
2 shallots, finely chopped
1 butternut squash, peeled, seeded and cubed, about 1 pound prepared weight
16 sage leaves
2 x 14-ounce cans chunky tomato sauce
4 ounces mozzarella cheese, sliced
4 ounces firm goat cheese
salt and freshly ground black pepper

1 Put 1¼ cups warm water in a measuring cup. Add the yeast and sugar and let sit 5–10 minutes, until mixture is frothy.

2 Sift the flour and salt into a large bowl and make a well in the center. Gradually pour in the yeast mixture and the olive oil. Mix to make a smooth dough. Knead on a lightly floured surface for about 10 minutes, until smooth, springy and elastic. Place the dough in a floured bowl, cover and let rise in a warm place for 1½ hours.

3 Preheat the oven to 400°F. Oil four baking sheets. Put the butter and oil in a roasting pan and heat in the oven for a few minutes. Add the shallots, squash and half the sage leaves. Toss to coat. Roast for 15–20 minutes, until tender.

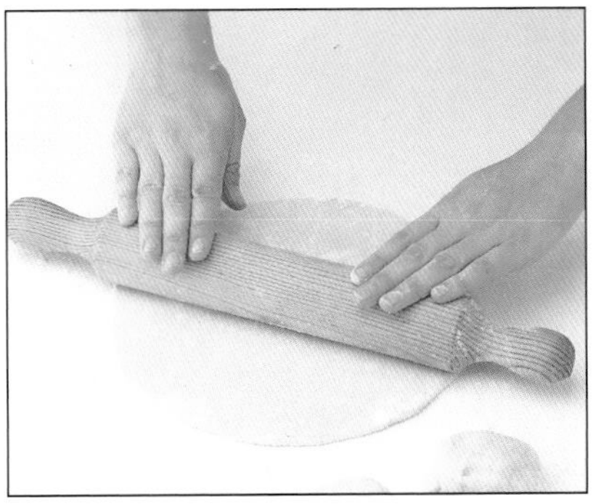

4 Raise the oven temperature to 425°F. Divide the dough into four equal pieces and roll out each piece on a floured surface to a 10-inch round.

5 Transfer each round to a baking sheet and spread with tomato sauce, leaving a ½-inch border all around. Spoon the squash and shallot mixture over the top.

6 Arrange the mozzarella over the squash mixture and crumble the goat cheese on top. Sprinkle with the remaining sage leaves and season with plenty of salt and pepper. Bake for 15–20 minutes, until the cheese has melted and the crusts are golden.

Eggplant, Shallot and Tomato Calzone

Eggplant, shallots and sun-dried tomatoes make an unusual filling for calzone. Add more or less crushed red pepper, depending on how fiery you like your food.

INGREDIENTS

Serves 2

- 1/4 teaspoon active dry yeast
- pinch of sugar
- 2 cups white bread flour
- 1 teaspoon salt
- 1/4 cup olive oil
- 4 baby eggplant
- 3 shallots, chopped
- 1 garlic clove, chopped
- 10 sun-dried tomatoes in oil, drained and chopped
- 1/4 teaspoon crushed red pepper
- 2 teaspoons chopped fresh thyme
- 3 ounces mozzarella cheese, cubed
- salt and freshly ground black pepper
- 1–2 tablespoons freshly grated Parmesan cheese, to serve

1 To make the dough, put 2/3 cup warm water in a measuring cup. Add the yeast and sugar and let sit for 5–10 minutes, until frothy.

2 Sift the flour and salt into a large bowl and make a well in the center. Gradually pour in the yeast mixture and 1 tablespoon oil. Mix to make a smooth dough. Knead the dough on a lightly floured surface for 10 minutes, until smooth. The dough should be springy and elastic.

3 Place the dough in a floured bowl, cover and let rise in a warm place for 1 1/2 hours. Preheat the oven to 425°F. Trim the eggplant, then cut into small cubes.

4 Heat 1 tablespoon of the oil in a frying pan and cook the shallots until soft. Add the eggplant, garlic, sun-dried tomatoes, crushed red pepper, thyme and seasoning. Cook for 4–5 minutes, stirring frequently, until the eggplant is beginning to soften.

5 Divide the dough in half and roll out each piece on a lightly floured surface to a 7-inch circle.

6 Spread the eggplant mixture over half of each round, leaving a 1-inch border, then top with the mozzarella cubes.

7 Dampen the edges with water, then fold over the other half of dough to enclose the filling. Press the edges firmly together to seal. Place the calzones on two greased baking sheets.

8 Brush with half the remaining olive oil and make a small hole in the top of each to allow the steam to escape. Bake for 15–20 minutes, until golden. Remove from the oven and brush with the remaining oil. Sprinkle with the Parmesan cheese and serve immediately.

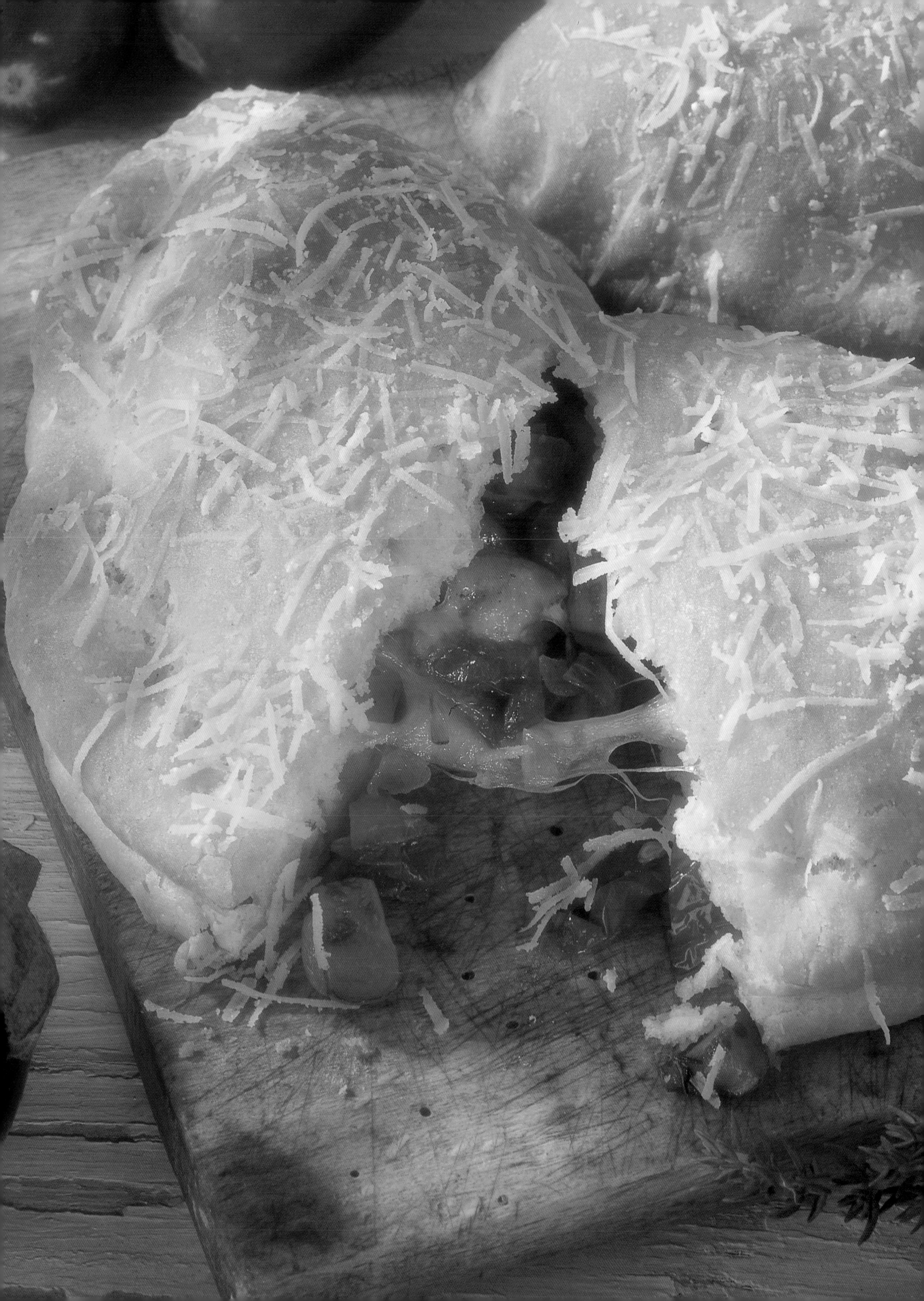

Ravioli with Ricotta and Spinach

Homemade ravioli are fun to make, and can be stuffed with different cheese or vegetable fillings. This filling is particularly easy to make.

INGREDIENTS

Serves 4

14 ounces fresh spinach or 6 ounces frozen spinach
¾ cup ricotta cheese
1 egg
½ cup grated Parmesan cheese
pinch of grated nutmeg
salt and freshly ground black pepper

For the pasta

1½ cups flour
3 eggs

For the sauce

6 tablespoons butter
5–6 sprigs of fresh sage

1 Wash the fresh spinach well in several changes of water. Place in a saucepan, cover and cook until tender, about 5 minutes. Drain. Cook frozen spinach according to the package instructions. When cool, squeeze out as much moisture as possible. Chop finely.

2 Combine the chopped spinach with the ricotta, egg, Parmesan and nutmeg. Season with salt and pepper. Cover and set aside.

3 To make the pasta, place the flour in the center of a clean smooth work surface. Make a well in the middle. Break the eggs into the well. Add a pinch of salt.

4 Start beating the eggs with a fork, gradually drawing the flour from the inside walls of the well. As the paste thickens, continue mixing with your hands.

5 Incorporate as much flour as possible until the mixture forms a mass. It will still be lumpy. If it still sticks to your hands, add a little more flour. Set the dough aside. Scrape off the dough from the work surface until it is smooth.

6 Lightly flour the work surface. Knead the dough. Work for about 10 minutes, or until the dough is smooth and elastic.

7 Divide the dough in half. Flour the rolling pin and the work surface. Pat the dough into a disk and begin rolling out into a flat circle. Roll until it is about ⅛ inch thick. Do the same with the second half of the dough.

8 Cut the dough into sheets. Place small teaspoons of filling along the pasta in rows 2 inches apart. Cover with another sheet of pasta, pressing down gently to expel any air pockets.

9 Use a fluted pastry wheel to cut between the rows to form small squares with filling in the center of each. If the edges do not stick well, moisten with milk or water and press together.

10 Place the ravioli on a lightly floured surface and allow to dry for at least 30 minutes. Turn occasionally so they are completely dry on both sides. Bring a large pan of salted water to a boil.

11 Heat the butter and sage together over very low heat, taking care that the butter melts but does not darken.

12 Drop the ravioli into the boiling water. Stir gently to prevent them from sticking together. They will be cooked in very little time, 4–5 minutes. Drain carefully and arrange in individual serving dishes. Spoon on the sauce and serve at once.

Cilantro Ravioli with Pumpkin Filling

A stunning pasta that combines fresh herbs with a superb creamy pumpkin and roast garlic filling.

INGREDIENTS

Serves 4–6

scant 1 cup unbleached bread flour
2 eggs
pinch of salt
3 tablespoons chopped cilantro
sprigs of cilantro, to garnish

For the filling

4 garlic cloves in their skins
1 pound pumpkin, peeled and seeds removed
½ cup ricotta cheese
4 sun-dried tomatoes in olive oil, drained and finely chopped (reserve 2 tablespoons of the oil)
freshly ground black pepper

1 Place the flour, eggs, salt and cilantro in a food processor. Pulse until combined.

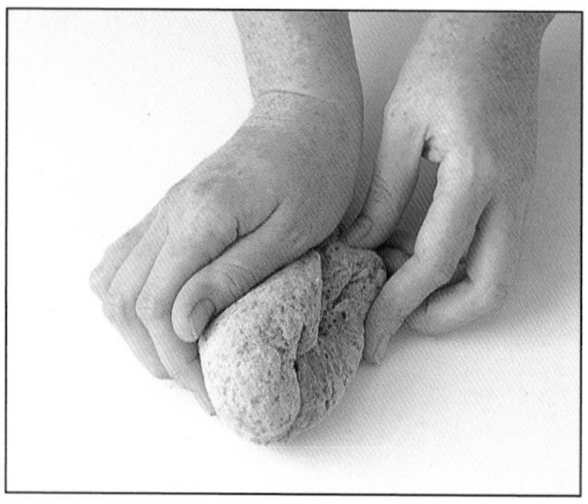

2 Knead the dough on a lightly floured board until smooth.

3 Wrap the dough in plastic wrap and let rest in the refrigerator for 20–30 minutes.

4 Preheat the oven to 400°F. Place the garlic cloves on a baking sheet and bake for 10 minutes, until softened. Steam the pumpkin for 5–8 minutes, until tender, and drain well.

5 Peel the garlic cloves and mash into the pumpkin together with the ricotta and sun-dried tomatoes. Season with plenty of black pepper.

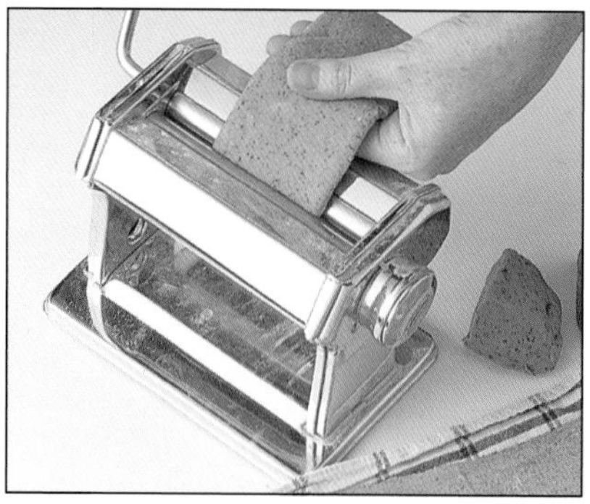

6 Divide the pasta into four pieces and flatten slightly. Using a pasta machine on its thinnest setting, roll out each piece. Lay the sheets of pasta on a clean dish towel until slightly dried.

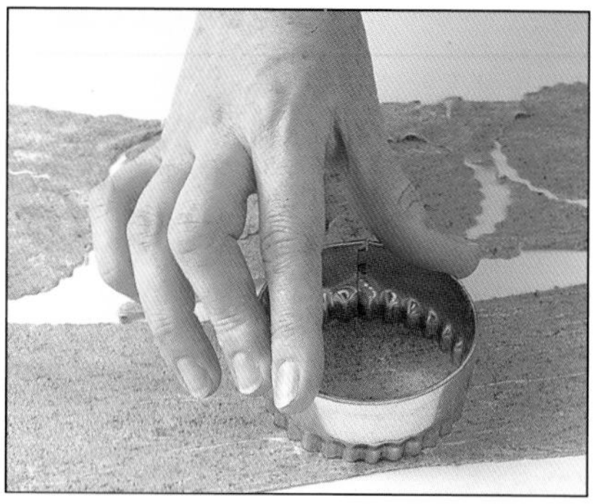

7 Using a 3-inch crinkle-edged round cutter, stamp out 36 rounds.

8 Top 18 of the rounds with a teaspoonful of the pumpkin mixture, brush the edges with water and place another round of pasta on top. Press firmly around the edges to seal. Bring a large pan of water to a boil, add the ravioli and cook for 3–4 minutes. Drain well and toss with the reserved tomato oil. Add pepper and serve garnished with cilantro sprigs.

VARIATION

For an alternative filling you could replace the ricotta cheese with 1 ounce grated Parmesan cheese mixed with 4 ounces cottage cheese. Serve with shavings of Parmesan.

Purée of Lentils with Baked Eggs

This unusual dish makes an excellent supper. For a nutty flavor you could add a 14-ounce can of unsweetened chestnut purée to the lentil mixture.

INGREDIENTS

Serves 4

2 cups washed brown lentils
3 leeks, thinly sliced
2 teaspoons coriander seeds, crushed
1 tablespoon chopped cilantro
2 tablespoons chopped fresh mint
1 tablespoon red wine vinegar
4 cups vegetable stock
4 eggs
salt and freshly ground black pepper
generous handful of chopped parsley to garnish

1 Put the lentils in a deep saucepan. Add the leeks, coriander seeds, cilantro, mint, vinegar and stock. Bring to a boil, then lower the heat and simmer for 30–40 minutes, until the lentils are cooked and have absorbed all the liquid.

2 Preheat the oven to 350°F.

3 Season the lentils with salt and pepper and mix well. Spread out in four lightly greased baking dishes about 6 inches in diameter and 2 inches deep.

4 Using the back of a spoon, make a hollow in the lentil mixture in each dish. Break an egg into each hollow. Cover the dishes with foil and bake for 15–20 minutes, or until the whites are set and the yolks are still soft. Sprinkle with plenty of parsley and serve at once.

Harvest Vegetable and Lentil Casserole

Take advantage of root vegetables in season to produce a hearty dish that's not only full of natural goodness but delicious, too.

INGREDIENTS

Serves 6

1 tablespoon sunflower oil
2 leeks, sliced
1 garlic clove, crushed
4 celery ribs, chopped
2 carrots, sliced
2 parsnips, diced
1 sweet potato, diced
8 ounces rutabaga, diced
6 ounces whole brown or green lentils
1 pound tomatoes, peeled, seeded and chopped
1 tablespoon chopped fresh thyme
1 tablespoon chopped fresh marjoram
3¾ cups vegetable stock
1 tablespoon cornstarch
salt and freshly ground black pepper
sprigs of fresh thyme, to garnish

1 Preheat the oven to 350°F. Heat the oil in a flameproof casserole over moderate heat. Add the leeks, garlic and celery and cook gently for 3 minutes.

2 Add the carrots, parsnips, sweet potato, rutabaga, lentils, tomatoes, herbs, stock and seasoning. Stir well. Bring to a boil, stirring occasionally.

3 Cover and bake for about 50 minutes, until the vegetables and the lentils are cooked and tender. While it is cooking, remove the casserole from the oven and stir the vegetable mixture once or twice so that it is evenly cooked.

4 Remove the casserole from the oven. Blend the cornstarch with 3 tablespoons cold water in a bowl. Stir into the casserole and heat, stirring constantly, until the mixture comes to a boil and thickens. Simmer gently for 2 minutes.

5 Spoon the vegetable mixture into bowls and serve garnished with thyme sprigs.

Vegetable Lasagne

This recipe uses fresh vegetables and herbs to create a delicious version of the favorite classic.

INGREDIENTS

Serves 8

15–18 fresh or precooked lasagne sheets
2 tablespoons olive oil
1 medium onion, very finely chopped
1¼ pounds tomatoes, fresh or canned, chopped
1½ pounds cultivated or wild mushrooms, or a combination of both
6 tablespoons butter
2 garlic cloves, finely chopped
juice of ½ lemon
4 cups béchamel sauce
1½ cups freshly grated Parmesan or Cheddar cheese, or a combination of both
salt and freshly ground black pepper

1 Butter a large, shallow, ovenproof baking dish, preferably rectangular or square.

2 Heat the oil in a small frying pan and sauté the onion until translucent. Add the chopped tomatoes and cook for 6–8 minutes, stirring often. Season with salt and pepper and set aside.

3 Wipe the mushrooms carefully with a damp cloth. Slice finely. Heat half the butter in a frying pan and, when it is bubbling, add the mushrooms. Cook until the mushrooms start to exude their juice. Add the garlic and lemon juice and season with salt and pepper.

4 Cook the mushroom mixture until nearly all the liquids have evaporated and the mushrooms are starting to brown. Set aside.

5 Preheat the oven to 400°F. Bring a pan of water to a boil and place a bowl of cold water near the stove. Add salt to the rapidly boiling water.

6 Drop in 3 or 4 of the lasagne sheets. Cook for about 30 seconds. Remove them from the pan and drop them into the cold water for 30 seconds. Remove and lay out to dry. Continue with the remaining pasta. If using pre-cooked lasagne, skip this step.

7 To assemble the lasagne, have all the elements at hand: the baking dish, fillings, pasta, cheeses and butter. Spread one large spoonful of the béchamel sauce over the bottom of the dish. Arrange a layer of pasta in the dish, cutting it with a sharp knife so that it fits well. Cover the pasta with a thin layer of mushrooms, then one of béchamel sauce. Sprinkle with a little cheese.

8 Make another layer of pasta and spread with a thin layer of tomatoes, then one of béchamel. Sprinkle with cheese.

9 Repeat the layers in the same order, ending with a layer of pasta and béchamel. Do not make more than about 6 layers. Use the pasta trimmings to patch any gaps in the pasta. Sprinkle with cheese and dot with the remaining butter.

10 Bake for 20 minutes. Remove from the oven and let stand for 5 minutes.

COOK'S TIP

Fresh pasta is not necessarily better than dried, but it takes much less time to cook, as it still contains moisture. Fresh pasta should always be stored in the refrigerator or freezer until ready for cooking.

Chile, Tomato and Spinach Pizza

This richly flavored topping with a hint of spice makes a colorful and satisfying pizza.

INGREDIENTS

Serves 3

1–2 fresh red chiles
3 tablespoons tomato oil (from jar of sun-dried tomatoes)
1 onion, chopped
2 garlic cloves, chopped
10 sun-dried tomatoes in oil, drained
14-ounce can chopped tomatoes
1 tablespoon tomato paste
6 ounces fresh spinach
1 pizza crust, 10–12 inches in diameter
3 ounces firm smoked cheese, grated
3 ounces aged Cheddar, grated
salt and freshly ground black pepper

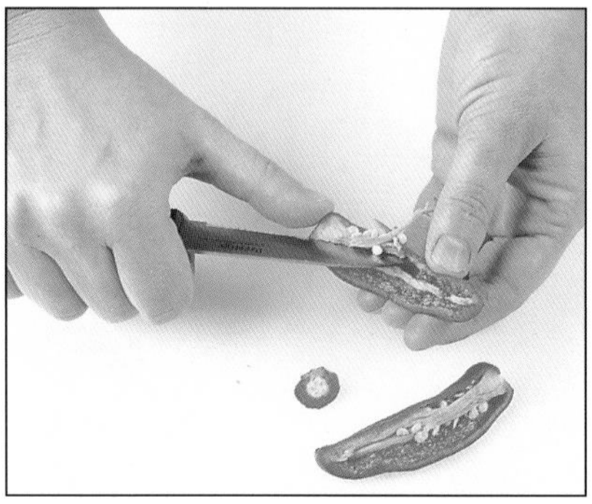

1 Seed and finely chop the chiles.

2 Heat 2 tablespoons of the tomato oil in a saucepan, add the onion, garlic and chiles and cook gently for about 5 minutes, until they are soft.

3 Roughly chop the sun-dried tomatoes. Add to the pan with the chopped tomatoes and tomato paste. Season with salt and pepper. Simmer, uncovered, stirring occasionally, for 15 minutes.

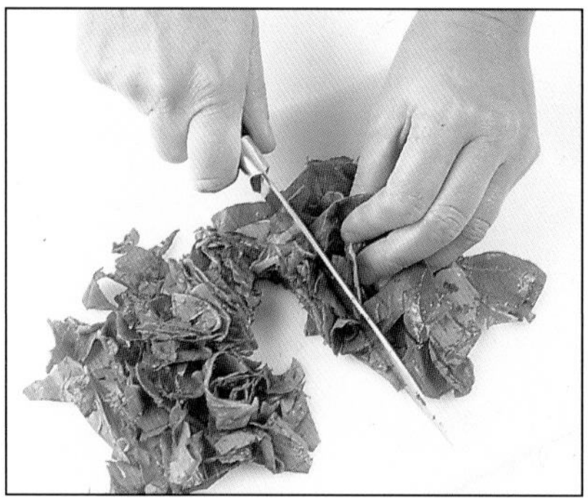

4 Remove the stalks from the spinach and wash the leaves in plenty of cold water. Drain well and pat dry with paper towels. Roughly chop the spinach.

5 Stir the spinach into the sauce. Cook, stirring, for another 5–10 minutes, until the spinach has wilted and no excess moisture remains. Let cool.

6 Meanwhile, preheat the oven to 425°F. Brush the pizza crust with the remaining tomato oil, then spoon the sauce over it. Sprinkle with the grated cheeses and bake for 15–20 minutes, until crisp and golden. Serve immediately.

COOK'S TIP

The smoked cheese used in this pizza topping creates an unusual, rich flavor, that complements the hot, spicy chiles. If you want to heighten this taste, replace the Cheddar with another 3 ounces of the smoked cheese.

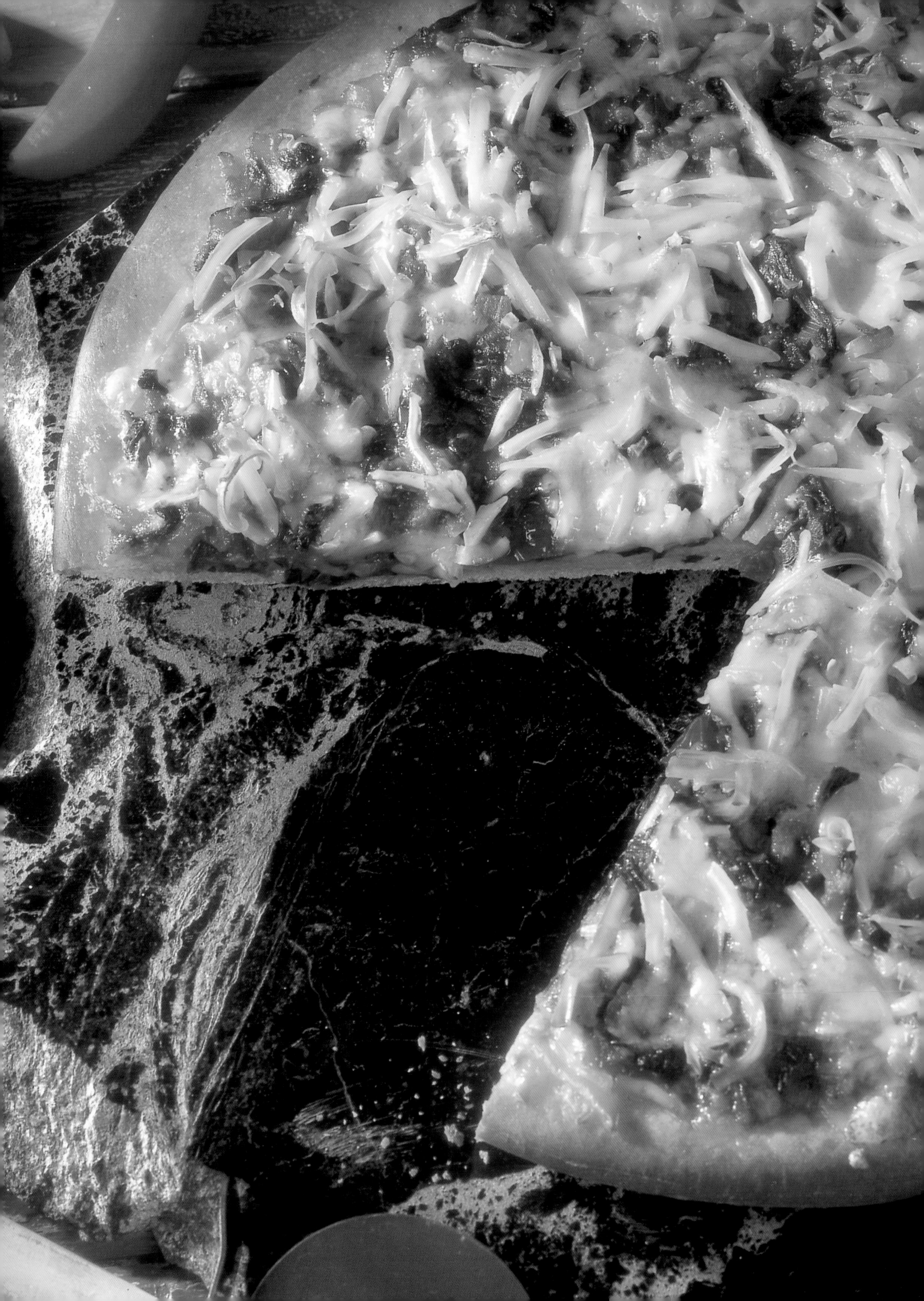

Tagliatelle with Spinach Gnocchi

Gnocchi are extremely smooth and light and make a delicious accompaniment to this pasta dish.

INGREDIENTS

Serves 4–6

1 pound mixed flavored tagliatelle
shavings of Parmesan cheese, to garnish

For the spinach gnocchi

1 pound frozen chopped spinach
1 small onion, finely chopped
1 garlic clove, crushed
¼ teaspoon ground nutmeg
14 ounces low-fat cottage cheese
4 ounces dried white bread crumbs
¾ cup semolina or all-purpose flour
½ cup grated Parmesan cheese
3 egg whites

For the tomato sauce

1 onion, finely chopped
1 celery rib, finely chopped
1 red bell pepper, seeded and diced
1 garlic clove, crushed
⅔ cup vegetable stock
14-ounce can whole peeled tomatoes
1 tablespoon tomato paste
2 teaspoons sugar
1 teaspoon dried oregano
salt and freshly ground black pepper

1 To make the tomato sauce, put the chopped onion, celery, pepper and garlic in a nonstick pan. Add the stock, bring to a boil and cook for 5 minutes, or until tender.

2 Add the tomatoes, tomato paste, sugar and oregano. Season to taste, bring to a boil and simmer, stirring occasionally, for 30 minutes, until thick.

3 Put the spinach, onion and garlic in a saucepan, cover and cook until the spinach is defrosted. Remove the lid and increase the heat. Season with salt, pepper and nutmeg. Cool in a bowl. Mix in the remaining ingredients. Shape into about 24 ovals and refrigerate for 30 minutes.

4 Cook the gnocchi in boiling salted water for about 5 minutes. Remove with a slotted spoon and drain. Cook the tagliatelle in a pan of boiling salted water until al dente. Drain. Transfer to serving plates and top with gnocchi, the tomato sauce and shavings of Parmesan cheese.

Pizza with Fresh Vegetables

This pizza can be made with any combination of fresh vegetables. Most will benefit from being blanched or sautéed before being baked on the pizza.

INGREDIENTS

Serves 4

14 ounces peeled plum tomatoes, fresh or canned, weighed whole, without extra juice
2 medium broccoli spears
8 ounces fresh asparagus
2 small zucchini
5 tablespoons olive oil
⅓ cup shelled peas, fresh or frozen
4 scallions, sliced
1 pizza crust, 10–12 inches in diameter
3 ounces mozzarella cheese, cut into small dice (about ⅓ cup)
10 leaves fresh basil, torn into pieces
2 cloves garlic, finely chopped
salt and freshly ground black pepper

1 Preheat the oven to 475°F for at least 20 minutes before baking the pizza. Strain the tomatoes through the medium disk of a food mill, scraping in all the pulp.

2 Peel the broccoli stems and asparagus and blanch with the zucchini in boiling water for 4–5 minutes. Drain. Cut the broccoli and asparagus into bite-size pieces and slice the zucchini lengthwise.

3 Heat 2 tablespoons of the olive oil in a small saucepan. Stir in the peas and scallions and cook for 5–6 minutes, stirring often. Remove from the heat.

4 Spread the puréed tomatoes over the pizza crust, leaving the rim uncovered. Add the other vegetables, spreading them evenly over the tomatoes.

5 Sprinkle with the mozzarella, basil, garlic, salt and pepper and remaining olive oil. Immediately place the pizza in the oven. Bake for about 20 minutes, or until the crust is golden brown and the cheese has melted.

Ricotta and Fontina Pizza

The earthy flavors of the mixed mushrooms perfectly complement the two creamy cheeses in this delectable recipe.

INGREDIENTS

Serves 4

½ teaspoon active dry yeast
pinch of sugar
4 cups white bread flour
1 teaspoon salt
2 tablespoons olive oil

For the tomato sauce

14-ounce can chopped tomatoes
⅔ cup passata or tomato sauce
1 large garlic clove, finely chopped
1 teaspoon dried oregano
1 bay leaf
2 teaspoons malt vinegar
salt and freshly ground black pepper

For the topping

2 tablespoons olive oil
1 garlic clove, finely chopped
12 ounces mixed mushrooms (cremini, portobello or button), sliced
2 tablespoons chopped fresh oregano, plus whole leaves, to garnish
generous 1 cup ricotta cheese
8 ounces Fontina cheese, sliced

1 To make the dough, put 1¼ cups warm water in a measuring cup. Add the yeast and sugar and let sit for 5–10 minutes, until frothy.

2 Sift the flour and salt into a large bowl and make a well in the center. Gradually pour in the yeast mixture and the olive oil. Mix to make a smooth dough. Knead on a lightly floured surface for about 10 minutes, until dough is smooth, springy and elastic. Place the dough in a floured bowl, cover and let rise in a warm place for 1½ hours.

3 Meanwhile, make the tomato sauce. Put all the ingredients in a saucepan, cover and bring to a boil. Lower the heat, remove the lid and simmer for 20 minutes, stirring occasionally, until reduced.

4 To make the topping, heat the oil in a frying pan. Add the garlic and mushrooms and season with salt and pepper. Cook, stirring, for about 5 minutes, or until the mushrooms are tender and golden. Set aside.

5 Preheat the oven to 425°F. Brush four baking sheets with oil. Knead the dough for 2 minutes, then divide into four equal pieces. Roll out each piece to a 10-inch round and place on a baking sheet.

6 Spoon the tomato sauce over each dough round. Brush the edge with a little olive oil. Add the mushrooms, oregano and cheeses. Season to taste. Bake for about 15 minutes, until golden brown and crisp. Garnish with oregano leaves.

COOK'S TIP

To freeze, allow to cool to room temperature after baking. Wrap in foil and freeze. Thaw completely and heat in a warm oven before serving.

Red Cabbage and Apple Casserole

The brilliant color and pungent flavor make this an excellent winter dish. Serve it with plenty of rye bread.

INGREDIENTS

Serves 6

1½ pounds red cabbage
3 onions, chopped
2 fennel bulbs, roughly chopped
2 tablespoons caraway seeds
3 large, tart eating apples or 1 large cooking apple
1¼ cups plain yogurt
1 tablespoon creamed horseradish
salt and freshly ground black pepper
crusty rye bread, to serve

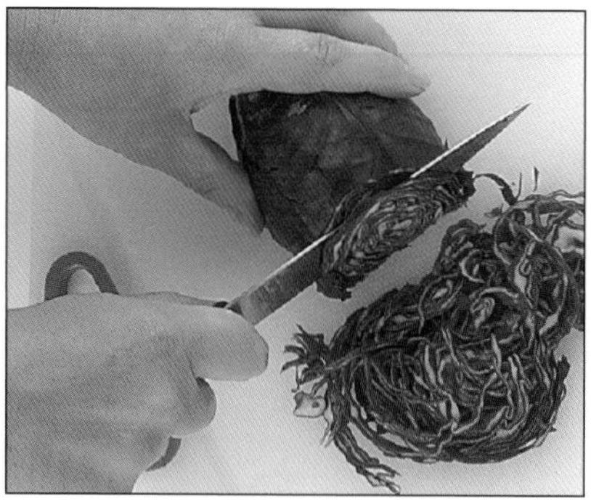

1 Preheat the oven to 300°F. Shred the cabbage finely, discarding any tough stalks. Mix with the onions, fennel and caraway seeds in a large bowl. Peel, core and chop the apples, then stir them into the cabbage mixture. Transfer the mixture to a casserole dish.

2 Mix the yogurt with the creamed horseradish. Stir the yogurt and horseradish mixture into the casserole, season with salt and pepper and cover tightly.

3 Bake for 1½ hours, stirring once or twice during cooking. Serve hot, with rye bread.

Mixed Vegetables with Artichokes

Baking a vegetable medley in the oven is a wonderfully easy way of producing a quick and simple, wholesome midweek meal.

INGREDIENTS

Serves 4

2 tablespoons olive oil
1½ pounds frozen fava or lima beans
4 turnips, peeled and sliced
4 leeks, sliced
1 red bell pepper, seeded and sliced
7 ounces fresh spinach leaves or 4 ounces frozen spinach
2 x 14-ounce cans artichoke hearts, drained
¼ cup pumpkin seeds
soy sauce
salt and freshly ground black pepper

1 Preheat the oven to 350°F. Pour the olive oil into a casserole. Cook the beans in a saucepan of boiling lightly salted water for about 10 minutes. Drain the beans and place them in the casserole with the turnips, leeks, pepper, spinach and canned artichoke hearts.

2 Cover the casserole and bake the vegetables for 30–40 minutes, or until the turnips are slightly soft.

3 Stir in the pumpkin seeds and soy sauce to taste. Season with salt and pepper to taste and serve immediately.

Vegetable Moussaka

This is a really flavorful main-course dish. It can be served with warm fresh bread for a hearty, satisfying meal.

INGREDIENTS

Serves 6

1 pound eggplant, sliced
4 ounces whole green lentils
2½ cups vegetable stock
1 bay leaf
3 tablespoons olive oil
1 onion, sliced
1 garlic clove, crushed
8 ounces mushrooms, sliced
14-ounce can chickpeas, rinsed and drained
14-ounce can chopped tomatoes
2 tablespoons tomato paste
2 teaspoons dried herbes de Provence
1¼ cups plain yogurt
3 eggs
½ cup grated aged Cheddar cheese
salt and freshly ground black pepper
sprigs of fresh flat-leaf parsley, to garnish

1 Sprinkle the eggplant slices with salt and place in a colander. Cover and place a weight on top. Let sit for at least 30 minutes, to allow the bitter juices to be extracted.

2 Meanwhile, place the lentils, stock and bay leaf in a saucepan, cover, bring to a boil and simmer for about 20 minutes, until the lentils are just tender but not mushy. Drain thoroughly and keep warm.

3 Heat 1 tablespoon of the oil in a large saucepan, add the onion and garlic and cook, stirring, for 5 minutes. Stir in the lentils, mushrooms, chickpeas, tomatoes, tomato paste, herbs and 3 tablespoons water. Bring to a boil, cover and simmer gently for 10 minutes, stirring occasionally.

4 Preheat the oven to 350°F. Rinse the eggplant slices, drain and pat dry. Heat the remaining oil in a frying pan and cook the slices in batches for 3–4 minutes, turning once so both sides are browned.

5 Season the lentil mixture with salt and pepper. Arrange a layer of eggplant slices in the bottom of a large, shallow, ovenproof dish or roasting pan, then spoon a layer of the lentil mixture on top. Continue the layers until all the eggplant slices and lentil mixture are used up.

6 Beat the yogurt, eggs and salt and pepper together and pour the mixture over the vegetables. Sprinkle generously with the grated Cheddar cheese and bake for about 45 minutes, until the topping is golden brown and bubbling. Serve immediately, garnished with the flat-leaf parsley.

VARIATION

Sliced and sautéed zucchini or potatoes can be used instead of the eggplant in this dish.

Eggplant Curry

A simple and delicious way of cooking eggplant that retains their full flavor.

INGREDIENTS

Serves 4

2 large eggplant, about 1 pound each
3 tablespoons oil
½ teaspoon black mustard seeds
1 bunch scallions, finely chopped
4 ounces button mushrooms, halved
2 garlic cloves, crushed
1 fresh red chile, finely chopped
½ teaspoon chili powder
1 teaspoon ground cumin
1 teaspoon ground coriander
¼ teaspoon ground turmeric
1 teaspoon salt
14-ounce can chopped tomatoes
1 tablespoon chopped cilantro
sprigs of cilantro, to garnish

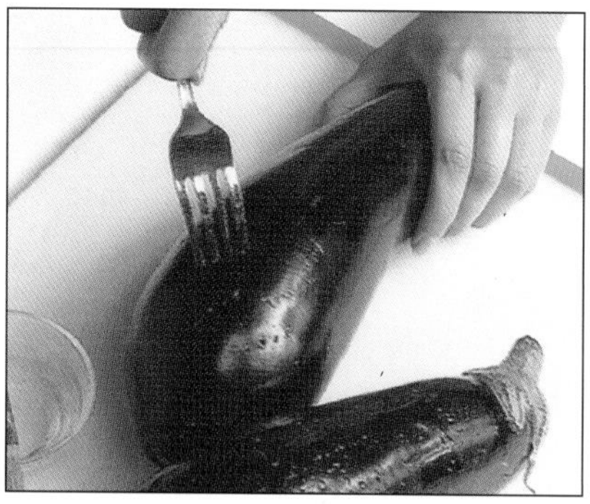

1 Preheat the oven to 400°F. Brush both of the eggplant with 1 tablespoon of the oil and prick with a fork. Bake for 30–35 minutes, until soft.

2 Meanwhile, heat the remaining oil in a saucepan and sauté the mustard seeds for 2 minutes, until they being to splutter.

3 Add the scallions, mushrooms, garlic and chile and cook for 5 minutes. Stir in the chili powder, cumin, coriander, turmeric and salt and cook for 3–4 minutes. Add the tomatoes and simmer for 5 minutes.

4 Cut each eggplant in half lengthwise and scoop out the soft flesh into a bowl. Mash the flesh briefly.

5 Add the mashed eggplant and chopped cilantro to the saucepan. Bring to a boil and simmer for 5 minutes, or until the sauce thickens. Serve garnished with cilantro sprigs.

COOK'S TIP

If you want to omit some of the oil, wrap the eggplants in foil and bake them for 1 hour.

Vegetable Korma

The blending of spices produces a subtle, aromatic curry.

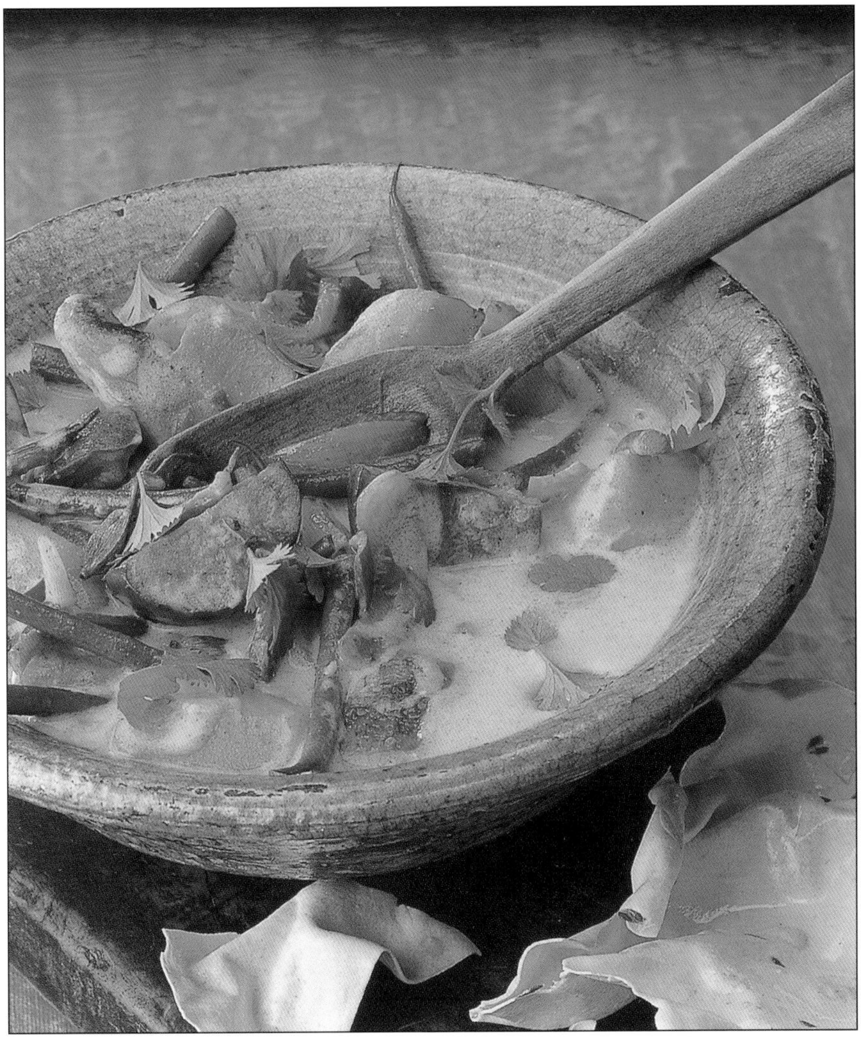

INGREDIENTS

Serves 4

4 tablespoons (1/2 stick) butter
2 onions, sliced
2 garlic cloves, crushed
1-inch piece of fresh ginger root, grated
1 teaspoon ground cumin
1 tablespoon ground coriander
6 cardamom pods
2-inch cinnamon stick
1 teaspoon ground turmeric
1 fresh red chile, seeded and finely chopped
1 potato, peeled and cut into 1-inch cubes
1 small eggplant, chopped
4 ounces mushrooms, thickly sliced
1 cup green beans, cut into 1-inch lengths
1/4 cup plain yogurt
2/3 cup heavy cream
1 teaspoon garam masala
salt and freshly ground black pepper
sprigs of cilantro, to garnish
pappadams, to serve

1 Melt the butter in a heavy saucepan. Add the onions and cook for 5 minutes, until soft. Add the garlic and ginger and cook for 2 minutes, then stir in the cumin, coriander, cardamom, cinnamon stick, turmeric and chile. Cook, stirring, for 30 seconds.

2 Add the potato, eggplant and mushrooms and about 3/4 cup water. Cover the pan, bring to a boil, then lower the heat and simmer for 15 minutes. Add the green beans and cook, uncovered, for 5 minutes.

3 With a slotted spoon, remove the vegetables to a warmed serving dish and keep hot. Allow the cooking liquid to bubble up until it reduces a little. Season with salt and pepper, then stir in the yogurt, cream and garam masala. Pour the sauce over the vegetables and garnish with cilantro. Serve with pappadams.

VARIATION

Any combination of vegetables can be used for this korma, including carrots, cauliflower, broccoli, peas and chickpeas.

Mushroom and Okra Curry

This simple but delicious curry with its fresh gingery mango relish is best served with plain basmati rice.

INGREDIENTS

Serves 4

4 garlic cloves, roughly chopped
1-inch piece of fresh ginger root, peeled and roughly chopped
1–2 fresh red chiles, seeded and chopped
¾ cup cold water
1 tablespoon sunflower oil
1 teaspoon coriander seeds
1 teaspoon cumin seeds
1 teaspoon ground cumin
2 green cardamom pods, seeds removed and ground
pinch of ground turmeric
14-ounce can chopped tomatoes
1 pound mushrooms, quartered if large
8 ounces okra, trimmed and cut into ½-inch slices
2 tablespoons chopped cilantro

For the mango relish
1 large ripe mango, about 1¼ pounds
1 small garlic clove, crushed
1 onion, finely chopped
2 teaspoons grated fresh ginger root
1 fresh red chile, seeded and finely chopped
pinch of salt and sugar

1 To make the mango relish, peel the mango and cut off the flesh from the pit.

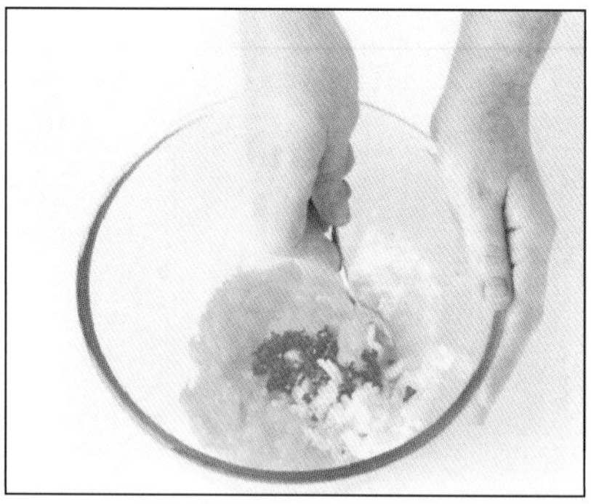

2 In a bowl, mash the mango flesh with a fork, or process in a food processor or blender. Mix in the rest of the relish ingredients. Set aside.

3 Place the garlic, ginger, chiles and 3 tablespoons of the water in a blender or food processor and process until smooth.

4 Heat the sunflower oil in a large saucepan. Add the whole coriander and cumin seeds and allow them to sizzle for a few seconds. Add the ground cumin, cardamom and turmeric and cook for about 1 minute more.

5 Add the garlic paste, tomatoes and remaining water. Stir to mix well, then add the mushrooms and okra. Stir again, then bring to a boil. Reduce the heat, cover and simmer for 5 minutes.

6 Remove the cover, turn up the heat slightly and cook for another 5–10 minutes, until the okra is tender but not too soft.

7 Stir in the chopped cilantro and serve with the mango relish and rice.

COOK'S TIP

When buying okra, choose firm, brightly colored pods that are less than 4 inches long.

Provençal Stuffed Peppers

Stuffed peppers are easy to make for a light and healthy supper.

INGREDIENTS

Serves 4

1 tablespoon olive oil
1 red onion, sliced
1 zucchini, diced
4 ounces mushrooms, sliced
1 garlic clove, crushed
14-ounce can chopped tomatoes
1 tablespoon tomato paste
scant 1/3 cup pine nuts
2 tablespoons chopped fresh basil
4 large yellow bell peppers
1/2 cup red Leicester or Cheddar cheese, finely grated
salt and freshly ground black pepper
fresh basil leaves, to garnish

1 Preheat the oven to 350°F. Heat the oil in a saucepan, add the onion, zucchini, mushrooms and garlic and cook gently for 3 minutes, stirring occasionally.

2 Stir in the tomatoes and tomato paste, then bring to a boil and simmer, uncovered, for 10–15 minutes, stirring occasionally, until thickened slightly. Remove from the heat and stir in the pine nuts, basil and seasoning.

3 Cut the peppers in half lengthwise and seed them. Blanch in a pan of boiling water for about 3 minutes. Drain.

4 Place the peppers in a shallow ovenproof dish and fill them with the vegetable mixture.

5 Cover the dish with foil and bake for 20 minutes. Uncover, sprinkle each pepper with grated cheese and bake for another 5–10 minutes, until the cheese is melted and bubbling. Garnish with basil leaves and serve.

VARIATION

Use the vegetable filling to stuff other vegetables, such as zucchini or eggplant, in place of the bell peppers.

Spicy Chickpea and Eggplant Stew

This is a Lebanese dish that's full of the spicy flavors of the Middle East.

INGREDIENTS

Serves 4

3 large eggplant, cubed
1 cup chickpeas, soaked overnight
¼ cup olive oil
3 garlic cloves, chopped
2 large onions, chopped
½ teaspoon ground cumin
½ teaspoon ground cinnamon
½ teaspoon ground coriander
3 x 14-ounce cans chopped tomatoes
salt and freshly ground black pepper

For the garnish

2 tablespoons olive oil
1 onion, sliced
1 garlic clove, sliced
sprigs of cilantro

1 Place the eggplant in a colander and sprinkle with salt. Set the colander in a bowl and let sit for 30 minutes to allow the bitter juices to escape. Rinse the eggplant with cold water and dry on paper towels.

2 Drain the chickpeas and put in a saucepan with enough water to cover. Bring to a boil and simmer for 1–1½ hours, or until tender. Drain.

3 Heat the oil in a large saucepan. Add the garlic and onion and cook until soft. Add the spices and cook, stirring, for a few seconds. Stir in the eggplant and cook for 5 minutes. Add the tomatoes and chickpeas and season with salt and pepper. Cover and simmer for 20 minutes.

4 To make the garnish, heat the oil in a frying pan and, when very hot, add the sliced onion and garlic. Fry until golden and crisp. Serve the stew with rice, topped with the onion and garlic and garnished with cilantro.

Vegetable Hot Pot with Cheese Triangles

Use a selection of your favorite vegetables, as long as the overall weight remains the same. Firm vegetables may need a little longer cooking time.

INGREDIENTS

Serves 6

2 tablespoons oil
2 garlic cloves, crushed
1 onion, roughly chopped
1 teaspoon mild chili powder
1 pound potatoes, peeled and roughly chopped
1 pound celeriac, peeled and roughly chopped
12 ounces carrots, roughly chopped
12 ounces trimmed leeks, roughly chopped
8 ounces cremini mushrooms, halved
¼ cup all-purpose flour
2½ cups vegetable stock
14-ounce can chopped tomatoes
1 tablespoon tomato paste
2 tablespoons chopped fresh thyme
14-ounce can kidney beans, drained and rinsed
salt and freshly ground black pepper
sprigs of fresh thyme, to garnish (optional)

For the topping

8 tablespoons (1 stick) butter
2 cups self-rising flour
4 ounces Cheddar cheese, grated
2 tablespoons snipped fresh chives
about 5 tablespoons milk

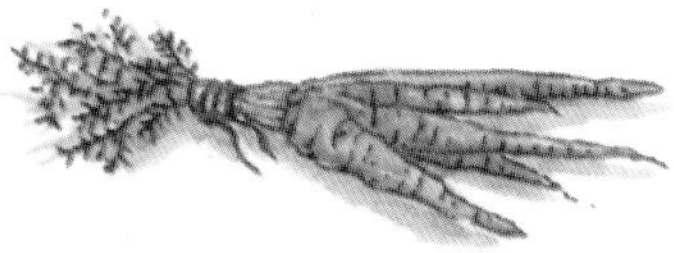

1 Preheat the oven to 350°F. Heat the oil in a large, flameproof casserole and sauté the garlic and onion for 5 minutes, or until beginning to brown. Stir in the chili powder and cook for 1 minute more.

2 Add the potatoes, celeriac, carrots, leeks and mushrooms. Cook for 3–4 minutes. Stir in the flour and cook for 1 minute.

3 Gradually stir in the stock with the tomatoes, tomato paste and thyme and season with plenty of salt and pepper. Bring to a boil, stirring. Cover and bake for 30 minutes.

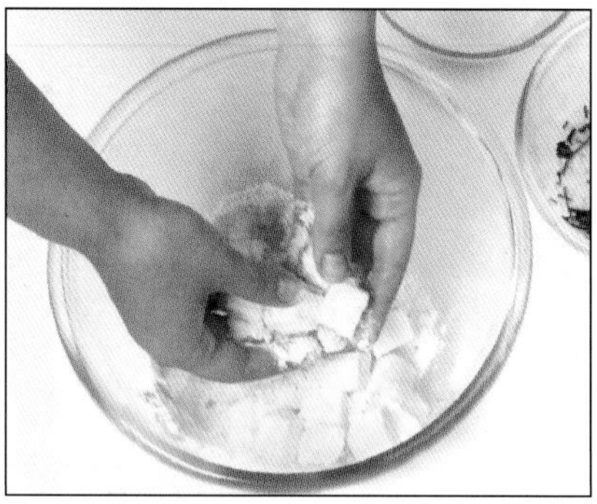

4 Meanwhile, make the topping. Rub the butter into the flour, then stir in half the cheese with the chives and plenty of salt and pepper. Add just enough milk to make a smooth dough.

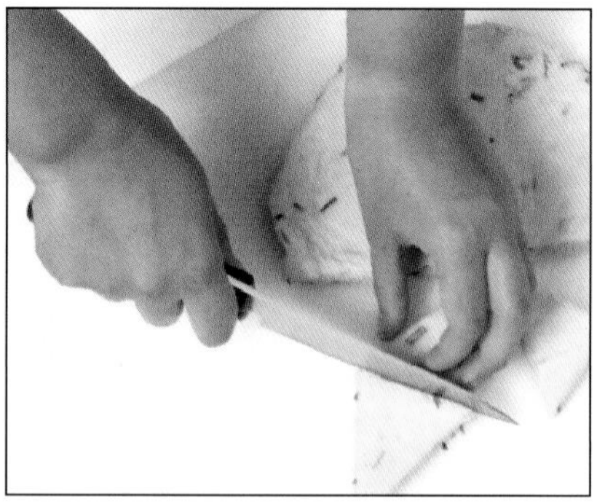

5 Roll out the dough until it is 1 inch thick. Cut into 12 triangles and brush with milk.

6 Remove the casserole from the oven, add the beans and stir to combine. Place the triangles on top and sprinkle with the remaining cheese. Return to the oven, uncovered, and bake for 20–25 minutes. Serve garnished with fresh thyme sprigs, if using.

Sweet and Sour Mixed Bean Hot Pot

An appetizing mixture of beans and vegetables in a tasty sweet and sour sauce, topped with potato.

INGREDIENTS

Serves 6

1 pound unpeeled potatoes
1 tablespoon olive oil
3 tablespoons butter
$\frac{1}{3}$ cup whole-wheat flour
1$\frac{1}{4}$ cups passata or tomato sauce
$\frac{2}{3}$ cup unsweetened apple juice
$\frac{1}{4}$ cup each light brown sugar, ketchup, dry sherry, cider vinegar and light soy sauce
14-ounce can lima beans
14-ounce can flageolet beans
14-ounce can chickpeas
6 ounces green beans, chopped and blanched
8 ounces shallots, sliced and blanched
8 ounces mushrooms, sliced
1 tablespoon each chopped fresh thyme and marjoram
salt and freshly ground black pepper
sprigs of fresh herbs, to garnish

1 Preheat the oven to 400°F. Thinly slice the potatoes and parboil them for 4 minutes. Drain the potatoes thoroughly, toss them in the oil so they are lightly coated all over and set aside.

2 Place the butter, flour, passata, apple juice, sugar, ketchup, sherry, vinegar and soy sauce in a saucepan. Heat gently, whisking constantly, until the sauce comes to a boil and thickens. Simmer gently for 3 minutes, stirring.

3 Rinse and drain the beans and chickpeas and add to the sauce with all the remaining ingredients except the herb garnish. Mix well.

4 Spoon the bean mixture into a casserole.

5 Arrange the potato slices over the top, overlapping them slightly and completely covering the bean mixture.

6 Cover the casserole with foil and bake for about 1 hour, until the potatoes are cooked and tender. Remove the foil for the last 20 minutes of the cooking time, to lightly brown the potatoes. Serve garnished with fresh herb sprigs.

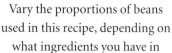

COOK'S TIP

Vary the proportions of beans used in this recipe, depending on what ingredients you have in your pantry.

Spicy Baked Potatoes

Simple baked potatoes take on an exciting new character with the addition of a few herbs and spices.

INGREDIENTS

Serves 2–4

2 large baking potatoes
1 teaspoon sunflower oil
1 small onion, finely chopped
1-inch piece fresh ginger root, grated
1 teaspoon ground cumin
1 teaspoon ground coriander
½ teaspoon ground turmeric
garlic salt
plain yogurt and sprigs of cilantro, to serve

1 Preheat the oven to 375°F. Prick the potatoes with a fork. Bake for 1 hour, or until soft.

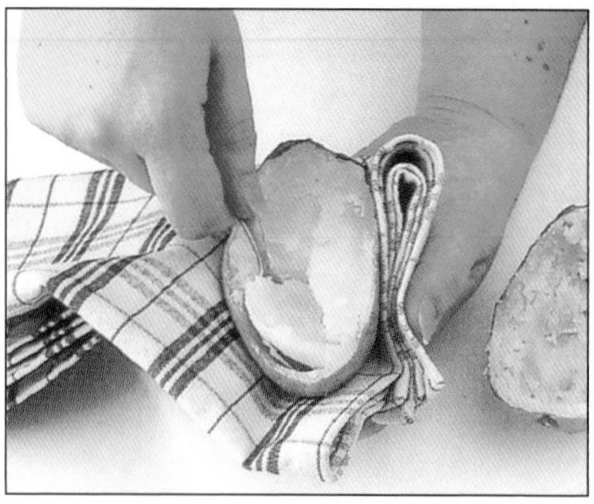

2 Cut the potatoes in half, scoop out the flesh and set aside. Heat the oil in a nonstick frying pan and fry the onion for a few minutes to soften. Stir in the ginger, cumin, coriander and turmeric.

3 Stir over low heat for about 2 minutes, then add the potato flesh and garlic salt to taste.

4 Cook the potato mixture for another 2 minutes, stirring occasionally. Spoon the mixture back into the potato shells and top each with a spoonful of plain yogurt and a sprig or two of cilantro. Serve hot.

Baked Leeks with Cheese and Yogurt

Like all vegetables, the fresher leeks are, the better their flavor, and the freshest leeks available should be used for this dish. Small, young leeks are around at the beginning of the season and are perfect to use here.

INGREDIENTS

Serves 4

2 tablespoons butter
8 small leeks, about 1½ pounds
2 small eggs or 1 large one, beaten
5 ounces fresh goat cheese
⅓ cup plain yogurt
½ cup grated Parmesan cheese
½ cup fresh white or brown bread crumbs
salt and freshly ground black pepper

1 Preheat the oven to 350°F. Butter a shallow ovenproof dish. Trim the leeks, cut a slit from top to bottom and rinse well under cold water.

2 Place the leeks in a saucepan of water, bring to a boil and simmer gently for 6–8 minutes, until just tender. Remove and drain well using a slotted spoon. Arrange in the prepared dish.

3 Beat the eggs with the goat cheese, yogurt and half the Parmesan cheese. Season well with salt and pepper.

4 Pour the cheese and yogurt mixture over the leeks. Mix the bread crumbs and remaining Parmesan cheese together and sprinkle over the sauce. Bake for 35–40 minutes, until the top is crisp and golden brown.

Tofu Stir-Fry with Egg Noodles

Sweet and delicately flavored, this is the perfect supper for lovers of Chinese food.

INGREDIENTS

Serves 4

8 ounces firm smoked tofu (bean curd)
2 tablespoons sherry or vermouth
3 tablespoons dark soy sauce
3 leeks, thinly sliced
1-inch piece fresh ginger root, peeled and finely grated
1–2 fresh red chiles, seeded and sliced in rings
1 small red bell pepper, seeded and sliced thinly
⅔ cup vegetable stock
2 teaspoons honey
2 teaspoons cornstarch
8 ounces medium Chinese egg noodles
salt and freshly ground black pepper

1 Cut the tofu into ¾-inch cubes. Put it in a bowl with the sherry or vermouth and the soy sauce. Toss to coat each piece and then let marinate for about 30 minutes.

2 Put the leeks, ginger, chiles, pepper and stock in a frying pan. Bring to a boil and cook quickly over high heat for 2–3 minutes, until all the ingredients are just soft.

3 Strain the tofu, reserving the marinade, and set the tofu aside. Mix the honey and cornstarch into the marinade.

4 Put the egg noodles into a large pan of boiling water. Remove from the heat and let stand for about 6 minutes, until cooked (or follow the package instructions).

5 Heat a nonstick frying pan and quickly sauté the tofu until lightly golden brown on all sides.

6 Place the vegetable mixture and the tofu in a saucepan with the marinade and stir well until the liquid is thick and glossy. Spoon onto the egg noodles and serve at once.

VARIATION

Tofu absorbs flavors readily when marinated. If you are not a great fan of tofu, you could substitute any type of firm smoked cheese and omit Step 5.

Beet, Wild Mushroom and Potato Casserole

This inexpensive dish captures the spirit of some traditional Polish autumn menus.

INGREDIENTS

Serves 4

2 tablespoons vegetable oil
1 medium onion, chopped
3 tablespoons all-purpose flour
1¼ cups vegetable stock
1½ pounds cooked beets, peeled and chopped
5 tablespoons light cream
2 tablespoons creamed horseradish
1 teaspoon hot mustard
1 tablespoon wine vinegar
1 teaspoon caraway seeds
2 tablespoons butter
1 shallot, chopped
8 ounces assorted wild and cultivated mushrooms, trimmed and sliced
3 tablespoons chopped fresh parsley

For the potato border
2 pounds floury potatoes, peeled
⅔ cup milk
1 tablespoon chopped fresh dill (optional)
salt and freshly ground black pepper

1 Preheat the oven to 375°F. Lightly oil a 9-inch round baking dish. Heat the oil in a large saucepan, add the onion and cook until soft, without coloring. Stir in the flour, remove from the heat and gradually add the stock, stirring until well blended.

2 Return to the heat, stir and simmer to thicken, then add the beets, cream, creamed horseradish, mustard, vinegar and caraway seeds.

3 To make the potato border, bring the potatoes to a boil in salted water and cook for 20 minutes. Drain well and mash with the milk. Add the dill, if using, and season with salt and pepper.

4 Spoon the potatoes into the prepared dish and make a well in the center. Spoon the beet mixture into the well and set aside.

5 Melt the butter in a large nonstick frying pan and cook the shallot until soft, without browning. Add the mushrooms and cook over moderate heat until their juices begin to run. Increase the heat and boil off the moisture. When quite dry, season with salt and pepper and stir in most of the chopped parsley.

6 Spread the mushrooms over the beet mixture, cover and bake for about 30 minutes. Serve at once, garnished with the reserved parsley.

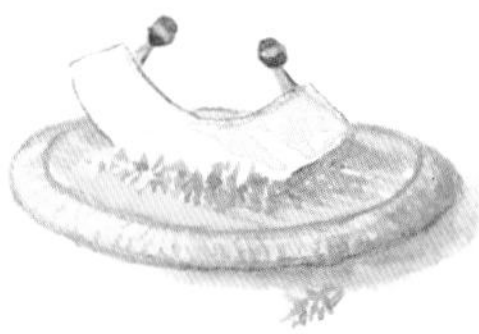

COOK'S TIP

If you are planning ahead, this entire dish can be made in advance and heated when needed. Allow 50 minutes baking time from room temperature.

Special Occasions

~

Breaded Eggplant with Hot Vinaigrette

Crisp on the outside, beautifully tender within, these eggplant slices taste wonderful with a spicy dressing flavored with chiles and capers.

INGREDIENTS

Serves 2

1 large eggplant
½ cup all-purpose flour
2 eggs, beaten
2 cups fresh white bread crumbs
vegetable oil, for frying
1 head of radicchio
salt and freshly ground black pepper

For the dressing

2 tablespoons olive oil
1 garlic clove, crushed
1 tablespoon drained capers
1 tablespoon white wine vinegar
1 tablespoon chili oil

1 Remove the ends from the eggplant. Cut it into ½-inch slices. Set aside.

COOK'S TIP

It is a good idea to salt the eggplant slices before frying in order to draw out some of their moisture. This will also reduce the amount of oil they absorb.

2 Season the flour with a generous amount of salt and pepper. Spread out in a shallow dish. Pour the beaten eggs into a second dish. Spread out the bread crumbs in a third.

3 Dip the eggplant slices in the flour, then in the beaten egg and finally in the bread crumbs, patting them on top to make an even coating.

4 Pour vegetable oil into a large frying pan to a depth of about ¼ inch. Heat the oil, then fry the eggplant slices for 3–4 minutes, turning once. Drain well on paper towels.

5 To make the dressing, heat the olive oil in a small pan. Add the garlic and capers and cook over gentle heat for 1 minute. Increase the heat, add the vinegar and cook for 30 seconds. Stir in the chili oil and remove the pan from the heat.

6 Arrange the radicchio leaves on two plates. Top with the hot eggplant slices. Drizzle with the vinaigrette and serve.

Broccoli Timbales

This elegant but easy-to-make dish can be made with almost any puréed vegetable, such as carrot or celeriac. To avoid last-minute fuss, make the timbales a few hours ahead and cook while the first course is being eaten. Or serve them on their own as an appetizer with a little white wine butter sauce.

INGREDIENTS

Serves 4

1 tablespoon butter
12 ounces broccoli florets
3 tablespoons crème fraîche or whipping cream
1 egg, plus one egg yolk
1 tablespoon chopped scallion
pinch of freshly grated nutmeg
salt and freshly ground black pepper
white wine butter sauce, to serve (optional)
fresh chives, to garnish (optional)

1 Preheat the oven to 375°F. Lightly butter four ¾-cup ramekins. Line the bottoms with waxed paper and butter the paper.

2 Steam the broccoli in the top of a covered steamer over boiling water for 8–10 minutes, until very tender.

3 Put the broccoli in a food processor fitted with the metal blade and process with the cream, egg and egg yolk until smooth.

4 Add the scallion and season with salt, pepper and nutmeg. Pulse to mix.

5 Spoon the purée into the ramekins and place in a roasting pan. Add boiling water to come halfway up the sides. Bake for 25 minutes, until just set. Invert onto warmed plates and peel off the paper. If serving as an appetizer, pour sauce around each timbale and garnish with chives.

Fonduta with Steamed Vegetables

Fonduta is a creamy cheese sauce from Italy. Traditionally, it is garnished with slices of white truffles and eaten with toasted bread rounds.

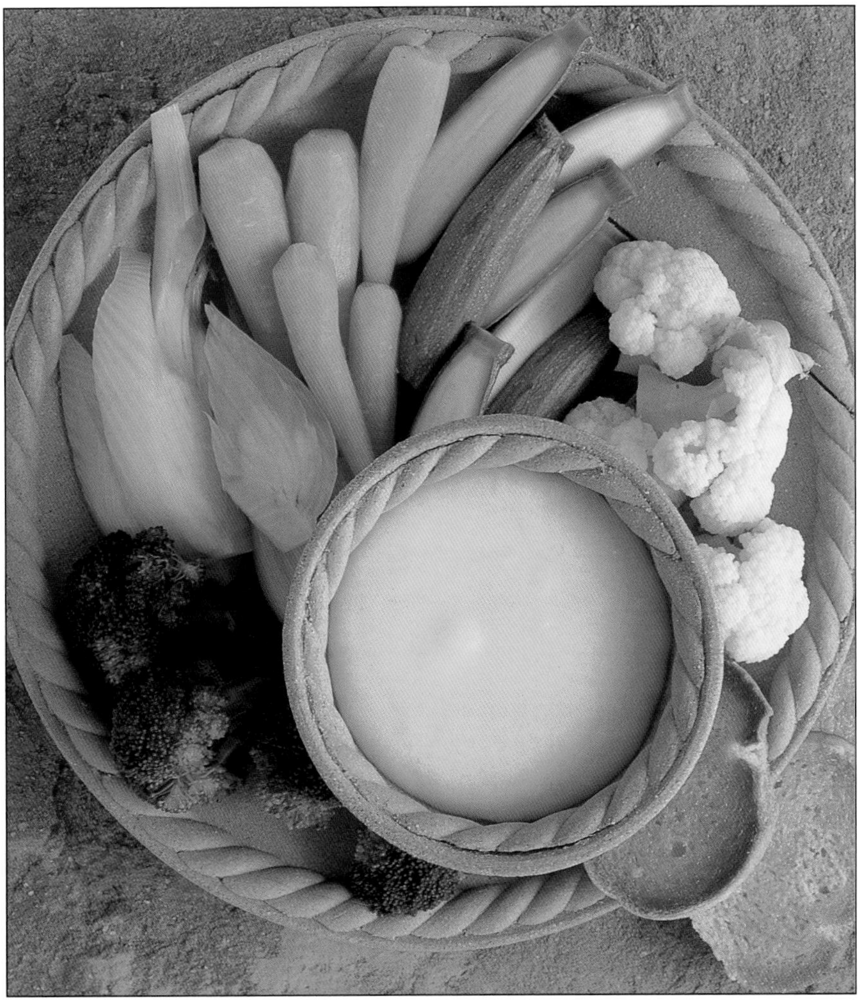

INGREDIENTS

Serves 4

assorted vegetables, such as fennel, broccoli, carrots, cauliflower and zucchini
8 tablespoons (1 stick) butter
12–16 rounds of Italian bread or French baguette

For the fonduta

11 ounces Fontina cheese
1 tablespoon flour
milk, as required
4 tablespoons butter
½ cup freshly grated Parmesan cheese
pinch of grated nutmeg
2 egg yolks, at room temperature
a few slivers of white truffle (optional)
salt and freshly ground black pepper

1 About 6 hours before you want to serve the fonduta, cut the Fontina into chunks and place in a bowl. Sprinkle with the flour. Pour in enough milk to barely cover the cheese and set aside in a cool place. The cheese should be at room temperature before being cooked.

2 Just before preparing the fonduta, steam the vegetables until tender. Cut into pieces. Place on a serving platter, dot with butter and keep warm.

3 Butter the bread and toast lightly in the oven or under the broiler. Pass the egg yolks through a sieve and set aside.

4 For the fonduta, melt the butter in a bowl set over a pan of simmering water, or in a double boiler. Strain the Fontina and add it with 3–4 tablespoons of its soaking milk. Cook, stirring, until the cheese melts. When it is hot and has formed a homogeneous mass, add the Parmesan and stir until melted. Season with nutmeg, salt and pepper.

5 Remove from the heat and immediately beat in the sieved egg yolks. Spoon into warmed individual serving bowls, garnish with white truffle slivers, if using, and serve with the vegetables and toasted bread.

Red Pepper and Watercress Phyllo Parcels

Peppery watercress combines well with sweet red pepper in these crisp little parcels.

INGREDIENTS

Makes 8

3 red bell peppers
6 ounces watercress
1 cup ricotta cheese
¼ cup blanched almonds, toasted and chopped
8 sheets phyllo pastry
2 tablespoons olive oil
salt and freshly ground black pepper
green salad, to serve

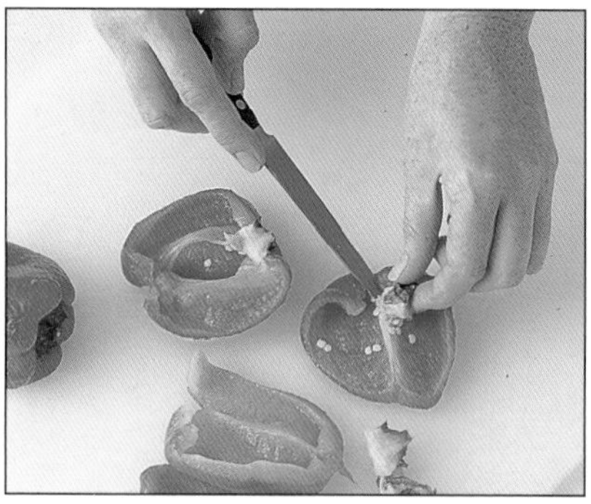

1 Preheat the oven to 375°F. Place the peppers under a hot broiler until blistered and charred. Place in a paper bag. When cool enough to handle, peel, seed and pat dry on paper towels.

2 Place the peppers and watercress in a food processor and pulse until coarsely chopped. Spoon into a bowl.

3 Gradually mix in the ricotta and almonds, and season with salt and pepper.

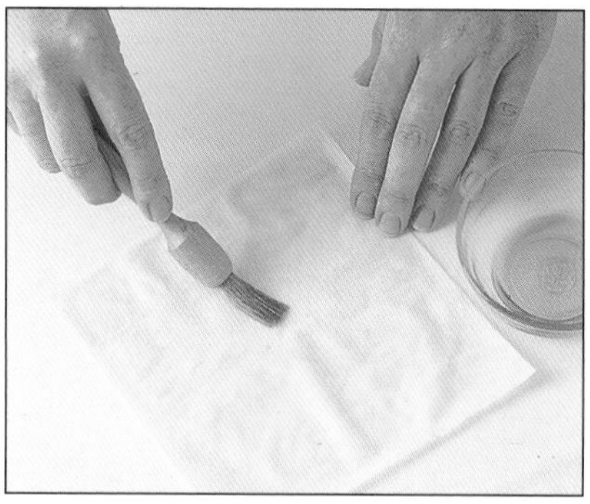

4 Working with 1 sheet of phyllo pastry at a time, cut out 2 x 7-inch rectangles and 2 x 2-inch squares from each sheet. Brush 1 of the large pieces with a little olive oil and place the second large piece at an angle of 90° to form a star shape.

5 Carefully place one of the squares in the center of the star shape. Brush lightly with olive oil and top with the second square.

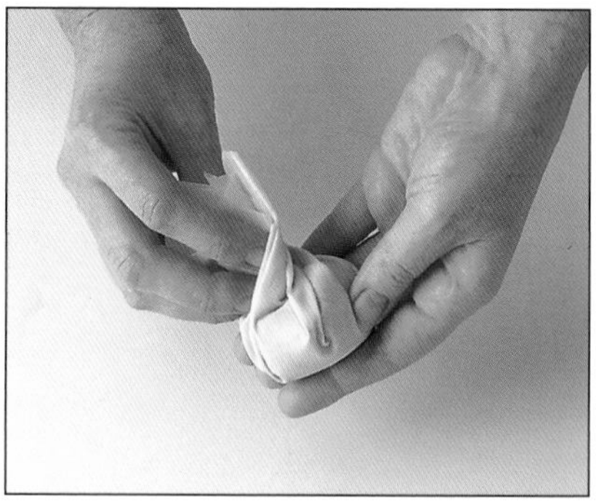

6 Top with one-eighth of the red pepper mixture. Bring the edges of the pastry together to form a purse shape and twist to seal. Place on a lightly greased baking sheet and cook for 25–30 minutes, until crisp and golden. Serve with green salad.

COOK'S TIP

Keep phyllo pastry refrigerated until you need to use it. When working with the pastry, try to handle it as little as possible, and keep the work area cool.

Buckwheat Blinis with Mushroom Caviar

These little Russian pancakes are traditionally served with fish roe caviar and sour cream. The term caviar is also given to fine vegetable mixtures called "ikry." This wild mushroom caviar has a rich and silky texture.

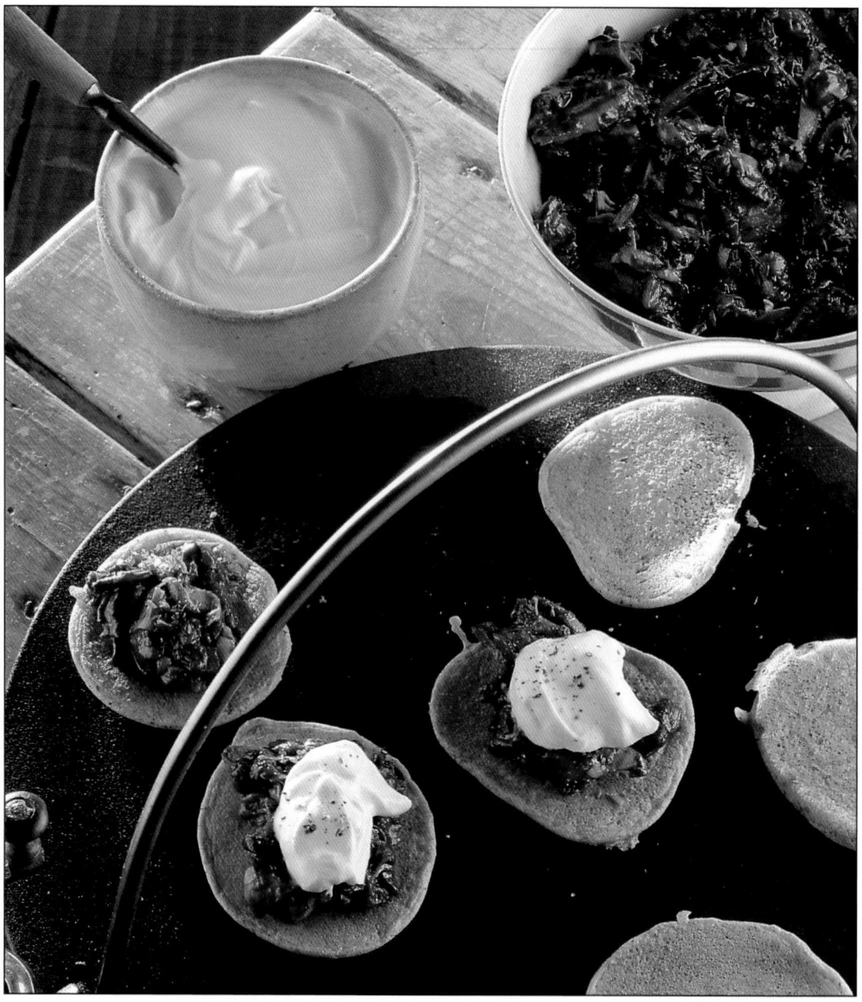

INGREDIENTS

Serves 4

1 cup white bread flour
⅓ cup buckwheat flour
½ teaspoon salt
1¼ cups milk
1 teaspoon active dry yeast
2 eggs, separated
1 cup sour cream or crème fraîche, to serve

For the caviar

12 ounces assorted wild mushrooms, such as cremini, porcini, oyster and portobello mushrooms
1 teaspoon celery salt
2 tablespoons walnut oil
1 tablespoon lemon juice
3 tablespoons chopped fresh parsley
freshly ground black pepper

1 To make the caviar, trim and chop the mushrooms and place them in a glass bowl. Toss with the celery salt and cover with a weighted plate.

2 Let the mushrooms sit for 2 hours, until the juices have run out into the bottom of the bowl. Rinse them thoroughly to remove the salt.

3 Drain the mushrooms and press out as much liquid as you can with the back of a spoon. Return them to the bowl and toss with the walnut oil, lemon juice and parsley. Season with pepper and chill until ready to serve.

4 For the blinis, sift the two flours together with the salt in a large mixing bowl. Warm the milk to lukewarm. Add the yeast to the milk, stirring until dissolved, then pour into the flour. Add the egg yolks and stir to make a smooth batter. Cover with a damp cloth and let sit in a warm place to rise for about 30 minutes.

5 Beat the egg whites in a clean bowl until stiff, then fold into the risen batter.

6 Heat a cast-iron pan to moderate. Moisten with oil, then drop spoonfuls of the batter onto the surface, turn them over and cook briefly on the other side. Spoon the mushroom caviar on top and serve with the sour cream.

Greek Phyllo Twists

Spinach and feta cheese make up the secret filling hidden inside these pretty phyllo parcels.

INGREDIENTS

Serves 4

1 tablespoon olive oil
1 small onion, finely chopped
10 ounces fresh spinach, stalks removed
4 tablespoons butter, melted
4 sheets phyllo pastry (each about 18 x 10 inches)
1 egg
pinch of grated nutmeg
1/4 cup crumbled feta cheese
1 tablespoon freshly grated Parmesan cheese
salt and freshly ground black pepper

1 Preheat the oven to 375°F. Heat the oil in a pan, add the onion and cook gently for 5–6 minutes, until softened.

2 Add the spinach leaves and cook, stirring, until the spinach has wilted and some of the liquid has evaporated. Let cool.

3 Brush four 4-inch-diameter removable-bottomed tartlet pans with a little melted butter. Take two sheets of the phyllo pastry and cut each into eight 4½-inch squares. Keep the remaining sheets covered.

4 Brush four squares at a time with melted butter. Line the first tartlet tin with one square, gently easing it into the bottom and up the sides. Leave the edges overhanging.

5 Lay the remaining three buttered squares on top of the first, turning them so the corners form a star shape. Repeat for the remaining tartlet pans.

6 Beat the egg with the nutmeg and season with salt and pepper. Stir in the cheeses and spinach. Divide the mixture among the pans and smooth the tops. Fold the overhanging pastry back over the filling.

7 Cut one of the remaining sheets of pastry into eight 4-inch rounds. Brush with butter and place two on top of each tartlet. Press around the edges to seal. Brush the remaining sheet of pastry with butter and cut into strips. Twist each strip and lay on top of the tartlets. Let stand for 5 minutes, then bake for 30–35 minutes. Serve hot or cold.

Grilled Vegetable Terrine

Impress your guests with a colorful layered terrine using a mixture of Mediterranean vegetables.

INGREDIENTS

Serves 6

2 large red bell peppers, quartered, cored and seeded
2 large yellow bell peppers, quartered, cored and seeded
1 large eggplant, sliced lengthwise
2 large zucchini, sliced lengthwise
6 tablespoons olive oil
1 large red onion, thinly sliced
½ cup raisins
1 tablespoon tomato paste
1 tablespoon red wine vinegar
1⅔ cups tomato juice
2 tablespoons agar-agar
fresh basil leaves, to garnish

For the dressing
6 tablespoons olive oil
2 tablespoons red wine vinegar
salt and freshly ground black pepper

1 Place the peppers skin side up under a hot broiler until blackened. Put in a bowl. Cover.

2 Arrange the eggplant and zucchini slices on separate baking sheets. Brush them with oil and cook under the broiler.

3 Heat the remaining olive oil in a frying pan. Add the onion, raisins, tomato paste and red wine vinegar. Cook until soft.

4 Line a 7½-cup terrine with plastic wrap.

5 Pour half the tomato juice into a saucepan. Sprinkle with the agar-agar. Dissolve over low heat.

6 Layer the red peppers in the terrine and cover with some of the tomato juice and agar-agar. Add the eggplant, zucchini, yellow peppers and onion mixture.

7 Pour tomato juice over each layer of vegetables and finish with another layer of red peppers.

8 Add the remaining tomato juice to any left in the pan and pour into the terrine. Give the terrine a sharp tap to disperse the juice. Cover and chill in the refrigerator until set.

9 To make the dressing, whisk together the oil and vinegar. Season with salt and pepper.

10 Turn out the terrine and remove the plastic wrap. Serve in thick slices, drizzled with dressing. Garnish with basil leaves.

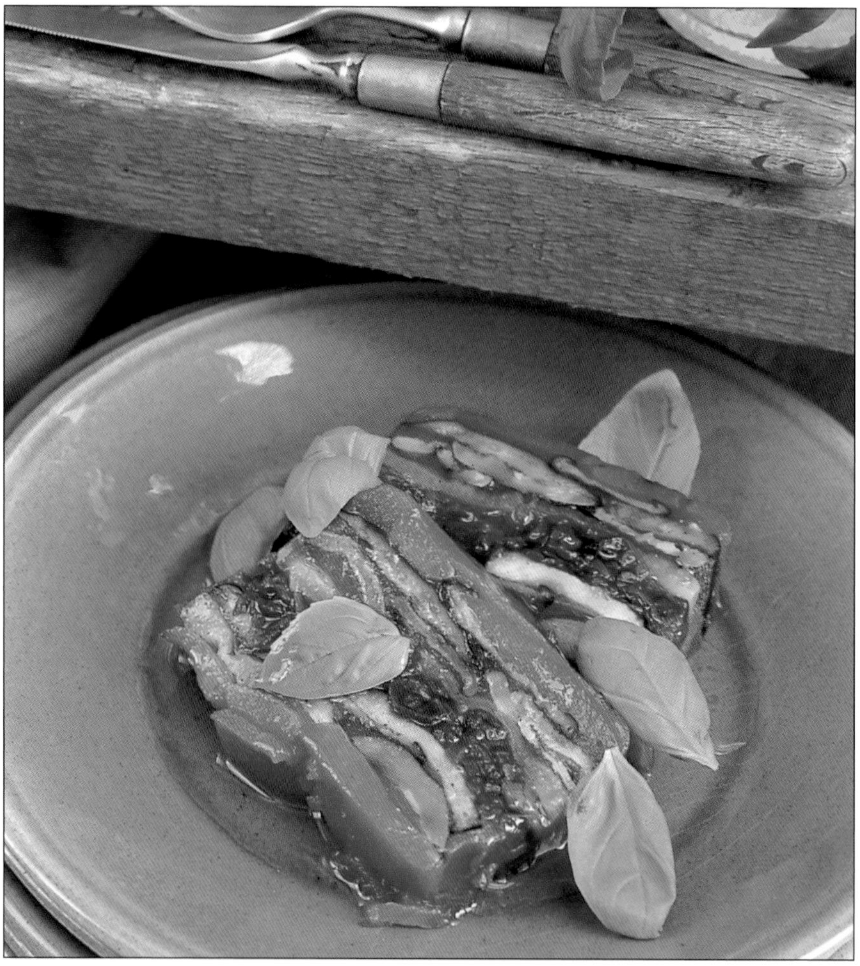

Leek Soufflé

Soufflés are a great way to impress guests at a dinner party. This one is simple to make but it looks very sophisticated.

INGREDIENTS

Serves 2–3

4 tablespoons (½ stick) butter
1 tablespoon sunflower oil
2 leeks, thinly sliced
about 1¼ cups milk
¼ cup all-purpose flour
4 eggs, separated
3 ounces Gruyère or Emmenthal cheese, grated
salt and freshly ground black pepper

1 Preheat the oven to 350°F. Grease a large soufflé dish with 1 tablespoon of the butter. Heat the sunflower oil and 1 tablespoon butter in a small saucepan or flameproof casserole and cook the leeks over gentle heat for 4–5 minutes, until soft but not brown.

2 Stir in the milk and bring to a boil. Cover and simmer for 4–5 minutes, until the leeks are tender. Strain the liquid through a sieve into a measuring cup.

3 Melt the remaining butter, stir in the flour and cook for 1 minute. Remove from the heat.

4 Add enough milk to the reserved liquid to make 1¼ cups. Gradually stir the milk into the flour mixture to make a smooth sauce. Return to the heat and bring to a boil, stirring. When thickened, remove from the heat. Cool slightly and beat in the egg yolks, cheese and leeks.

5 Beat the egg whites until stiff and, using a large metal spoon, fold into the leek and egg mixture. Pour into the prepared soufflé dish and bake for about 30 minutes, until puffed and golden brown. Serve immediately.

Broccoli and Chestnut Terrine

Served hot or cold, this versatile terrine is equally suitable for a dinner party or for a picnic. A light salad makes an ideal accompaniment.

INGREDIENTS

Serves 4–6

1 pound broccoli, cut into small florets
8 ounces cooked chestnuts, roughly chopped
1 cup fresh whole-wheat bread crumbs
¼ cup plain yogurt
2 tablespoons finely grated Parmesan cheese
2 eggs, beaten
pinch of grated nutmeg
salt and freshly ground black pepper
new potatoes, to serve

For the salad and dressing (optional)

¼ cup olive oil
1 tablespoon lemon juice
½ teaspoon sugar
salt and freshly ground black pepper
1 tablespoon chopped fresh thyme or dill
9 ounces mixed salad greens

1 Preheat the oven to 350°F. Line a 9 x 5 x 3-inch (8-cup) loaf pan with baking parchment.

2 Blanch or steam the broccoli for 3–4 minutes, until just tender. Drain well. Reserve one-fourth of the smallest florets and chop the rest finely.

3 Mix together the chestnuts, bread crumbs, yogurt and Parmesan. Season with salt, pepper and nutmeg.

4 Gradually fold in the chopped broccoli, reserved florets and the beaten eggs.

5 Spoon the broccoli mixture into the prepared pan.

6 Place in a roasting pan and pour in boiling water to come halfway up the sides of the loaf pan. Bake for 20–25 minutes.

7 Meanwhile, to make the salad dressing, if using, mix together the olive oil, lemon juice and sugar. Season with salt and pepper and stir in the thyme or dill. Arrange the salad greens on a plate. Pour the dressing over the salad.

8 Remove the roasting pan from the oven and turn the terrine out onto a plate. Cut into even slices and serve with new potatoes.

Goat Cheese Soufflé

Make sure everyone is seated before the soufflé comes out of the oven, because it will begin to deflate almost immediately. This recipe works equally well with strong blue cheeses, such as Roquefort.

INGREDIENTS

Serves 4–6

3 tablespoons butter
1/4 cup all-purpose flour
3/4 cup milk
1 bay leaf
freshly grated nutmeg
grated Parmesan cheese, for sprinkling
1 1/2 ounces herb and garlic soft cheese
5 ounces firm goat cheese, diced
6 egg whites, at room temperature
1/4 teaspoon cream of tartar
salt and freshly ground black pepper

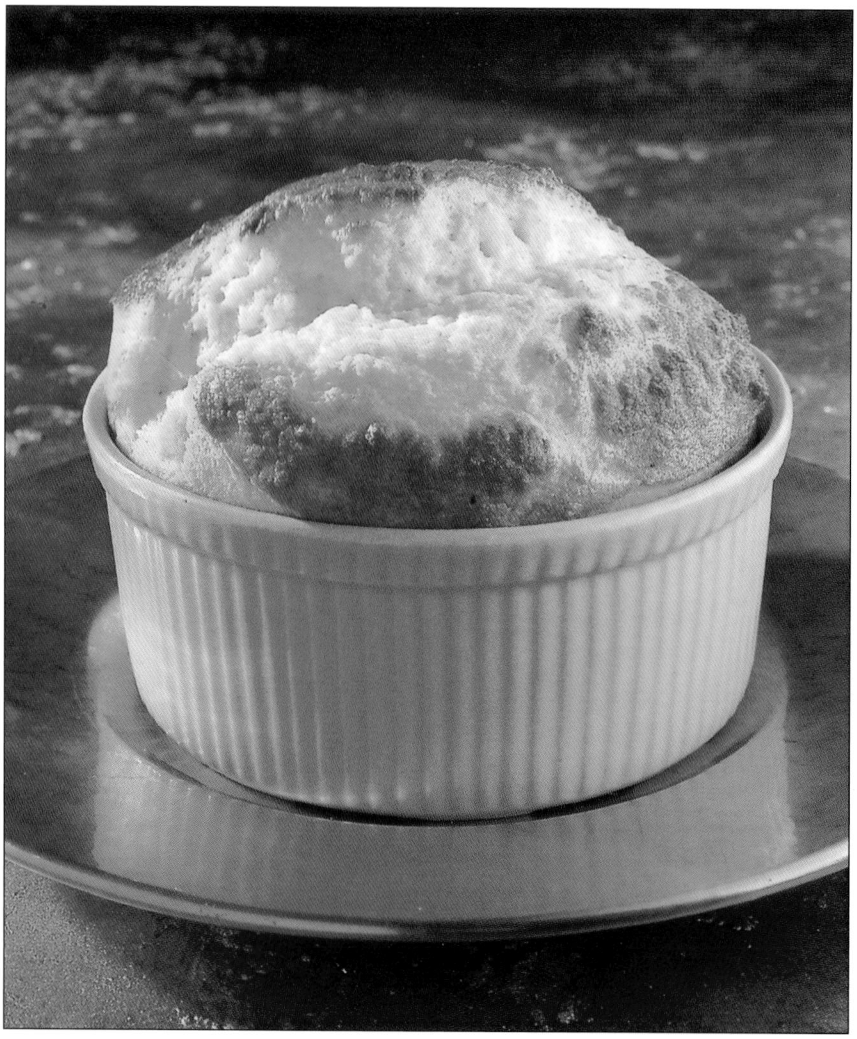

1 Melt 2 tablespoons butter in a heavy saucepan over medium heat. Add the flour and cook until golden, stirring occasionally.

2 Pour in half the milk, stirring vigorously until smooth. Stir in the remaining milk and add the bay leaf. Season with a pinch of salt and plenty of pepper and nutmeg. Reduce the heat to medium low, cover and simmer gently for about 5 minutes, stirring occasionally.

3 Preheat the oven to 375°F. Generously butter a 6 1/4-cup soufflé dish and sprinkle with Parmesan cheese.

4 Remove the sauce from the heat and discard the bay leaf. Stir in both cheeses.

5 In a clean, grease-free bowl, using an electric mixer or balloon whisk, beat the egg whites slowly until they become frothy. Add the cream of tartar, increase the speed and continue beating until they form soft peaks, then stiffer peaks that just flop over a little at the top.

6 Stir a spoonful of beaten egg whites into the cheese sauce to lighten it, then pour the cheese sauce over the remaining whites. Using a large metal spoon, gently fold the sauce into the whites until the mixtures are just combined.

7 Pour the soufflé mixture into the prepared dish and bake for 25–30 minutes, until puffed and golden brown. Serve at once.

Celeriac and Blue Cheese Roulade

Celeriac adds a delicate and subtle flavor to this attractive dish.

INGREDIENTS

Serves 6

1 tablespoon butter
8 ounces cooked spinach, drained and chopped
⅔ cup light cream
4 large eggs, separated
2 tablespoons grated Parmesan cheese
pinch of nutmeg
salt and freshly ground black pepper

For the filling

8 ounces celeriac
lemon juice
3 ounces Gorgonzola cheese
4 ounces fromage frais

1 Preheat the oven to 400°F. Line a 13 x 9-inch jelly roll pan with baking parchment.

2 Melt the butter in a saucepan and add the spinach. Cook until all the liquid has evaporated. Remove the pan from the heat. Stir in the cream, egg yolks, Parmesan and nutmeg. Season.

3 Beat the egg whites until stiff, fold them gently into the spinach mixture and then spoon into the prepared pan. Spread the mixture evenly and use an icing spatula to smooth the surface.

4 Bake for 10–15 minutes, until the roulade is firm to the touch. Turn out onto a sheet of waxed paper and peel away the lining paper. Roll up the roulade with the waxed paper inside and let cool slightly.

5 To make the filling, peel the celeriac and grate it into a bowl. Sprinkle with lemon juice to taste. Blend the Gorgonzola cheese and fromage frais together and mix with the celeriac and a little black pepper.

6 Unroll the roulade, spread with the filling and roll up again, this time without the paper. Serve at once or wrap loosely and chill.

Spinach and Wild Mushroom Soufflé

Wild mushrooms combine especially well with eggs and spinach in this sensational soufflé. Almost any combination of mushrooms can be used for this recipe, although the firmer varieties provide the best texture for the dish.

INGREDIENTS

Serves 4

8 ounces fresh spinach, washed, or 4 ounces frozen chopped spinach
4 tablespoons (½ stick) unsalted butter, plus extra for greasing
1 garlic clove, crushed
6 ounces assorted wild mushrooms such as porcini, cremini, oyster and portobello mushrooms
1 cup milk
3 tablespoons all-purpose flour
6 eggs, separated
pinch of grated nutmeg
¼ cup grated Parmesan cheese
salt and freshly ground black pepper

1 Preheat the oven to 375°F. Steam the spinach over moderate heat for 3–4 minutes. Cool under running water, then drain. Press out as much liquid as you can with the back of a large spoon and chop finely. If using frozen spinach, defrost and prepare following the package instructions. Squeeze dry in the same way.

2 Melt the butter in a saucepan and cook the garlic and mushrooms over low heat until softened. Turn up the heat and evaporate the juices. When dry, add the spinach and transfer to a bowl. Cover and keep warm.

3 Measure 3 tablespoons of the milk into a bowl. Bring the remainder to a boil. Stir the flour and egg yolks into the cold milk in the bowl and blend well. Stir the boiling milk into the egg and flour mixture, return to the pan and simmer to thicken. Add the spinach mixture to the pan. Season with salt, pepper and nutmeg.

4 Butter a 4-cup soufflé dish, paying particular attention to the sides. Sprinkle with a little of the Parmesan. Set aside.

5 Beat the egg whites until stiff. Bring the spinach mixture back to a boil. Stir in a spoonful of beaten egg white, then fold the mixture into the remaining egg white.

6 Turn the mixture into the soufflé dish, spread level, sprinkle with the remaining cheese and bake in the oven for about 25 minutes, until puffed and golden brown. Serve immediately, before the soufflé has a chance to deflate.

COOK'S TIP

The soufflé base can be prepared up to 12 hours in advance and reheated before the beaten egg whites are folded in.

Sweet Potato Roulade

Sweet potato works particularly well as the base for this roulade. Serve in thin slices for a truly impressive dinner party dish.

INGREDIENTS

Serves 6

1 cup low-fat cream cheese
5 tablespoons plain yogurt
6–8 scallions, finely chopped
2 tablespoons chopped Brazil nuts, roasted
1 pound sweet potatoes, peeled and cubed
12 allspice berries, crushed
4 eggs, separated
¼ cup finely grated Edam cheese
1 tablespoon sesame seeds
salt and freshly ground black pepper
green salad, to serve

1 Preheat the oven to 400°F. Grease and line a 13 x 10-inch jelly roll pan with baking parchment, snipping the corners with scissors to fit.

COOK'S TIP

Choose the orange-fleshed variety of sweet potato for the most striking color.

2 In a small bowl, mix together the cheese, yogurt, scallions and Brazil nuts. Set aside.

3 Boil or steam the sweet potatoes until tender. Drain well. Place in a food processor with the allspice and blend until smooth. Spoon into a bowl and stir in the egg yolks and Edam. Season with salt and pepper.

4 Beat the egg whites until stiff but not dry. Fold one-third of the egg whites into the sweet potatoes to lighten the mixture before gently folding in the rest.

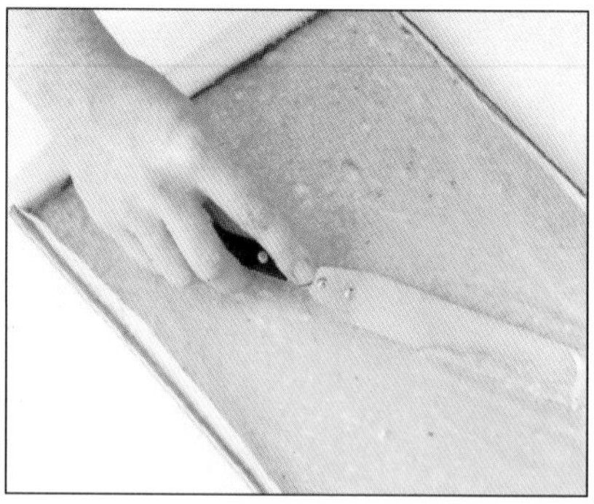

5 Pour into the prepared pan, tipping it to get the mixture into the corners. Smooth gently with a spatula and bake for 10–15 minutes.

6 Meanwhile, lay a large sheet of waxed paper on a clean dish towel and sprinkle with the sesame seeds. When the roulade is cooked, turn it out onto the paper, trim the edges and roll it up. Let cool. When cool, carefully unroll, spread with the cheese filling and roll up again. Cut into slices and serve with a green salad.

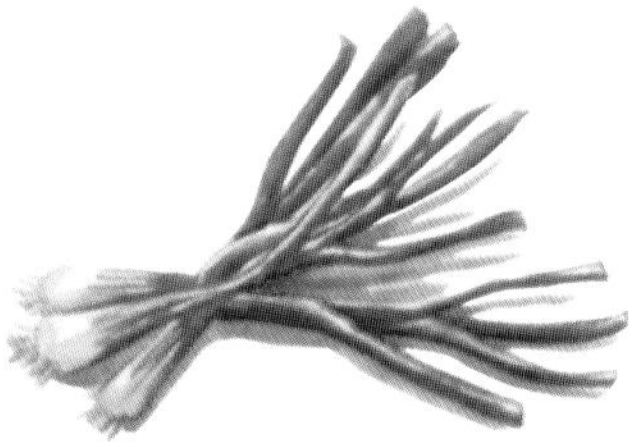

Asparagus Tart with Ricotta

A delightful tart filled with the delicate flavors of mixed cheeses and fresh asparagus.

INGREDIENTS

Serves 4

6 tablespoons (3/4 stick) butter
1 1/2 cups all-purpose flour
pinch of salt

For the filling

8 ounces asparagus
2 eggs, beaten
1 cup ricotta cheese
2 tablespoons strained plain yogurt
6 tablespoons grated Parmesan cheese
salt and freshly ground black pepper

1 Preheat the oven to 400°F. Rub the butter into the flour and salt. Stir in enough cold water to form a smooth dough and knead lightly on a floured surface.

2 Roll out the pastry and line a 9-inch tart pan. Press firmly into the pan and prick all over with a fork. Bake for about 10 minutes, until the pastry is firm but still pale. Remove from the oven and reduce the temperature to 350°F.

3 Trim the asparagus if necessary. Cut 2 inches from the tops and chop the remaining stalks into 1-inch pieces. Bring a pan of water to a boil.

4 Add the asparagus stalks, then the tips, to the boiling water. Simmer for 4–5 minutes. Drain.

5 Beat together the eggs, ricotta, yogurt and Parmesan. Season, stir in the asparagus stalks and pour into the pastry shell. Place the tips on top. Bake for 35–40 minutes, until golden. Serve warm or cold.

Asparagus with Tarragon Hollandaise

This is the perfect appetizer for an early summer dinner party, when the new season's asparagus is just in and at its best. Making hollandaise sauce in a blender or food processor is incredibly easy and virtually foolproof!

INGREDIENTS

Serves 4

1 1/4 pounds fresh asparagus

For the hollandaise sauce

2 egg yolks
1 tablespoon lemon juice
8 tablespoons (1 stick) butter
2 teaspoons finely chopped fresh tarragon
salt and freshly ground black pepper

1 Prepare the asparagus, lay it in a steamer or in an asparagus steamer and place over a saucepan of rapidly boiling water. Cover and steam for 6–10 minutes, until tender (the cooking time will depend on the thickness of the asparagus stems).

2 To make the hollandaise sauce, place the egg yolks and lemon juice in a blender or food processor. Season with salt and pepper and process briefly. Melt the butter in a small pan until foaming and then, with the blender or food processor running, pour it onto the egg mixture in a slow and steady stream.

3 Stir in the tarragon by hand or process it (for a sauce speckled with green or a pale green sauce, respectively).

4 Arrange the asparagus on small plates, pour some of the hollandaise sauce on top and sprinkle with pepper. Serve the remaining sauce in a pitcher.

Spring Vegetable Boxes with Pernod Sauce

Pernod is the perfect companion for the tender taste of early vegetables in crisp pastry shells. This is a very impressive dish for a dinner party, and it tastes as good as it looks.

INGREDIENTS

Serves 4

8 ounces puff pastry, thawed if frozen
1 tablespoon freshly grated Parmesan cheese
1 tablespoon chopped fresh parsley
beaten egg to glaze
6 ounces shelled fava beans
4 ounces baby carrots, scraped
4 baby leeks, cleaned
generous 1/2 cup peas, thawed if frozen
2 ounces snow peas, trimmed
salt and freshly ground black pepper
sprigs of fresh dill, to garnish

For the sauce

7-ounce can chopped tomatoes
2 tablespoons butter
2 tablespoons all-purpose flour
pinch of sugar
3 tablespoons chopped fresh dill
1 1/4 cups water
1 tablespoon Pernod

1 Preheat the oven to 425°F. Lightly grease a baking sheet.

2 Roll out the pastry very thinly. Sprinkle the grated cheese and parsley over the surface of the pastry sheets, fold and roll once more, so that the cheese and parsley are mixed into the pastry. Cut into four 3 x 4-inch rectangles.

3 Lift the rectangles onto the baking sheet. With a sharp knife, score an inner rectangle about 1/2 inch from the edge of each rectangle, cutting halfway through. (This will be removed once the boxes are cooked.) Score crisscross lines on the inner rectangles, brush with egg and bake for 12–15 minutes, until golden.

4 Meanwhile, make the sauce. Press the tomatoes through a sieve into a pan, add the remaining ingredients and bring to a boil, stirring all the time. Lower the heat and simmer until required. Season with salt and pepper.

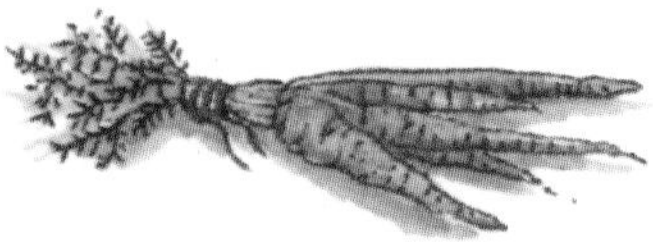

5 Cook the fava beans in a pan of lightly salted boiling water for about 8 minutes. Add the carrots, leeks and peas and cook for another 5 minutes. Add the snow peas and cook for 1 minute more. Drain all the vegetables thoroughly.

6 Using a knife, remove the notched inner rectangles from the pastry boxes. Set them aside to use as lids. Spoon the vegetables into the pastry boxes, pour the sauce over them, put the pastry lids on top and serve garnished with dill.

COOK'S TIP

If there is time, chill the pastry boxes for 20 minutes before baking.

Vegetable Kashmiri

This is a delicious vegetable curry, in which a variety of fresh mixed vegetables are cooked in a spicy, aromatic yogurt sauce.

INGREDIENTS

Serves 4

2 teaspoons cumin seeds
8 black peppercorns
2 green cardamom pods, seeds only
2-inch cinnamon stick
½ teaspoon grated nutmeg
3 tablespoons oil
1 fresh green chile, chopped
1-inch piece of fresh ginger root, grated
1 teaspoon chili powder
½ teaspoon salt
2 large potatoes, cut into 1-inch chunks
8 ounces cauliflower, broken into florets
8 ounces okra, thickly sliced
⅔ cup plain yogurt
⅔ cup vegetable stock
toasted sliced almonds and sprigs of cilantro, to garnish

1 Grind the cumin seeds, peppercorns, cardamom seeds, cinnamon stick and nutmeg to a fine powder using a blender or a mortar and pestle.

2 Heat the oil in a large saucepan and cook the chile and ginger for 2 minutes, stirring all the time.

3 Add the chili powder, salt and ground spice mixture and cook for 2–3 minutes, stirring all the time to prevent the spices from sticking.

4 Stir in the potatoes, cover and cook for 10 minutes over low heat, stirring occasionally.

5 Add the cauliflower and okra and cook for 5 minutes.

6 Add the yogurt and stock. Bring to a boil, then reduce the heat. Cover and simmer for 20 minutes, or until all the vegetables are tender. Garnish with toasted almonds and cilantro sprigs.

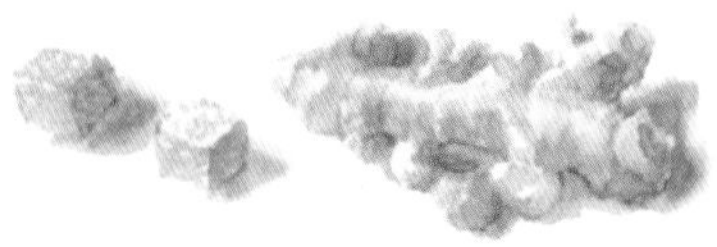

COOK'S TIP

This curry tastes good using most vegetables. Try to choose vegetables that have contrasting colors and textures.

Phyllo Vegetable Pie

This is a memorable main course.

INGREDIENTS

Serves 6-8

8 ounces leeks
11 tablespoons (1 stick plus 3 tablespoons) butter
8 ounces carrots, cubed
8 ounces mushrooms, sliced
8 ounces Brussels sprouts, quartered
2 garlic cloves, crushed
4 ounces (½ cup) cream cheese
4 ounces Roquefort or Stilton cheese
⅔ cup heavy cream
2 eggs, beaten
8 ounces cooking apples
8 ounces (1 cup) cashew nuts or pine nuts, toasted
12 ounces frozen phyllo pastry, thawed
salt and freshly ground black pepper

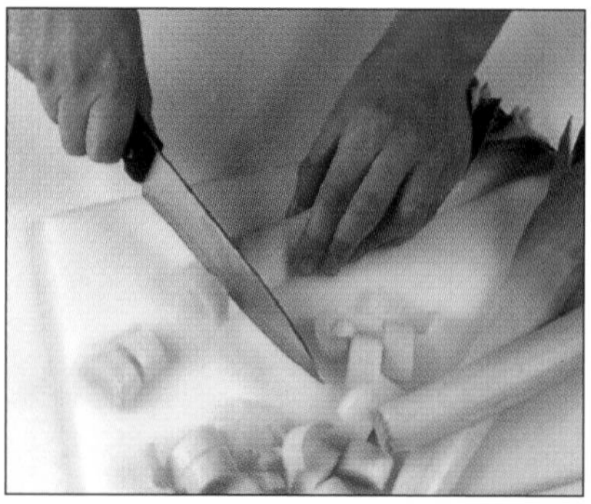

1 Preheat the oven to 350°F. Cut the leeks in half through the root and wash them to remove any soil, separating the layers slightly to check that they are clean. Slice into ½-inch pieces, drain and dry on paper towels.

2 Heat 3 tablespoons of the butter in a large pan and cook the leeks and carrots over medium heat for 5 minutes. Add the mushrooms, Brussels sprouts and garlic and cook for another 2 minutes. Turn the vegetables out into a bowl and let them cool.

3 Whisk the cream cheese, blue cheese, cream and eggs in a bowl. Season with salt and pepper. Pour over the vegetables.

4 Peel and core the apples and cut into ½-inch cubes. Add them to the vegetables with the toasted nuts.

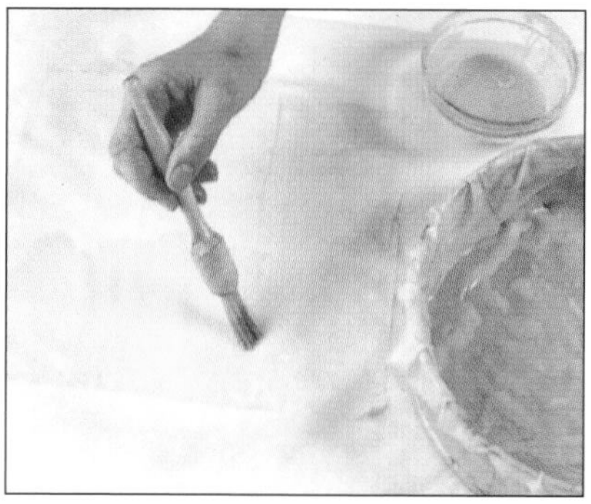

5 Melt the remaining butter in a pan. Brush the inside of a 9-inch springform pan with melted butter. Brush two-thirds of the pastry sheets with butter, one at a time, and use them to line the bottom and sides of the pan, overlapping the layers so that there are no gaps.

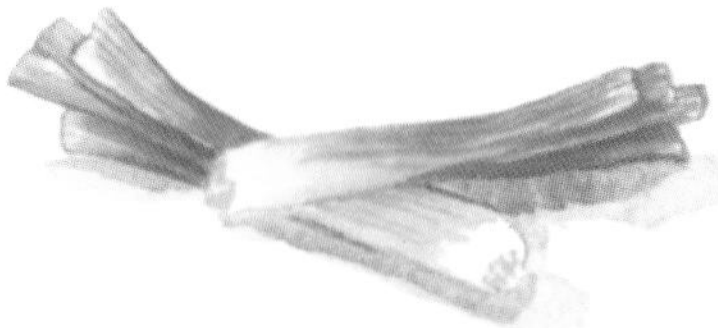

6 Spoon in the vegetable mixture and fold the excess phyllo pastry over toward the center to cover the filling.

7 Brush the remaining phyllo sheets with butter and cut them into 1-inch strips. Cover the surface of the pie with the strips, arranging them decoratively in a rough mound.

8 Bake for 35–40 minutes, until golden brown and crisp all over. Let stand for 5 minutes to cool, then carefully remove the pan and transfer the pie to a serving plate.

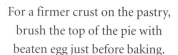

COOK'S TIP

For a firmer crust on the pastry, brush the top of the pie with beaten egg just before baking.

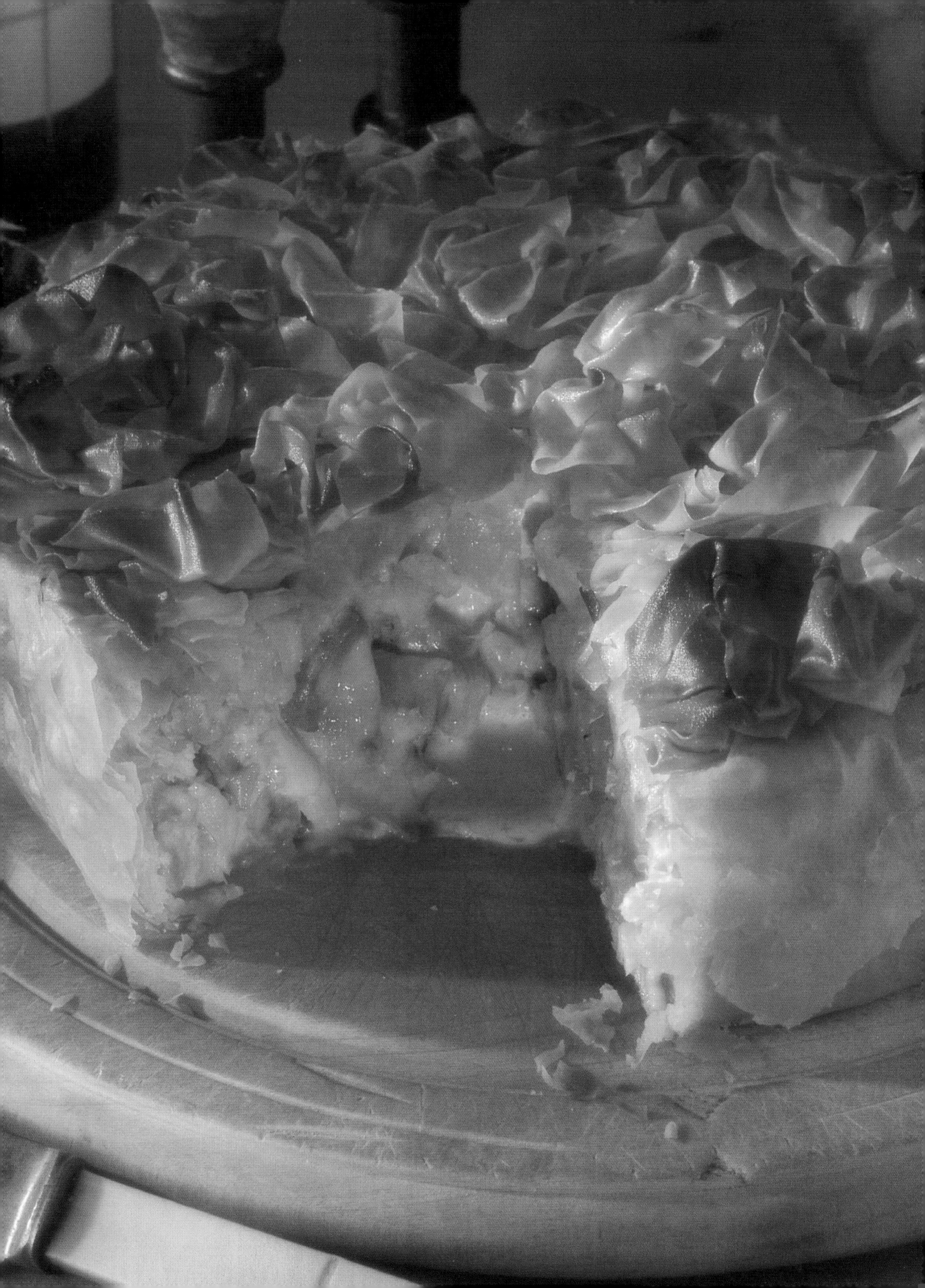

Cauliflower and Mushroom Gougère

This puffy, golden brown, cheese-flavored pastry shell filled with lovely fresh vegetables is a wonderful dinner party dish.

INGREDIENTS

Serves 4–6

8 tablespoons (1 stick) butter
1¼ cups all-purpose flour
4 eggs
4 ounces Gruyère or Cheddar cheese, finely diced
1 teaspoon Dijon mustard
salt and freshly ground black pepper

For the filling

1 small head cauliflower
7-ounce can tomatoes
1 tablespoon sunflower oil
1 tablespoon butter
1 onion, chopped
4 ounces button mushrooms, halved if large
sprig of fresh thyme

1 Preheat the oven to 400°F. Butter a large ovenproof dish. Place 1¼ cups water and the butter together in a large saucepan and heat until the butter has melted. Remove from the heat and add all the flour at once. Beat well with a wooden spoon for about 30 seconds, until smooth. Allow to cool slightly.

2 Beat in the eggs, one at a time, and continue beating until the mixture is thick and glossy. Stir in the cheese and mustard and season with salt and pepper. Spread the mixture around the sides of the ovenproof dish, leaving a hollow in the center for the filling.

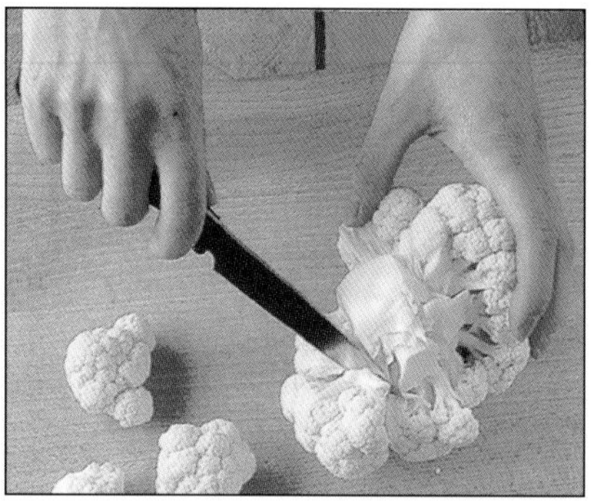

3 To make the filling, cut the cauliflower into florets, discarding the woody, hard stalk.

4 Purée the tomatoes in a blender or food processor, then pour into a measuring cup. Add enough water to make 1¼ cups of liquid.

5 Heat the oil and butter in a nonstick frying pan. Sauté the onion for 3–4 minutes. Add the mushrooms and cook for 2–3 minutes. Add the cauliflower and stir-fry for 1 minute. Add the tomato liquid and thyme. Season. Cook over low heat for 5 minutes.

6 Spoon into the hollow in the ovenproof dish. Bake for 40 minutes, until the pastry has risen.

Potato, Spinach and Pine Nut Gratin

Pine nuts add a satisfying crunch to this gratin of wafer-thin potato slices and spinach in a creamy cheese sauce. Serve with a simple lettuce and tomato salad.

INGREDIENTS

Serves 2

1 pound potatoes
1 garlic clove, crushed
3 scallions, thinly sliced
⅔ cup light cream
1 cup milk
8 ounces frozen chopped spinach, thawed
1 cup grated Cheddar cheese
scant ¼ cup pine nuts
salt and freshly ground black pepper
lettuce and tomato salad, to serve

1 Peel the potatoes and cut them carefully into wafer-thin slices. Spread them out in a large, heavy nonstick frying pan.

2 Sprinkle the crushed garlic and sliced scallions evenly over the potatoes.

3 Pour the cream and milk over the potatoes. Place the pan over gentle heat, cover and cook for 8 minutes, or until the potatoes are tender.

4 Using your hands, squeeze the spinach dry. Add the spinach to the potatoes, mixing lightly. Cover the pan and cook for 2 minutes more.

5 Season with salt and pepper, then spoon the mixture into a shallow flameproof casserole. Preheat the broiler.

6 Sprinkle the grated cheese and pine nuts over the spinach mixture. Heat under the broiler for 2–3 minutes, until the topping begins to turn golden. Serve with a lettuce and tomato salad.

Spinach and Ricotta Conchiglie

Large pasta shells are designed to hold a variety of delicious stuffings. Few are more pleasing than this mixture of chopped spinach and ricotta cheese.

INGREDIENTS

Serves 4

12 ounces large conchiglie
scant 2 cups passata or tomato pulp
10 ounces frozen chopped spinach, thawed
2 slices crustless white bread, crumbled
½ cup milk
¼ cup olive oil
2¼ cups ricotta cheese
pinch of grated nutmeg
1 garlic clove, crushed
½ teaspoon black olive paste (optional)
¼ cup freshly grated Parmesan cheese
2 tablespoons pine nuts
salt and freshly ground black pepper

1 Preheat the oven to 350°F. Bring a large saucepan of salted water to a boil. Add the pasta and cook according to the package instructions. Refresh under cold water, drain and reserve until needed.

2 Pour the passata or tomato pulp into a nylon sieve over a bowl and strain to thicken. Place the spinach in another sieve and press out any excess liquid with the back of a spoon.

3 Place the bread, milk and 3 tablespoons of the oil in a food processor and process. Add the spinach and ricotta and season with salt, pepper and nutmeg. Process briefly to combine.

4 Mix together the sieved passata or tomato pulp, garlic, remaining oil and olive paste, if using. Spread the sauce evenly over the bottom of a flameproof dish.

5 Spoon the spinach mixture into a pastry bag fitted with a large plain nozzle and fill the pasta shells (alternatively, fill with a spoon). Arrange the pasta shells over the sauce.

6 Heat the pasta in the oven for 15 minutes. Preheat the broiler to moderate. Sprinkle pasta with Parmesan cheese and pine nuts and finish under the broiler to brown the cheese.

COOK'S TIP

Choose a large saucepan when cooking pasta, and give an occasional stir to prevent the shapes from sticking together. If passata is not available, use a can of chopped tomatoes, sieved and puréed.

Index

Acknowledgments

The publishers would like to thank the following for their contributions to this book:

RECIPE CONTRIBUTORS

Michelle Berridale-Johnson, Angela Boggiano, Carla Capalbo, Jacqueline Clark, Carole Clements, Matthew Drennan, Sarah Edmonds, Joanna Farrow, Christine France, Silvana Franco, Sarah Gates, Shirley Gill, Shehzaid Husain, Christine Ingram, Peter Jordan, Manisha Kanani, Elizabeth Lambert Ortiz, Ruby Le Bois, Lesley Mackley, Sue Maggs, Sallie Morris, Annie Nichols, Anne Sheasby, Stephen Wheeler, Kate Whiteman, Elizabeth Wolf-Cohen, Jenni Wright.

PHOTOGRAPHERS

Karl Adamson, William Adams-Lingwood, Edward Allwright, Steve Baxter, James Duncan, Michelle Garrett, Amanda Heywood, Janine Hosegood, David Jordan, Patrick McLeavey, Thomas Odulate, Peter Reilly.

STYLISTS

Madeleine Brehaut, Michelle Garrett, Amanda Heywood, Clare Hunt, Marian Price, Kirsty Rawlings, Judy Williams.

HOME ECONOMISTS

Hilary Guy, Jane Hartshorn, Wendy Lee, Lucy McKelvie, Jane Stevenson, Stephen Wheeler.